EU Informal Debt-Collection Regulation

EU Informal Debt-Collection Regulation

Failure by Design?

CĂTĂLIN-GABRIEL STĂNESCU
Associate Professor in Private International Law,
University of Southern Denmark

OXFORD
UNIVERSITY PRESS

OXFORD
UNIVERSITY PRESS

Great Clarendon Street, Oxford, OX2 6DP,
United Kingdom

Oxford University Press is a department of the University of Oxford.
It furthers the University's objective of excellence in research, scholarship,
and education by publishing worldwide. Oxford is a registered trade mark of
Oxford University Press in the UK and in certain other countries.

Published in the United States of America by Oxford University Press
198 Madison Avenue, New York, NY 10016, United States of America.

British Library Cataloguing in Publication Data
Data available

Library of Congress Control Number: 2025930978

ISBN 978–0–19–896615–9

DOI: 10.1093/oso/9780198966159.001.0001

Printed and bound by
CPI Group (UK) Ltd, Croydon, CR0 4YY

MIX
Paper | Supporting
responsible forestry
FSC® C013604

The manufacturer's authorised representative in the EU for product safety is
Oxford University Press España S.A. of El Parque Empresarial San Fernando de
Henares, Avenida de Castilla, 2 – 28830 Madrid (www.oup.es/en or
product.safety@oup.com). OUP España S.A. also acts as importer into Spain
of products made by the manufacturer.

Minunii mele, Alexandra

Foreword

Consumer credit, consumer insolvency and informal (sic) debt-collection

Hans-W. Micklitz
Part-time Professor at the European University Institute, Law Department

The regulation of consumer credit dates to the 1960s and 1970s and was primarily aimed at facilitating access to money on reasonable terms and conditions. Consumer credit remained an area for specialists on both sides of the market; consumer advocates; and bank lawyers. The sharp rise in consumer credit gradually brought the dark side of credit into the political spotlight. Who should bear the loss if the consumer can no longer pay the loan, not because they no longer want to but because they no longer can, because they have lost their job or because they have divorced? The legal response was to establish a new field of law: consumer insolvency. Many Western countries introduced special regulations with widely diverging requirements. Some focus on the moral obligation to pay off debts and insist on categorically narrow conditions of economically sound behaviour, while others, especially in the Anglo-American region, want to give consumers a second chance, which necessarily reduces and de-moralizes the requirements. In recent years, there has been a tendency towards the latter variant. Both approaches are united by putting individual behaviour into the limelight, even if the second chance approach allows for a stronger connection between individual behaviour and market rationality.

The collapse of Lehman Brothers fundamentally changed the perspective. In the EU, two problems dominated the discussion: in Spain, buyers could no longer pay their mortgage loans and had to leave their homes under pressure from the banks; in the member states that were not part of the eurozone, interest rates on loans in foreign currencies exploded. To this day, many legal issues, but also many economic and social problems, remain unresolved, all of which revolve around the search for a fair distribution of risks. On a positive note, the collapse of Lehman Brothers has brought consumer credit and consumer debts from the periphery to the centre of public attention.

The legal literature has swelled considerably over the years. Dozens of books deal with consumer credit, consumer insolvency, and indebtedness. However, the issues on which Cătălin Gabriel Stănescu focuses in this book, with the provocative title *EU's Informal Debt-Collection Regulation: Failure by Design?*, remained under-investigated for a long time—one in which the boundaries between legal and illegal behaviour quickly become blurred. What possibilities and rights do banks have to induce their debtors to repay their debts with the help of third parties, such as debt-collection agencies? Can banks sell the outstanding debt, write it off against tax, and outsource the risk to private companies, which then might even use aggressive methods to force the debtor to pay? There are lots of stories in the newspapers, but there is little serious research which provides a clearer picture of the strategies, their impact, the costs, and the legal benchmarks. The painful search for an answer requires deep insight into market mechanisms and business practices, but also into the so far rather modest attempts by national legislators or the European legislator to set a legal framework that creates a fair balance between consumers, banks, and third-party companies. Cătălin Gabriel Stănescu closes a huge gap in the long discussion on consumer credit and consumer debt, empirically and legally dogmatically, with a strong emphasis on European regulation. The subtitle 'Failure by Design?' tells the message. The author looks at the deeper purpose of legal regulations, whether designed to protect consumers from abusive practices or whether the law is used primarily to ensure the functioning of the consumer credit market. The author delves deeply into the difficult questions of how to define abusive practices; what kind of practices have to be submitted under scrutiny; if there is a borderline between legal and illegal, between fair and abusive; who deserves to be protected and by whom; and whether special rules are needed in consumer credit regulation—or are the general requirements for protection against unfair market practices sufficient? The author presents a well-researched book full of facts and fine legal analyses. It is a book that has been needed for a long time and that now provides all those involved in informal debt-collection with data and analyses in the search for a fair solution.

Acknowledgements

This book represents the culmination of a personal journey, one that has been shaped by over a decade of passion for its subject. In the past five years, I have dedicated myself to rigorous research, and the three years of writing and reflection that followed have been a rewarding, albeit challenging, process. As I look back on this journey, I feel immense gratitude for the many people and institutions that made this book possible.

First and foremost, I want to express my sincere thanks to the Talent Track Program at the University of Southern Denmark. The financial support I received allowed me to undertake crucial research abroad at the European University Institute. Immersing myself in such a rich and diverse academic environment profoundly shaped this work, and I am deeply grateful for the opportunity and faith placed in me. Extra layers of knowledge and a deeper understanding of the topic have been added during my research stays at the Centre for Finance and Banking Law (National University of Singapore) and Max Planck Institute for Comparative and International Private Law (Hamburg).

At the European University Institute, I was fortunate to work with Professors Hans Micklitz and Peter Drahos. Their thoughtful feedback and countless discussions throughout the writing process were invaluable. Their insights sharpened my research and inspired me to think more critically and creatively. Our conversations were not only intellectually stimulating but also moments of genuine connection and friendship that I will always cherish. My gratitude and respect for both of them run deep, and no words could fully capture how much their guidance and mentorship have meant to me.

I also owe a debt of gratitude to those who took the time to read, critique, and help me improve my work. Liviu Damşa, Asress Adimi Gikay, Jodi Gardner, Maxim Usyinin, Christian Bergqvist, and Petruța Pârvan—their feedback was instrumental in refining my arguments and clarifying my ideas. Their thoughts and suggestions enriched the final manuscript in ways I could not have achieved alone.

During the inevitable difficult moments, I was sustained by the unwavering support of my mother, Petruța Anisia, and my friends, many of whom I have already mentioned: Hans, Peter, Liviu, and Asress. Their encouragement during tough times, whether through late-night conversations or simple gestures of kindness, reminded me to keep going. When I felt my strength wane, they were there to lift me, and I am endlessly grateful for that.

I am also thankful to my Oxford University Press editors, Charlotte Kershaw, Kim Vollrodt and Rachel Mullaly, for their support, professionalism, and flexibility in turning the manuscript into reality. Above all, I appreciate their willingness to accommodate my needs and to navigate the challenges of a speedy publication with me. It has been a pleasure working with such a dedicated and thoughtful team.

Finally, my deepest thanks go to my wife, Nataliia, and daughter, Alexandra. Their patience, understanding, and love, especially during my prolonged absences and extended work hours, kept me grounded. Without their tremendous support, this book would not have been possible. In many ways, this work belongs to them as much as it does to me.

Contents

Tables of Cases

INTERNATIONAL CASE LAW:

ECHR CASE LAW

EU CASE LAW:

Tables of Legislation

EU LEGISLATION:

European Directives:

European Regulations:

Other Legislation:

1

INFORMAL DEBT-COLLECTION IN THE EUROPEAN UNION: UNFAIR PRACTICES, PRIVACY CONCERNS, AND INADEQUATE REGULATION

1.1 Abuse in Debt-collection: A European Union Challenge

In December 2022, Bloomberg reported that debt-collectors in Spain had found success in an unconventional approach to their business. They would dress in undertaker garments and arrive at debtors' homes in fake hearses bearing the words 'Undertaker of Debt-collection'. This tactic aimed to shame and intimidate debtors into making repayments.[1]

Abusive informal debt-collection practices are widespread across the European Union (EU), although not all are spectacular enough to attract media attention. For example, in Croatia, individuals reported being contacted by debt-collection agencies on their private mobile phone numbers to relay messages to their neighbours about their debts.[2] In Greece, it is common for debtors or their close ones to be contacted at their workplace and for offensive language to be used.[3] In Estonia, the names of debtors have been publicly displayed on billboards or buildings in Tallinn, the capital city, as well as in business-oriented newspapers and on special websites.[4] Furthermore, the pursuit of non-existent debts has been documented

[1] Charles Penty, 'Debt Collectors in Hearses Are a Rare Booming Business in Spain' (*Bloomberg*, 13 December 2022) <https://www.bloomberg.com/news/articles/2022-12-13/for-debt-collectors-driving-fake-hearses-business-is-booming> accessed 7 February 2024.

[2] Paula Poretti, 'Regulation of Abusive Informal Debt Collection in Croatia' in Cătălin Gabriel Stănescu (ed), *Regulation of Debt Collection in Europe: Understanding Informal Debt Collection* (Routledge 2023) 55.

[3] Eleni Kaprou, 'Abusive Informal Debt Collection Practices in Greece' in Cătălin Gabriel Stănescu (ed), *Regulation of Debt Collection in Europe: Understanding Informal Debt Collection* (Routledge 2023) 90.

[4] Karin Sein, 'Abusive Debt Recovery Practices in Estonia' in Cătălin Gabriel Stănescu (ed), *Regulation of Debt Collection in Europe: Understanding Informal Debt Collection* (Routledge 2023) 110.

EU Informal Debt-Collection Regulation. Cătălin-Gabriel Stănescu, Oxford University Press.
 DOI: 10.1093/oso/9780198966159.003.0001

in the Netherlands[5] and Romania.[6] In Poland, receiving intimidating messages from banks or debt-collectors threatening physical violence is not unusual.[7] Additionally, in Sweden, there have been reports of scammers and rogue debt-collectors attempting to collect debts without proper authorization.[8] The issues of hidden and/or inflated costs and misleading representations are prevalent throughout the continent, indicating that the aforementioned examples are not confined to the specific countries cited.

Turning private debts into a public spectacle or scaring people to extract payment may appear as nothing more than a (well-deserved) nuisance for the defaulting debtor. So why should one care? After all, people must pay their debts.

Debt-collection is closely interlinked with consumer credit and utility markets (see Chapter V). Generally, defaulted debts trigger debt-collection efforts, which can be either judicial (formal), that is, involving some state-sanctioned agents (e.g. courts, bailiffs, and notaries), or non-judicial (informal), implying that they will be undertaken by either the creditor (including subsequent creditors, such as debt buyers) or third parties (e.g. debt-collection agencies, factors) (see Chapters II and III).

Judicial debt-collection poses fewer issues because it is more regulated. Due-process requirements and procedural laws are available in all member states (MS). Moreover, Article 6 of the European Convention of Human Rights, restated in Article 47 of the EU Charter of Fundamental Rights, has given considerable substance to individuals' right to a fair trial. Thus, EU intervention in the area is limited to cross-border matters and harmonization efforts, such as the Order for Payment Regulation.[9] Conversely, informal debt-collection entails more considerable risks due to the high potential for abusive practices that could be detrimental

[5] Candida Leone and Joanna van Duin, 'Doubling Down on Debt?' in Cătălin Gabriel Stănescu (ed) *Regulation of Debt Collection in Europe: Understanding Informal Debt Collection* (Routledge 2023) 119.

[6] Author's own practice. See also: Antonia Popescu, 'Sunteti hartuit de recuperatorii de creante? Un avocat va spune ce trebuie sa faceti' *DC Business* < https://www.dcbusiness.ro/sunteti-hartuit-de-recuperatorii-de-creante-un-avocat-va-spune-ce-trebuie-sa-faceti_648279.html> (20 September 2022).

[7] Jakub Kepinski, 'Regulation of Abusive Informal Debt Collection Practices: Poland' in Cătălin Gabriel Stănescu (ed), *Regulation of Debt Collection in Europe: Understanding Informal Debt Collection* (Routledge 2023) 142, 146.

[8] Hajo Michael Holtz, 'Regulation of Abusive Informal Debt Collection Practices: Sweden' in Cătălin Gabriel Stănescu (ed), *Regulation of Debt Collection in Europe: Understanding Informal Debt Collection* (Routledge 2023) 193.

[9] Regulation (EC) No 1896/2006 creating a European order for payment procedure [2006] OJ L399/1.

to the debtor's well-being and economic or privacy interests[10] and to the economic environment,[11] the judiciary,[12] and society.[13]

International institutions, such as the World Bank, suggest that states should regulate abusive informal debt-collection practices.[14] In the wake of the COVID-19 pandemic and in the current economic and geopolitical situation, this need has become even more pressing. However, a more holistic approach to consumer credit and market regulation would be required to regulate informal debt-collection. In the case of the EU, this involves discussions regarding its regulatory competencies (and process) and the daunting task of balancing the various interests of many stakeholders, especially considering the vast amounts of money involved (see Chapters VII and IX).

1.2 Stigma and Abuse: The Harsh Realities of Debt-collection

Debtors have faced harsh treatment throughout history. They were often publicly shamed, subjected to violence, and even forced into slavery.[15] Public rituals associated with being in too much debt, defaulting on loans, or declaring bankruptcy led to a loss of privacy and personal dignity, which intensified debtors' sense of

[10] Udo Reifner, Johanna Niemi-Kiesiläinen, Nik Huls, and Helga Springeneer, *Overindebtedness in European Consumer Law: Principles from 15 European States* (Books on Demand 2012); Elizabeth Warren, Jay Lawrence Westbrook, Katherine Porter, and John AE Pottow, *The Law of Debtors and Creditors: Text, Cases, and Problems* (Aspen Casebook Series 2014); Cătălin Gabriel Stănescu, *Self-Help, Private Debt Collection and the Concomitant Risks. A Comparative Law Analysis* (Springer 2015); Hans-W Micklitz and Irina Domurath, *Consumer Debt and Social Exclusion in Europe* (Taylor and Francis 2016); Iain Ramsay, 'Changing Policy Paradigms of EU Consumer Credit and Debt Regulation' in Dorota Leczykiewicz and Stephen Weatherill (eds), *The Involvement of EU Law in Private Law Relationships* (Hart Publishing 2013); Federico Ferretti and Daniela Vandone, *Personal Debt in Europe* (Cambridge UP 2019); Joseph Spooner, *Bankruptcy: The Case for Relief in an Economy of Debt* (Cambridge UP 2019); Jodi Gardner, Mia Gray, and Katharina Moser, *Debt and Austerity: Implications of the Financial Crisis* (Edward Elgar 2020).

[11] Stănescu (n 10); Olivier Jérusalmy, Paul Fox, and Nicolas Hercelin, 'Is the Human Dignity of Individual Debtors at Risk?' (*Finance Watch*, 2020) <https://www.finance-watch.org/wp-content/uploads/2020/01/Report_Human-dignity_final_with-annex.pdf> accessed 22 July 2024; Cătălin Gabriel Stănescu, 'Regulation of Abusive Debt Collection Practices in the EU Member States: An Empirical Account' (2021) 44(1) Journal of Consumer Policy 179.

[12] Ferretti and Vandone (n 10); Remo Caponi and Janek Novak, 'Access to Justice' in Burkhard Hess and Stephanie Law (eds), *Implementing EU Consumer Rights by National Procedural Law. Luxembourg Report on European Procedural Law Volume II*, (Beck, Hart, Nomos 2019).

[13] Cătălin Gabriel Stănescu and Camelia Bogdan, 'Regulatory Arbitrage and Non-Judicial Debt Collection in Central and Eastern Europe—Tax Sheltering and Money Laundering' (2021) 11(2) Accounting, Economics and Law: A Convivium 119.

[14] World Bank, 'Good Practices for Financial Consumer Protection' (*World Bank*, 2017).

[15] Teresa A Sullivan, Elizabeth Warren, and Jay Lawrence Westbrook, 'Less Stigma or More Financial Distress: An Empirical Analysis of the Extraordinary Increase in Bankruptcy Filings' (2006) 59(2) Stanford Law Review 213; Rafi Efrat, 'The Evolution of Bankruptcy Stigma' (2006) 7(2) Theoretical Inquiries in Law 365; MD Sousa, 'Bankruptcy Stigma: A Socio-Legal Study' (2013) 87(4) The American Bankruptcy Law Journal 435; Daniel Lord Smail, *Legal Plunder: Households and Debt Collection in Late Medieval Europe* (Harvard UP 2016).

shame.[16] In the nineteenth century, debtors' prisons were common, and even though the practice was eventually outlawed, people could still be imprisoned for their debts in 1970s Britain[17] or in the present-day US.[18]

However, modern studies show that subjecting debtors to stigmatization, humiliation, constant pressure, and harassment can have severe negative effects on their psychological well-being,[19] leading to stress, anxiety, and even suicide.[20] Nagging practices can quickly become abusive, violating individual rights, affecting material interests, leading to financial exclusion, and breaching societal peace.[21] Furthermore, the debt-collection process allows creditors to add costs for the debtors, increasing their burden and pushing them further into indebtedness,[22] from which they might never find a way out. In other words, although valid, a claim must be collected only legally, and debtors should be granted some protection against abusive behaviour.

Conventional wisdom tends to equate protection against abusive debt-collection with protection against repayment, although they are different. Two problems arise. One is finding and maintaining the right balance between the creditor's expectation to be paid and the debtor's expectation to be treated fairly. If debt prisons, debt bondage, and chattel slavery were commonly accepted 200 years ago, the increased emphasis on individual rights has created new rights and expectations, including vis-à-vis debt default. However, the humanization of debt-collection may be only apparent given that modern slavery and other forms of exploitation still exist, albeit to a lesser extent. The other problem is that, in many cases, the creditor has already disposed of the original debt by selling it at a discount to financial

16 Sousa (n 15); Smail (n 15).

17 Rock Paul, *Making People Pay* (Routledge 1973) Chapter 7, n 3; Joe Deville, *Lived Economies of Default* (Routledge 2015) 78.

18 Eli Hager, 'Debtors' Prisons, Then and Now: FAQ' (*The Marshall Project*, 24 February 2015) <https://www.themarshallproject.org/2015/02/24/debtors-prisons-then-and-now-faq> accessed 26 June 2024; Anne J Manning, 'Thinking of Jailing Debtors as Dickensian? Think Again' (*The Harvard Gazette*, 19 September 2023) <https://news.harvard.edu/gazette/story/2023/09/how-common-is-debt-imprisonment-in-u-s-today/> accessed 26 June 2024; The Debtors' Prisons Project <https://policylab.hks.harvard.edu/debtors-prisons/> accessed 26 June 2024.

19 Mark Hosley, *Dark Side of Prosperity. Late Capitalism's Culture of Indebtedness* (Routledge 2016) 10, 119, 132.

20 Denis Campbell, 'Aggressive Debt Collectors Raise Risk of Suicide' (*The Guardian*, 3 December 2018) <https://www.theguardian.com/society/2018/dec/03/aggressive-debt-collectors-raise-risk-of-suicide> accessed 7 February 2024; Noh Amit, Rozmi Ismail, Abdul Rahim Zumrah, Mohd Azmir Mohd Nizah, Tengku Elmi Azlina Tengku Muda, Edbert Chia Tat Meng, Norhayati Ibrahim, and Normah Che Din, 'Relationship Between Debt and Depression, Anxiety, Stress, or Suicide Ideation in Asia: A Systematic Review' (2020) 11 Frontiers in Psychology 1.

21 Heikki Hiilamo, *Household Debt and Economic Crisis. Causes, Consequences, Remedies* (Edward Elgar 2018) 29, 35, 102.

22 Nadja Jungmann and André Moerman, 'Schulden klein houden en perspectief bieden' (*Schuldenkleinhouden*, 2023) <https://www.schuldenkleinhouden.nl/index.php?id=2> accessed 22 July 2024. For English, see Nadja Jungmann, 'Dutch Debt Collection System Requires Major Reform, Experts Say' (*NL Times*, 5 October 2023) <https://nltimes.nl/2023/10/05/dutch-debt-collection-system-requires-major-reform-experts-say> accessed 22 July 2024.

speculators, which raises the question of whether the enforcement of the assigned debt still has a connection to the original one or is only a method of mass wealth extraction.

1.3 The Lack of Regulatory Oversight

Despite the impact of informal debt-collection on consumers, there is a noticeable lack of regulatory oversight in the EU. One would expect greater control and supervision of this industry, but it has largely been absent at the EU and state levels. My 2021 empirical study showed that only a third of EU MS had sector-specific informal debt-collection legislation.[23] In the remaining grey area, debt-collectors flew under the regulatory radar and operated with relative impunity as traditional remedies were ineffective in addressing them. Inadequate supervision and control mechanisms can lead to abusive behaviour affecting hundreds of thousands of consumers, even in cases where regulation is present. For example, in Denmark, Danske Bank's unfair debt-collection practices, uncovered in 2020, affected more than 150,000 consumers, prompting the Financial Supervision Authority to outsource the investigation to a private actor due to insufficient in-house resources.[24]

The situation is similar at the EU level. Despite the European Commission's commitment to ensuring a high level of consumer protection[25] and a safer market for retail financial services, consumer trust and empowerment levels remain low.[26] Consumer protection rules against informal debt-collection have only been

[23] Stănescu (n 11).

[24] Cătălin Gabriel Stănescu, 'Is There a Scandinavian Model for Regulating Abusive Informal Debt Collection Practices?' in Caroline Heide-Jørgensen, Ingrid Lund-Andersen, and Jesper Lau Hansen (eds), *Festskrift til Linda Nielsen* (Djøf Forlag 2022).

[25] Since the advent of the Single European Act and the introduction of Article 100a (now Article 95) into the EC Treaty, the Commission's proposals regarding the approximation of laws affecting the internal market must be based on a high level of consumer protection. A number of texts have been based on this article, notably the directives on package travel, package holidays, and package tours (1990) and unfair terms in consumer contracts (1993). A further impetus was given by the Inter-Governmental Conference preceding the adoption of the Treaty on European Union, with the introduction of a specific title on consumer protection into the EC Treaty. See 'Consumer protection' at <https://eur-lex.europa.eu/legal-content/EN/ALL/?uri=legissum:a17000> accessed 22 July 2024. Currently, the legal basis is formed by Articles 114 and 169 of the Treaty on the Functioning of the European Union.

[26] European Commission, '2018 Consumer Markets Scoreboard. Consumers Remain Positive about Key Markets but Trust in Services still Lacking' (*European Commission*, October 2018) <https://commission.europa.eu/document/download/be5c03bf-1244-4176-8e13-dbbeb928f3e8_en?filename=eujus15a-1816-i02_-_factsheet_2_pages_-_the_consumer_markets_scoreboard_2018-final-lr.pdf> accessed 22 July 2024; European Commission, '2023 Consumer Conditions Scoreboard' (*European Commission*, 27 March 2023) <https://commission.europa.eu/document/download/89ea35fe-728f-4749-b95d-88544687583c_en?filename=consumer_conditions_scoreboard_2023_v1.1.pdf> accessed 22 July 2024; European Commission, 'Consumer Vulnerability across Key Markets in the European Union' (*European Commission*, January 2016) 312 <https://commission.europa.eu/document/download/1356644b-16e3-41a0-b1e2-74acaaa85ec0_en?filename=consumers-approved-report_en.pdf> accessed 22 July 2024; European

incidental. EU lawmakers are more inclined to support neo-liberal perspectives promoting a laissez-faire approach that permits investors in debt portfolios and debt-collectors to continue their profitable trade.

The rationale is that the debt-collection industry performs valuable market functions. It (a) allows banks to clear their books and resume lending and (b) reinjects substantial amounts of money into the economy.[27] The 2021 Credit Servicers and Credit Purchasers Directive (CSCPD; see Chapters XIV–XVI), which is supposed to regulate the debt purchase and debt-collection industry, is a perfect example of this reasoning.[28] However, the legal framework fostering the development of the debt industry via harmonized, simplified, and effective procedures is not balanced by one that adequately protects against egregious recovery practices. Given these considerations, one might wonder why legislators have not banned such practices or regulated an industry of this size and significance.

1.4 Two Defining Moments

Understanding the paradigms surrounding debt-collection regulation at the EU level requires attention to its history and the influence of interest groups, institutions, and ideas. Two defining moments have presented significant opportunities for the EU to regulate and harmonize informal debt-collection practices: the 2002 Consumer Credit Directive (CCD) Proposal[29] and the adoption of the compromise text of the CSCPD in 2021[30] (see Chapter IX). However, both efforts failed due to the staunch opposition of the financial industry and a lack of institutional power or will.

Several contentions derive from the above and will be evident throughout the book. First, the available data reveals that the existing legal framework and economic system promote a system of traded and escalated debts. Banks create a debt and sell it for a fraction of its face value once defaulted. It is then recovered at face value to allow banks to create more debt that will re-enter the cycle and enable

Commission, 'Study on Measuring Consumer Detriment in the European Union' (*European Commission*, February 2017) <https://commission.europa.eu/document/download/a48e1d90-6728-4e46-bf64-6f0e9f15a935_en?filename=consumer-detriment-study-final-report_en.pdf> accessed 22 July 2024.

[27] According to figures provided by the industry's representatives, 45–55 billion euros are pumped back into the economy annually. FENCA <https://fenca.eu/> accessed 5 December 2023.

[28] Directive (EU) No 2021/2167 on credit servicers and credit purchasers [2021] OJ L438 (CSCPD) recital 6.

[29] Proposal for a Directive of the European Parliament and of the Council on the harmonisation of the laws, regulations and administrative provisions of the Member States concerning credit for consumers (2002/C 331 E/39), COM(2002) 443, 31 December 2002.

[30] CSCPD (n 28).

financial speculators to extract as much profit as possible. Second, this system is not only unsustainable but also morally questionable. It will ultimately lead to ruin, pauperism, and systemic issues similar to those seen in the 2008 financial crisis. Therefore, it should be closely monitored and tightly regulated. Third, notwithstanding all the above, as a matter of practice, the EU debt-collection market regulation is heavily influenced by the financial industry that profits from it. Finally, despite consumer protection claims, the reality shows that EU institutions lean towards and support the industry's interests regarding informal debt-collection.

1.5 Uncovering the Discrepancy: A Purposeful Failure

The book argues that the regulatory framework against abusive informal debt-collection activities at the EU and national levels is affected by a systemic and intentional failure of the EU's legislative machinery.

Systemic failure manifests in the fragmented, complex, and inefficient legal framework for protecting consumers. At the EU level, these issues are caused by scattered rules, such as the Unfair Commercial Practices Directive (UCPD),[31] the 2008 CCD,[32] the Unfair Contract Terms Directive (UCTD),[33] or the General Data Protection Regulation (GDPR),[34] which consumers have to navigate to exercise their rights or seek protection (see Chapters X–XIII).

Concomitantly, the few consumer protection rules contained in the CSCPD lack specificity and appear ineffective in light of a diverse and convoluted institutional framework, making redress almost impossible in a cross-border setting. This starkly contrasts with the CSCPD's provisions regulating the debt-collection profession, easing, harmonizing, and incentivizing the industry's growth across the Union (see Chapters XIV–XVI).

Without pan-EU regulation, consumer protection remains primarily a national effort. However, research indicates that national legal frameworks are also dispersed, fragmented,[35] and inefficient in addressing systemic violations or cross-border matters. Even if each MS were to implement its legislation, without a harmonized approach to regulation and enforcement and sufficient incentives for

[31] Directive No 2005/29/EC concerning unfair business-to-consumer commercial practices in the internal market [2005] OJ L149/22 (UCPD).

[32] Directive No 2008/48/EC on credit agreements for consumers and repealing Council Directive 87/102/EEC [2008] OJ L133/66.

[33] Council Directive No 93/13/EEC of 5 April 1993 on unfair terms in consumer contracts [1993] OJ L95.

[34] Regulation (EU) No 2016/679 on the protection of natural persons with regard to the processing of personal data and on the free movement of such data [2016] OJ L119.

[35] Stanescu (n 11); Jérusalmy, Fox, and Hercelin (n 11).

consumer action the system would likely remain ineffective. Notably, this ineffectiveness predominantly impacts consumer-debtors rather than the industry.

Intentional failure stems from the lack of adequate private remedies and the EU's unwillingness to adopt sectoral regulation due to the powerful opposition of the debt-collection industry. The substantial disparity between the benefits for debt-collectors and debt purchasers and the limitations to consumer protection is not merely a matter of poor governance but also the result of regulatory capture by the financial industry via powerful lobby groups, which manipulate EU and national institutions to serve their interests. The CSCPD appears deliberately crafted to fail in its purpose, further solidifying the industry's dominance. The task of safeguarding consumers is left to the MS, each with varying levels of leverage in negotiating with the financial industry.

The combined effect is an enormous gap between the consumer-friendly statements of EU officials and reality. Consequently, millions of consumers are transformed into lifetime debtors, trapped in debt peonage and facing substantial social costs due to psychological damage, poverty, and homelessness.

1.6 Challenges in Regulating the Debt-collection Industry

The absence of comprehensive informal debt-collection regulation may be attributed to the structural power of the financial industry but also to the prevailing belief in the inviolable nature of debt repayment, which is a fundamental tenet of contract and law, with a predominant emphasis on protecting creditors over debtors. Moreover, this ideological stance is reinforced by concerns that introducing debtor protections could lead to moral hazard and disrupt payment discipline,[36] potentially escalating credit costs. These notions remain influential, although recent research has largely discredited them.[37] States' vested interests in maintaining the status quo could also explain the leniency observed in regulation.

[36] International Monetary Fund, 'Romania: Letter of Intent, Memorandum of Economic and Financial Policies, and Technical Memorandum of Understanding' (*International Monetary Fund*, 10 June 2013) para 22 <https://www.imf.org/external/np/loi/2013/rou/061013.pdf> accessed 22 July 2024; European Commission, *Post-Programme Surveillance Report. Greece, Spring 2023* (Institutional paper 203, May 2023) <https://economy-finance.ec.europa.eu/system/files/2023-05/ip203_en.pdf> accessed 21 December 2023.

[37] Charles J Romeo and Ryan Sandler, 'The Effect of Debt Collection Laws on Access to Credit' (2021) 195 Journal of Public Economics 1; Viktar Fedaseyeu, 'Debt Collection Agencies and the Supply of Consumer Credit' (2020) 138 Journal of Financial Economics 193. Romeo and Sandler concluded that tightening debt-collection laws has only a limited adverse effect on credit access and debtor repayment. Meanwhile, Fedaseyeu found no conclusive evidence that debt-collection laws hurt credit access and consumer welfare, although it did lead to a reduction in the number of debt-collectors.

1.6.1 The moral argument for debt repayment

Our social order is built on the principle that financial obligations must be met.[38] Therefore, paying bills for services and consumer goods—whether for utilities (water, heating, electricity, internet, and telephone), credit cards, memberships, subscriptions, or car or house payments—continues to be regarded as a legal and moral obligation. Across the economy, these unpaid bills convert into millions of (often uncontested) small-value enforcement claims, which must be collected quickly and cheaply[39]—just not by any means.

Some have questioned whether the moral argument for paying debts is as absolute as the financial industry and its supporters would have one believe. It may be so in stark form, and modern legislation has been designed and constructed for this purpose. However, not all agree. In his monumental history of debt, David Graeber challenged the idea that debt repayment should be associated with morality. Instead, he showed that it is more rooted in state-sanctioned[40] violence,[41] slavery,[42] and colonialism,[43] and that debt enforcement remains vital to maintaining the political power relationships that persist today.[44]

Similarly, Johnna Montgomerie suggests that abolishing household debts could have positive effects.[45] Drawing on modern examples and the logic of debt jubilees,[46] she argued that cancelling household debts could end austerity and the unsustainable growth path based on credit and debt. Her views are not as radical as they seem: she merely suggested that after the 2008 financial crisis, instead of bailing out banks, half of the money could have been used to bail out households through a household debt cancellation fund. Additionally, she proposed affordable refinancing options and writing off the most pernicious elements of household debt, such as non-performing loans (NPLs).[47] In her view, such measures could create a fairer economy, address the enduring effects of the housing crisis, and reduce inequality. Furthermore, these actions would hurt the most exploitative parts of the financial sector, such as the debt-collection industry.[48]

[38] Hiilamo (n 21) 5; Guido Comparato, *The Financialisation of the Citizen: Social and Financial Inclusion through European Private Law* (Hart Publishing 2018) 1.

[39] Georgia Harley and Svetozara Petkova, 'What happens if you don't pay your bill? Lessons from Central and Eastern Europe' (*World Bank Blogs*, 18 July 2017) <https://blogs.worldbank.org/europeandcentralasia/what-happens-if-you-don-t-pay-your-bill-lessons-central-and-eastern-europe> accessed 5 December 2023.

[40] David Graeber, *Debt: The First 5,000 Years* (Melville House 2014) 50.

[41] ibid 19.

[42] ibid 291.

[43] ibid 268.

[44] ibid 269–70, 279.

[45] Johnna Montgomerie, *Should We Abolish Household Debts?* (Polity 2019) Introduction and Conclusion.

[46] ibid Chapter 5.

[47] ibid Chapters 2 and 5.

[48] ibid Chapter 5.

There is a growing emphasis on providing services responsibly to prevent people from becoming heavily indebted. This includes creditors providing loans responsibly.[49] The moral and legal aspects of debt repayment are being re-evaluated, and service providers must consider the ethical implications of their actions. Otherwise, the financial industry's moral hazard argument can cut both ways: under the guise of absolute obligations and without accountability for creditors, what would stop a lender from taking more chances in lending, knowing they can sell the non-performing debt to another market player?[50]

This book recognizes all these arguments, and some of them will be used throughout the text. However, the objective is not to completely reconsider the moral or legal grounds for debt repayment but to examine the underlying legal mechanisms that enable debt purchasers and collectors to profit from speculating on defaulted debt. Additionally, the book seeks to uncover the reasons that have thus far prevented the regulation of abusive informal debt-collection.

1.6.2 The industry's structural power

Another conceivable explanation is the considerable profitability and expansion of the debt-collection business over the past two decades, coupled with close ties to the credit and financial markets. In 2022, the debt-collection market in just twelve EU MS exceeded 505 billion euros, nearly three times the EU's budget for the same year.[51] This dynamic may elucidate the substantial influence of the financial industry on legislatures.

Debt-collectors increasingly assume a secondary role, namely, that of debt purchasers. More significant secondary markets and higher volumes of commercialized NPL portfolios translate into larger players. Small local debt-collection agencies have mutated into multinational conglomerates with speculating appetites and potent financial investors behind them. For example, two European leaders, the Swedish Intrum and the German EOS, started as debt-collection agencies but are now some of the largest debt purchasers in the EU (see Chapter VIII).[52]

[49] Vanessa Mak, 'What is Responsible Lending? The EU Consumer Mortgage Directive in the UK and the Netherlands' (2015) 38 Journal of Consumer Policy 411.

[50] Montgomerie (n 45), Chapter 5. On the issue of moral hazard, she writes: 'The "moral hazard" of bailouts dictates that individuals whose debts are cancelled will make everyone worse off, because the relief will only be temporary: these individuals will simply borrow again, anticipating that debts will be cancelled in the future. But in 2008 banks took bailouts for lending too much, only to keep overlending to households in order to revive profits since then. This moral hazard of bailouts is ignored because the financial system is considered too important and banks "too big to fail". None of the vocal opponents to abolishing household debts will be found denouncing unconventional monetary policy or bank bailouts. Instead of giving relief to both lenders and borrowers, together, we are indoctrinated to believe that bank bailouts are prudent and strategic but the bailout of debtors is abhorrent and crazy.'

[51] Data compiled by the author. See Chapter 7.

[52] Eleanor Duncan and Abhinav Ramnarayan, 'Debt Collectors' Awkward Moment: Their Own Debt Is Now Sinking', (*Bloomberg*, 23 June 2023) <https://www.bloomberg.com/news/articles/

The perverse effects of market concentration and expansion are already noticeable, leading to worries that instead of fostering competition, they stifle it.[53] Empirical evidence shows that the growing debt market has not led to increased competition but to mergers and creations of debt champions acting cross-border.[54] Therefore, a limited number of stakeholders can dominate MS markets while the remaining players settle for the crumbs.

Historically, post-classical Roman law provided special protection against professional debt purchasers trying to benefit from a bad economic climate. If they had paid less than the actual amount of the debt when purchasing the claim, they could not recover more from the debtor than they had paid themselves.[55] Despite its inherent logic and fairness, modern legislation, which is subordinated to business interests, did not maintain this remedy and continues to oppose it (see Chapter III).

1.6.3 States' vested interests

Similarly, states may exhibit leniency towards abusive debt-collection practices due to their direct vested interests. Their own aggressive methods in tax collection[56] and public debt recovery[57] illustrate a proclivity for harsh enforcement. Furthermore, states stand to gain from increased debt-collection profits through taxation, leading to a conflict of interest. This financial incentive can dissuade regulatory bodies from embracing and enforcing more humane practices.

2023-06-23/debt-collectors-awkward-moment-their-own-debt-is-now-sinking?embedded-checkout=true> accessed 22 February 2024.

[53] Gábor Koltay and Szabolcs Lorincz, *Industry Concentration and Competition Policy* (Competition Policy Brief Issue 2021/02, November 2021) <https://competition-policy.ec.europa.eu/system/files/2021-12/Competition%20Policy%20Brief%202-2021_Industry%20concentration%20and%20competition%20policy.pdf> accessed 22 July 2023.

[54] Reuters, 'Debt collectors make Europe's bad loans pay again' (*Financial Express*, June 14 2017) <https://www.financialexpress.com/policy/economy-debt-collectors-make-europes-bad-loans-pay-again-717307/> accessed 22 July 2023.

[55] Lex Anastasiana C 4, 35, 22, cited in Reinhard Zimmermann, *The Law of Obligations. Roman Foundations of the Civilian Tradition* (Oxford UP 1990/96) 57–58, n 233.

[56] In 1991, a Danish local authority purchased a vehicle, marked it with the words 'Debt-collection', and parked it in front of citizens' residences to shame them into repaying their taxes. At the same time, the authority started mailing payment reminders, replacing unobtrusive envelopes with special ones printed with 'Debt-collection' in white on a red background. These practices, banned in private debt-collection since 1976, were challenged in front of the Parliamentary Ombudsman, who issued a decision that rendered it illegal. See: Hans Gammeltoft-Hansen, *The Danish Ombudsman 2005—50 Years—50 Cases* (Folketingets Ombudsman 2005) 139–140.

[57] One of the most egregious examples comes from Australia, where between 2015 and 2019, more than 440,000 welfare recipients were targeted by an unlawful debt-recovery scheme in what came to be known as the Robodebt scandal. The scheme was set up to boost the country's budget bottom line by recovering 1.7 billion Australian dollars in 'overpayments' to welfare recipients. Royal Commission into the Robodebt Scheme, 'Full Report' (*Commonwealth of Australia*, 7 July 2023) <https://robodebt.royalcommission.gov.au/system/files/2023-09/rrc-accessible-full-report.PDF> accessed 22 July 2024.

1.7 Methodology and Limits

This monograph employs a rigorous and multifaceted mixed-methods approach, befitting its aim to provide a definitive analysis of informal debt-collection in the EU. The methodology integrates exhaustive analysis of black letter laws, judicial decisions, and policy frameworks with extensive empirical research. It encompasses quantitative and qualitative data about the consumer credit market, the EU's NPL and debt markets, and the financial metrics of the debt-collection industry.

The study leverages a diverse array of data sources to shed light on the complex dynamics between the debt-collection industry and legislative bodies. These include official correspondences and surveys circulated among a broad spectrum of stakeholders, such as regulatory and supervisory agencies, debt-collection associations, and consumer protection organizations. Additionally, the methodology incorporates interviews and informal discussions with high-ranking representatives of EU institutions, specifically the Directorate-General for Financial Stability, Financial Services, and Capital Markets Union, members of the European Parliament, and prominent figures in the debt-collection sector.

Given the sensitivity and opacity of certain topics, this monograph transcends conventional academic sources by utilizing non-traditional channels. These include social media analyses, investigative journalism, and data mining techniques, ensuring a comprehensive examination of the subject matter.

The book deliberately features overlapping sections, reflecting the interconnected nature of the topics discussed. For instance, references to the 2002 CCD Proposal and the 2021 CSCPD appear throughout the text, underscoring the multifaceted influences and relationships among regulatory and industry practices. This approach enhances the coherence and depth of the analysis, illustrating the pervasive impact of legislative and regulatory frameworks on informal debt-collection practices.

This monograph aims to illuminate critical issues affecting the governance of informal debt-collection in the EU and its MS while being aware of the potential of exhaustive legal and policy analysis to veer into dogmatism. The ultimate objective is to provoke a meaningful legislative response that addresses these issues with precision and efficacy.

1.8 Roadmap

The remainder of the monograph is structured into four parts, comprising fifteen chapters and culminating in a conclusion. Every chapter meticulously dissects one fundamental aspect of the overarching argument.

In **Part I: Conceptual Foundation**, Chapters II–IV introduce readers to informal debt-collection and its role within the broader contexts of finance, credit, and enforcement. It establishes the conceptual grounds necessary for understanding the subsequent analytical sections, underscoring the theoretical and practical significance of the topic. Chapter II traces the evolution of debt-collection practices from ancient times to the present day, highlighting critical transitions from body-based to asset-based enforcement. It also examines the development of modern debt-collection agencies and the impact of technological advancements. The chapter explores the foundational concepts of money, credit, and security interests, explaining their interconnections and relevance to debt-collection. Chapter III delves into debt assignment and commodification, explaining how debts are transformed into tradeable assets. It examines the legal, ethical, and social implications of treating debt as property, emphasizing the role of legal fictions in facilitating debt commodification. The chapter also comprehensively analyses the legal framework governing debt commodification in the EU, including the Court of Justice of the European Union's (CJEU) stance on trading debts. Chapter IV concludes the conceptual framework by discussing the general role of debt-collection in the financial system, differentiating between formal and informal practices. The chapter addresses the impact of debt-collection on financial stability, consumer protection, and the broader economy, emphasizing the importance of regulatory oversight to prevent abusive practices and ensure fair treatment of debtors.

Part II: Empirical Landscape comprises Chapters V–IX. This part provides a comprehensive empirical background, detailing the key actors—consumers, businesses, and industry associations—and the landscape of credit and utility markets. It examines the socioeconomic effects of indebtedness on the economy and individual lives, highlighting the interplay between these markets and the financial system, with a particular focus on the regulatory needs of informal debt-collection. It also reveals the influence of the debt-collection industry and how it has been used to curb potentially threatening regulation. Chapter V initiates the discussion by examining the growth and impact of consumer credit and utility markets in Europe, from the emergence of consumer credit markets in the 1980s to the contemporary era. It investigates the role of consumer credit in economic development and the challenges posed by over-indebtedness. The chapter scrutinizes the impact of utility bill debt claims and the financial crisis on European economies, highlighting the need for responsible arrears management and regulatory intervention. Chapter VI addresses the issue of consumer over-indebtedness in the EU and the lack of adequate legislative responses at the MS level. It explores the profile of over-indebted consumers, the impact of the 2008 financial crisis, and proposed measures for responsible arrears management. Additionally, it discusses the exacerbation of abusive industry practices and the effects of the COVID-19 pandemic on consumer debt, presenting policy recommendations for handling debtors fairly. Chapter VII offers an overview of the debt markets, focusing on the NPL and debt-collection markets. It scrutinizes the growth of secondary markets for NPLs and the role of debt purchasers in the financial system. In direct continuation, Chapter

VIII identifies the key actors in the debt-collection market, including regional and national associations, multinational corporations, and debt-collection agencies. It examines the role of prominent players in shaping industry practices and influencing regulatory policies. The chapter also considers the impact of market concentration on competition and consumer protection. It comprehensively analyses the market structure and key actors' influence on debt-collection regulation. Finally, Chapter IX examines the challenges to reform and the role of industry lobbying in hindering effective regulation. It presents a detailed analysis of regulatory failures at the EU level, emphasizing the need for greater transparency and accountability in the legislative process.

Part III: Legal Analysis consists of Chapters X–XIII and offers a thorough legal examination of debt-collection regulation at the EU level. The analysis reveals how fragmented regulations, institutional weaknesses, and inconsistent enforcement mechanisms compromise consumer protection against abusive informal debt-collection. Each chapter addresses a specific legal instrument applicable to informal debt-collection practices. Chapter X looks at abusive informal debt-collection practices within the framework of the UCPD. It explores the CJEU's interpretation of the UCPD concerning informal debt-collection and its implications for consumer protection. Chapter XI analyses the influence of the CCD on debt-collection practices, focusing on the role of debt-collectors as credit intermediaries. It examines a key CJEU ruling concerning debt-collection agencies' potential obligations towards consumers and its implications for future regulation. Chapter XII investigates the connection between the UCTD and debt-collection practices. It thoroughly discusses the CJEU's interpretation of unfairness regarding contract terms in the context of debt-collection. Chapter XIII dissects the influence of the GDPR on informal debt-collection practices, emphasizing privacy concerns and data-protection issues. It considers the GDPR's implications for consumer protection and the necessity of regulatory oversight to prevent the misuse of personal data.

Part IV: Policy Implications encompasses Chapters XIV–XVI and delves into policy issues engendered by the CSCPD. It discusses the rationale behind the directive, the legal intricacies it introduces for consumers, and the challenges associated with its enforcement. The analysis extends to broader policy implications, advocating for comprehensive reforms to enhance consumer protection and regulatory oversight. Chapter XIV analyses the CSCPD's impact on debt-collection practices and consumer protection. It emphasizes that the directive's primary goal is to facilitate the growth of secondary debt markets, with consumer protection measures taking on a secondary role. Chapter XV furthers this argument by examining the prohibited behaviours outlined in the CSCPD and their implications for debt-collection regulation and consumer protection. Lastly, Chapter XVI explores the supervision and compliance mechanisms delineated in the CSCPD, including contractual and administrative supervision requirements and enforcement challenges related to consumer protection.

Instead of merely summarizing the book's findings, the Conclusion applies Ehrlich and Posner's economic theory of law-making to critically evaluate the regulatory landscape. It explores alternative explanations for the EU and national legislators' reluctance to implement sectoral regulations for informal debt-collection, offering well-founded policy recommendations to address the systemic deficiencies identified throughout the study.

II
HISTORICAL AND CONCEPTUAL BACKGROUND OF DEBT-COLLECTION

2.1 A Brief History of Debt-collection

Exploring their historical development facilitates a better understanding of present-day informal debt-collection methods and their lasting influence on society. From the very inception of money, the practice of collecting debts without resorting to legal or official channels has been prevalent. Those to whom money was owed often found it more convenient and expedient to handle debt-collection on their own, bypassing formal procedures.

In Europe, evidence of this phenomenon dates back to the Roman Empire, where state claims were bought by public companies, known as *societas publicanorum*, who used non-judicial methods to recover them.[1] This led to the introduction of the first rules for safeguarding debtors from abusive debt-collection practices.[2]

The Middle Ages witnessed the continuation of debt recovery, marked by the widespread employment of self-help methods. Recent scholarly investigations have highlighted the persistent efforts of creditors to seek repayment, indicating that they

> [d]id not have to seek the services of the court ... they simply walked into the houses of their debtors and took all that they fancied, daring their victims to do something about it ... whatever the frequency, the mere existence of the practice is a reminder that debt-collection ... was hardly a monopoly of the courts of law ... The process was swift and unfussy. It may have been deeply satisfying as well.[3]

[1] Juan Javier del Granado, 'The Genius of Roman Law from a Law and Economics Perspective' (2011) 13 San Diego International Law Journal 301, 322.

[2] Hanina Ben-Menahem and Neil S. Hecht, *Topics in Jewish Law* (The Open University of Israel Publishing House 1993) 648.

[3] Daniel Lord Smail, *Legal Plunder: Households and Debt Collection in Late Medieval Europe* (Harvard UP 2016) 137.

EU Informal Debt-Collection Regulation. Cătălin-Gabriel Stănescu, Oxford University Press.
 DOI: 10.1093/oso/9780198966159.003.0002

The historical evidence demonstrates that economic coercion, such as repossession of movable property or houses, evictions, and the large body of repo men and debt-collection agencies have a long-standing presence.[4] Although informal debt-collection practices have always existed, what has changed is the degree to which they impact debtors' lives.[5]

2.1.1 From body-based to asset-based debt enforcement (1850–1900)

The shift from body-based to asset-based debt enforcement was a pivotal moment that laid the groundwork for modern debt-collection practices. Understanding this evolution is essential for analysing current regulatory challenges.

From the mid-1800s, the organized debt-collection industry began to take shape in Europe, with businesses emerging to assist creditors in recouping debts. During this period, nearly all European states eliminated debtor prisons.[6] Before this shift, creditors wielded the authority to imprison, enslave, or use force to compel debtors or their loved ones to repay their debt.[7] Prisons were tasked with monitoring and pressuring inmates to pay, coercing debtors into selling their property to cover the debt, or persuading their family and friends to pay on their behalf.[8]

During the mid-1800s, debtor prisons, which were prevalent across various regions, religions, and forms of governance, began to be widely seen as a tradition incompatible with the principles of enlightened societies.[9] In addition to this ethical consideration, there was a practical drawback: the cost of incarcerating debtors had to be borne by the creditor or the state. This became economically untenable, primarily when the debtor could not repay the debt in the first place. Furthermore, imprisonment hindered debtors from contributing to society through work, making it impossible for them to generate funds and undermining the original justification for their confinement.

France was the first of the current European Union (EU) member states (MS) to permanently ban debtor prisons, in 1867,[10] after having previously attempted to do so during the Revolution (1793–97) and the Second Republic (1848).[11]

[4] ibid 14.

[5] Joe Deville, *Lived Economies of Default* (Routledge 2015) 80–81.

[6] Gustav Peebles, 'Washing Away the Sins of Debt: The Nineteenth-Century Eradication of the Debtors' Prison' (2013) 55(3) Comparative Studies in Society and History 701.

[7] Finance Watch, 'From Debtor Prisons to Being Prisoners of Debt. Making the Case for Harmonised EU Consumer Insolvency Rules' (*Finance Watch*, January 2022) <https://www.finance-watch.org/wp-content/uploads/2022/01/Personal-insolvency-paper-january-2022.pdf> accessed 30 January 2024.

[8] Sarah Balakrishnan, 'The Jailhouse Divergence: Why Debtors' Prisons Disappeared in 19th Century Europe and Flourished in West Africa' (2022) 24(5) Punishment & Society 807, 812.

[9] Peebles (n 6) 715.

[10] ibid 702, n 5. See also: Julie Claustre, 'La dette, la haine et la force: les débuts de la prison pour dette à la fin du Moyen Âge' (2007) 644 Revue historique 797, 797.

[11] Jacques Hillairet, *Gibets, piloris et cachots du vieux Paris* (Éditions de Minuit 1956).

Following France's lead, several other nations also ended the practice: Germany in 1868,[12] England in 1869,[13] Austria and Belgium in 1871,[14] Denmark in 1872,[15] and Finland in 1895.[16]

However, not all countries were as progressive in this regard. For example, three years before France permanently abolished debtors' prisons, the new state of Romania[17] passed a law establishing them in 1864.[18] It was not until 1912 that Romania abolished debtor prisons.[19] England also provides an interesting example. Although debtors could no longer be incarcerated for non-payment of debts after 1869, they could still be imprisoned for failing to comply with a court order to settle a debt (in legal terms, for 'contempt of court').[20] This continued until the early 1970s.[21] Remarkably, this practice endures in Ireland to this day.[22]

Despite the exceptions noted above, debtor prisons had become outdated in Europe by the late 1800s. Consequently, creditors had to develop alternative approaches to recover debts. Instead of incarcerating debtors, attention turned to their income and property, which could be more readily seized through new legal mechanisms.[23]

The transition from focusing on the debtor's person to their assets proved more financially beneficial, signalling the onset of a new phase in debt recovery. Nowadays, the limited number of scholars researching this era often credit this significant shift with the swift ascent of the debt-collection industry, implying a direct correlation rather than mere coincidence.

The emergence of European collection agencies also dates back to the late 1800s. In France, there are indications that Eugene Francois Vidocq, a reformed criminal turned criminalist, may have used his private detective agency for debt-collection.[24] In Germany, these agencies evolved from credit-reporting organizations based on American and English models, with the first agency being established in 1872.[25] In

[12] Peebles (n 6) 702, n 5.
[13] ibid.
[14] ibid.
[15] ibid.
[16] ibid.
[17] The modern state of Romania is the direct result of the union of Walachia and Moldova in 1859.
[18] Law No 1124/1864 published in the Official Gazette of Romania, Part I of 1 September 1864 (Romania).
[19] Law No 1124/1864 was abrogated on 21 October 1912.
[20] Paul Rock, Making People Pay (Routledge 1973) 156, n 3, 190.
[21] Deville (n 5) 78.
[22] Finance Watch (n 7) 4.
[23] Daisy Sainsbury, 'Eugène-François Vidocq and the Birth of the Detective' (*The Public Domain Review*, 7 February 2024) <https://publicdomainreview.org/essay/eugene-francois-vidocq-and-the-birth-of-the-detective/> accessed 22 July 2024.
[24] Bertrand Mazuir, 'Le recouvrement à travers l'Histoire—Partie 1' (*Le Blog du Recouvrement*, 2016) <http://www.leblogdurecouvrement.com/le-recouvrement-a-travers-lhistoire-partie-1/> accessed 20 December 2023.
[25] Timo Raffael Beck, *Inkassounternehmen und der Erfolg beim Forderungseinzug* (Springer 2013) 23.

Denmark, the oldest debt-collection agency, Købmandsstandens Inkassoservice As, can be traced back to 1870.[26]

2.1.2 The emergence of the modern debt-collection agency (1900–50)

Debt-collection became more widespread before and after the First World War, primarily due to changing economic conditions and the growing popularity of instalment sales. Although commonplace in modern society, buying in instalments was a new concept, allowing purchasers to make payments at regular intervals instead of paying the total cost upfront. Initially, this option was only accessible to the wealthy as credit and trade still relied on personal connections, reputation, and income.[27] It was a privilege and a convenience, not a necessity. Like banking, debt-collection was carried out through personal interactions such as letters and in-person visits.[28]

In this era, debt-collection agencies focused on recovering overdue amounts, making it their core business. Some of today's leading companies in the European debt-collection industry were established during this time. Swedish company Intrum, the largest debt-collection company in the EU (see Chapter VIII, Subsection 8.3.1), was founded in 1923.[29] Independent debt-collection entities also emerged in France and Germany in the 1920s.[30] Around the same time, debt-collectors began to establish industry associations, signalling their increasing recognition as a legitimate industry, with national associations forming in France in 1936.[31]

2.1.3 Post-war expansion (1950–90)

Following the Second World War, debt-collection industries experienced substantial growth on both sides of the Atlantic, with the United States (US) taking the lead.[32] The expansion of consumer credit led to a rise in late payments, creating favourable conditions for debt-collectors. Credit historians emphasize that

[26] Jørn Busch Olsen, 'Købmandstandens OplysningsBureau' (*Den Store Danske*) <https://denstoredanske.lex.dk/Købmandstandens_OplysningsBureau> accessed 22 July 2024.

[27] Scott B MacDonald and Albert L Gastman, *A History of Credit & Power in the Western World* (Routledge 2017) 6–7, 193. See also: Rosa-Maria Gelpi and François Julien-Labruyère, *The History of Consumer Credit. Doctrines and Practices* (Palgrave Macmillan 2000) 113, 129.

[28] Deville (n 5).

[29] Intrum, *Leading the Way to a Sound Economy since 1923* (Business History Publishing 2023) 18.

[30] Waldemar Koch, *Das Abzahlungsgeschäft in Handel und Industrie und seine Finanzierung* (Springer 1931) 136–38; Mazuir (n 24).

[31] FIGEC, 'Nos Missions' (*FIGEC*) https://www.figec.com/nos-missions/ accessed 22 July 2024.

[32] Deville (n 5) 81–89.

the introduction of credit cards profoundly impacted the consumer credit market, gaining widespread use in the US in the 1960s[33] and later in Europe in the 1990s.[34]

The accessibility of credit for consumption, once exclusive to the upper classes, resulted in a 'democratization of credit'.[35] This trend coincided with substantial growth in the debt-collection industry and clientele. As more companies grappled with late payments or non-payment from customers, they sought assistance from debt-collection agencies.

The evolution of recovery methods mirrored the growth and change in the industry. While letters remained a common form of communication, they became more standardized and less personalized.[36] The telephone began to play a more significant role in long-distance collection, gradually replacing in-person visits. In Europe, telephones were adopted in the 1960s, whereas they were already used in the 1940s in the US.[37] The US debt-collection industry was an early adopter of automation, with evidence showing that IBM machines were used to assist in the debt recovery process in the 1960s.[38] The computerization of debt-collection became a reality in Europe in the 1980s, but it was not fully embraced until the 2000s.[39]

In the 1940s, the US debt-collection industry began to integrate principles of psychology and behaviourism into its strategies.[40] This shift led to more sophisticated training for debt-collectors and recovery rates. Additionally, collectors learned to structure their interactions to evoke emotional responses, often leading to heightened anxiety for debtors, which pressured them to repay.[41]

In this regard, Europe fell behind the US. The continent was recovering from the aftermath of the Second World War, and its consumer credit industry did not emerge until the late 1970s.[42] During this time, several debt-collection agencies gained prominence in the European market, such as the German champion EOS, which was established in 1974 (see Chapter VIII, Subsection 8.3.2).[43] The first

[33] Jonathan Levy, *Ages of American Capitalism. A History of the United States* (Random House 2021); Deville (n 5) 84.

[34] Sarah Brown, *The Regulation of Consumer Credit. A Transatlantic Analysis* (Edward Elgar 2019) 22–23; Akos Rona-Tas and Alya Guseva, *Plastic Money. Constructing Markets for Credit Cards in Eight Postcommunist Countries* (Stanford UP 2014) 13.

[35] MacDonald and Gastman (n 27) 217–35; Lendol Calder, *Financing the American Dream. A Cultural History of Consumer Credit* (Princeton UP 1999) 37; Gelpi and Julien-Labruyère (n 27) 100; Steven Finlay, *Consumer Credit Fundamentals* (Palgrave Macmillan 2005) 23, 25.

[36] Deville (n 5) 90–91, 131.

[37] ibid 84.

[38] ibid 85–87.

[39] ibid 88–89.

[40] ibid 92–103.

[41] ibid 98–102.

[42] Gelpi and Julien-Labruyère (n 27) 129–48; Rebecca Belvederesi-Kochs, 'Moral or Modern Marketing? Sparkassen and Consumer Credit in West Germany' in Jan Logemann (ed), *The Development of Consumer Credit in Global Perspective: Business, Regulation, and Culture* (Palgrave Macmillan 2012) 46–55.

[43] EOS, 'Homepage' (*EOS*) <https://de.eos-solutions.com/en/eos-deutschland-b2c> accessed 22 July 2024.

sector-specific laws dedicated to informal debt-collection were enacted in Sweden (1974)[44] and the United Kingdom (1974).[45]

The advancement of technology within the industry, along with its workforce's increasing knowledge and skills, allowed collectors to efficiently reach many debtors with reduced resources, resulting in a significant increase in revenues. Once the correlation between technology and profitability was recognized, the shift from using computers to automate and handle collection notices to employing statistical modelling and econometric analysis to evaluate collection probabilities and project returns became relatively seamless.

2.1.4 The era of technology and new business models (1990–present)

As the turn of the millennium approached, collectors' business models expanded significantly. This growth was fuelled not only by the widespread global adoption of consumer credit (referred to by academics as 'globalization' and 'financialization') but also by the rapid expansion of the internet, advancements in technology, and the enactment of national legislation. The late twentieth century saw a revolutionary transformation in the debt-collection industry with the rise of debt purchasing.

One noteworthy outcome of this development was the appearance of European debt-purchasing companies. These companies were a new type of entity, modelled after American ones.[46] Previously, lenders had two choices: handle the debt-collection themselves or transfer it to a collection agency operating on commission. In the traditional setup, the lender retained ownership of the debt while the collector received a percentage of the recovered amount on the creditor's behalf. Debt buyers operated differently: they purchased portfolios of 'bad' debt, effectively becoming the creditor, and then used collection agencies, often after employing sophisticated statistical and econometric tools to identify the receivables most likely to be collected,[47] or pursued the accounts themselves.

In the early days, debt purchasers were primarily investment funds seeking quick and substantial returns. However, today's debt-collection agencies assume

44 Inkassolag (1974:182) (Sweden) <http://rkrattsbaser.gov.se/sfst?bet=1974:182> accessed 22 July 2024.

45 Consumer Credit Act 1974 (United Kingdom) <https://www.legislation.gov.uk/ukpga/1974/39/contents/enacted> accessed 22 July 2024.

46 Deville (n 5) 113.

47 Lukasz A Drozd and Ricardo Serrano-Padial, 'Modelling the Revolving Revolution: The Debt Collection Channel' (2017) 107(3) The American Economic Review 897, 898–99; Johannes Kriebel and Kevin Yam, 'Forecasting Recoveries in Debt Collection: Debt Collectors and Information Production' (2020) 26 European Financial Management 537.

a dual role and rely on intricate corporate structures to acquire debt portfolios, which they then endeavour to collect while minimizing or evading taxation on their profits.[48] Since the late 1990s, they have gained a significant foothold in the European debt-collection market.

Another significant change is that debt-collection, whether carried out by debt buyers or collection agencies, has become less personal. This shift to remote collection is driven by technological advancements and logistical constraints, particularly the large number of debtors being pursued. The days of debt-collectors knocking on doors are all but over, although there are exceptions, as will be detailed in Chapter XII, Subsection 12.1. Furthermore, collectors seek to avoid legal action for as long as possible, especially if the outstanding amounts are small. Instead, they attempt to secure payments through letters, phone calls, and, more recently, social media, even though the latter is still frowned upon in Europe.[49]

As the twentieth century drew to a close, debt-collection became a global industry. The collapse of communism in 1989 and the subsequent disintegration of the former Soviet bloc opened up Eastern European markets to credit products, paving the way for the establishment of debt-collection agencies in the region. Taking advantage of limited oversight, inexperienced supervisory bodies, and a lack of regulation, these agencies flourished. Furthermore, the expansion of the EU in the following decades led to cross-border consolidation and mergers of debt-collection agencies seeking to access international markets.

Today's debt-collection groups see all of Europe as their domain. The Swedish group Intrum is present in twenty European countries.[50] The German EOS, a competitor, has a network covering twenty-four European countries.[51] Generally, multinational debt-collection companies dominate the European market.[52] These companies heavily utilize big data and advanced algorithms to optimize their debt recovery rates.[53] Additionally, they continue to incorporate psychology and econometrics to gain insights into consumer-debtor behaviour. Contemporary collection methods rely on extensive data gathering and interpretation, standardization,

48 Cătălin Gabriel Stănescu and Camelia Bogdan, 'Regulatory Arbitrage and Non-Judicial Debt Collection in Central and Eastern Europe—Tax Sheltering and Money Laundering' (2021) 11(2) Accounting, Economics and Law: A Convivium 119.

49 Danish Consumer Ombudsman, Case 15/03102, 29 May 2015 (Denmark) <https://www.forbrugerombudsmanden.dk/find-sager/markedsfoeringsloven/sager-efter-markedsfoeringsloven/oevrige/kontakt-til-skyldnere-paa-facebook/> accessed 22 July 2024. The case held that contacting debtors via Facebook is contrary to good debt-collection practice.

50 Intrum, 'About our company' (*Intrum*) <https://www.intrum.com/about-us/company-info/about-our-company/> accessed 22 July 2024.

51 EOS, 'EOS Worldwide' (*EOS*) <https://eos-solutions.com/worldwide-companies> accessed 22 July 2024.

52 A counterexample, however, is that of Germany. The country has more than 926 debt-collection agencies, most domestic, small (five or fewer employees), and regionally active, retaining their traditional local character. See: Listflix, 'Inkassounternehmen Statistik Deutschland' (*Listflix*) <https://listflix.de/statistik/inkassounternehmen/> accessed 22 July 2024.

53 Drozd and Serrano-Padial (n 47) 898–99.

algorithmic scoring, and debtor profiling (see Chapter VIII, Section 8.3 and Chapter XIII).[54]

However, some debt-collectors have exploited technological innovation to circumvent old, static legal protections.[55] Present-day deceptive practices and breaches of privacy include the use of devices that conceal or alter the caller's ID, deceptive data gathering, leveraging social media to shame consumers into paying debts, outsourcing consumer-debtor databases, and targeting specific groups of debtors who are more likely to pay, such as women and elderly individuals.[56] As regulatory responses often lag behind technological advancements, these emerging threats remain unresolved within existing legal frameworks, and consumer-debtors are vulnerable to targeted and abusive practices not yet covered by the law. While some in the industry aim to modernize and humanize their collection methods, others operate at the fringes of legality and ethical standards.

Against this historical backdrop, I now turn to the concepts of money and credit, which are essential to grasping the broader economic implications of debt and the various forms it can take.

2.2 Money and Credit

The legal concept of money has been extensively studied.[57] Although the book does not aim to explore this concept thoroughly, it is essential to understand the functions of money concerning credit, security interests, and enforcement, including debt-collection. Scholars have identified three main functions of money: (a) a means of exchange; (b) a measure of value; and (c) a store of value.[58] The first two are particularly relevant to our topic. Money has supplanted barter as a means of exchange, serving as a tool for making payments for goods and services. Additionally, as a measure of value, money can represent records in an account, such as debts owed to a customer when the account is in credit or a loan to be repaid by the customer when the account is in debit.

Originally, money existed in physical forms, such as coins or banknotes, for trading purposes. Despite the constant increase in the amount of money in circulation, the demand for money continued to rise, leading to the rapid expansion of credit.[59] In essence, credit has been an integral part of markets for as long as they

[54] Kriebel and Yam (n 47).

[55] Cătălin Gabriel Stănescu, 'Digital Debt Collection. Opportunities, Abuses and Concerns' in Cătălin Gabriel Stănescu and Adimi A. Gikay (eds), *Discrimination, Vulnerable Consumers and Financial Inclusion. Fair Access to Financial Services and the Law* (Routledge 2021) 185–205.

[56] Lauren Goldberg, 'Dealing in Debt: The High-Stakes World of Debt Collection after FDCPA' (2006) 79 Southern California Law Review 736, 736–38.

[57] Simon Gleeson, *The Legal Concept of Money* (OUP 2018).

[58] ibid 7–8. See also: Alastair Hudson, *The Law of Finance* (Sweet & Maxwell 2009) 39–51.

[59] Craig Muldrew, *The Economy of Obligation: The Culture of Credit and Social Relations in Early Modern England* (Basingstoke 1998) 100; Gleeson (n 57) 49.

have existed, and it is crucial for economic growth because the number of transactions surpasses the available physical currency.[60] This underscores the consequential connection between money and credit.[61] Given that physical money is always insufficient, the importance of credit grows, serving as a bridge between people and businesses.

If credit was considered a convenience in its early days, in the second half of the twentieth century, borrowing began to be viewed as a necessity to achieve better living standards and economic growth. This shift attracted commercial banks to the personal credit market, making them the primary credit providers to consumers. However, it also brought challenges, such as vulnerability, over-indebtedness (see Chapter VI), and exploitation through unfair practices and contract terms (see Chapters X and XII). As a result, legislators must establish consumer protection regulations ensuring a fair balance between the rights of creditors to conduct business and be paid and the rights of debtors to be treated fairly before, during, and after entering a credit agreement.[62]

Hence, scholars have concluded that the settlement of economic transactions involves a complex web of credit and obligation.[63] In cases where cash is unavailable,[64] debts remain unsettled and the web becomes more complex with each transaction. Any missing link threatens the entire system because, in a credit-driven economy, all economic actors rely on each other.[65] For instance, when A owes money to B and B owes money to C, if A cannot pay B, then B cannot pay C.

Consequently, any default will likely affect more than one actor and may trigger a chain reaction with severe economic consequences, especially when debtors are consumers.[66] This may be why many societies deem debt repayment not just a legal but also a moral obligation.[67] The moral stance legitimizes the debt-collection industry. It adds further pressure on the debtors because not only the creditor but also society itself expects them to repay their debts, whether or not they can.[68]

In general, every individual is, to some extent, involved in providing and receiving credit. This implies that depending on the situation, one may act as a lender, a borrower, neither, or both. The credit supply can be illustrated as follows.

[60] Gleeson (n 57) 48.

[61] The term 'credit' has multiple meanings. However, in this context, it is understood to mean either a loan of money (loan credit) or the deferment of a payment obligation (sale credit).

[62] Brown (n 34) 38–39.

[63] Muldrew (n 59) 95.

[64] Lack of cash can result from the physical unavailability of fiat money, which is insufficient to cover the sum of the transactions, or, more importantly, from the fact that debts exceed the available income (in which case penalties start to accrue), leading to missed payments.

[65] Gleeson (n 57) 49.

[66] Brown (n 34) 1. According to Brown, the inability to pay debts can lead to insolvency, hardship for individuals and families, loss of homes, and a significant decrease in quality of life.

[67] Gleeson (n 57) 49. For a very long time, default on debt was also considered a crime. Brown (n 34) 21; Deville (n 5) 74–81.

[68] Guido Comparato, *The Financialisation of the Citizen: Social and Financial Inclusion through European Private Law* (Hart Publishing 2018) 1.

Due to the rapid increase in international trade and technological development, the pool of potential business partners has expanded considerably. However, this reduces the willingness of both companies and consumers to extend credit due to trust issues.[69] When offering credit to a known local debtor within the same jurisdiction, the creditor faces manageable risks. However, the situation is different when dealing with an unknown foreign debtor situated in a distant jurisdiction.[70] Any credit transaction that goes beyond the local knowledge and trust of the creditor is encumbered by risks that the creditor is unwilling to assume.[71] One solution to this issue is to secure payment.[72]

In conclusion, credit plays a pivotal role in fostering economic growth, although it is accompanied by inherent risks that require the implementation of robust debt-collection mechanisms. The next section presents an in-depth analysis of security interests, examining the measures employed by creditors to mitigate these risks.

2.3 Security Interests

Understanding the mechanisms that ensure debt repayment is crucial for explaining the significance of creditor protections and their role in maintaining financial stability. As evidenced in the previous section, if a debtor lacks financial resources, the creditor will not receive payments. The creditor's risk is thus essentially tied to the debtor's capacity to pay. To protect themselves against the debtor's insolvency or refusal to pay, creditors can establish a legal mechanism, namely, a security interest giving them recourse to specific property owned by the debtor to satisfy their right to receive payment.[73]

Various forms of security, such as mortgages, charges, liens, and pledges, can be categorized into two groups: the reified *promise to pay* and the reified *instruction to pay*.[74] The crucial aspect is the transferability of the reified promise to pay to a third

[69] Brown (n 34) 69.

[70] This issue is one of the main obstacles to completing the banking union: even if secured, creditors remain reluctant to grant credits outside their national boundaries. Among the reasons invoked is the uncertainty and difficulty of monitoring or enforcing against the collateral due to differences between legal systems. Thus, financiers push for more harmonization of enforcement to ease and speed up recovery in case of default. At the same time, a market where consumers are free to choose among financial products based on the best offered terms would not benefit the financial sector, which makes significant profits from hedging loans. Credit institutions borrow cheaply and loan expensively, pocketing the difference. Some also expatriate the profits back to their mother companies, which have no incentive to compete at the EU level.

[71] Gleeson (n 57) 56. See also: Tibor Tajti, *Comparative Secured Transactions Law* (Akademiai Kiado 2002) 65–66.

[72] Tajti (n 71) 66–67 and the literature referenced there.

[73] Hudson (n 58) 19–20.

[74] Gleeson (n 57) 56–57. See also: Roy Goode and Ewan McKendrick, *Commercial Law* (Penguin 2016) 501.

party without restriction.[75] This means that although the third party may still have to pursue the original promisor, there is no requirement for a prior relationship between them. Transferability underpins all debt assignments or transfers (see Chapter III), which are also seen as the potential solution for restoring stability to the EU's financial system under the Credit Servicers and Credit Purchasers Directive.[76]

Irrespective of their form or nature, securities serve multiple functions: (a) a security function; (b) a marketing function; (c) an economic function; and (d) a remedial function.[77] The security and remedial functions are particularly relevant to the present book. The *security* function ensures that in the event of a default, the secured creditor will have a preferred claim over other creditors or the debtor's trustee, thereby reducing the risk of non-payment. The *remedial* function allows the creditor to ascertain their rights and remedies through the agreement entered with the debtor. Their combination places the debtor under a constant threat of enforcement, strengthening the latter's commitment to repay. Additionally, depending on the applicable law, the secured creditor may be permitted to take possession of the collateral without having to involve the court or employ the services of a state agent, which increases the efficiency of enforcement while reducing its costs.

Securities also play a crucial role in secured debt financing, which appears in various forms in market economies and even forms entire industries, such as factoring.[78] In this scenario, the collateral can take the form of receivables, which can be outright discharged to reduce indebtedness, discounted, or used as security to obtain immediate cash.[79]

Building on this discussion of security interests, the next section examines how debts are enforced, covering the various debt enforcement methods and highlighting the differences and implications of judicial and non-judicial approaches.

[75] Gleeson also shows that moneylenders are traders in credit risk and their fundamental business proposition is exactly that of a bookmaker or an insurance policy: the amount they receive for taking a portfolio of risks will exceed the losses resulting from the crystallization of some of those risks. Conversely, if participants in the economy can transfer their debts to a specialist debt trader, and the specialist debt trader can construct a properly diversified portfolio, the cost of credit provision by that credit trader will be substantially lower—at least in theory. In other words, the possibility to trade debt portfolios is beneficial for all parties involved. Gleeson (n 57) 62, 63.

[76] Directive (EU) No 2021/2167 on credit servicers and credit purchasers [2021] OJ L438 recitals 3, 5, and 18.

[77] Tajti (n 71) 68–76.

[78] ibid 77.

[79] ibid 78.

2.4 Enforcement

During any commercial transaction, a time gap may exist between the performance of its parts. This time gap gives rise to credit risk and necessitates efficient and affordable enforcement in case of default.

There are two types of enforcement. The rule is *judicial* enforcement, where interested parties bring their claims to court and, if successful, can use state agents to collect the debt. The exception is *non-judicial enforcement* (also referred to as *self-help*), where, if allowed by the law and agreed upon by the parties, the creditor can collect the debt or the collateral without court authorization and state agents' assistance.

Judicial enforcement is a last resort option and a stage where the creditor suffers greater vulnerability, especially in cases where the self-help option is unavailable. This is because creditors already face challenges due to the debtor's non-payment.

When creditors opt to pursue debtors in court, they incur additional expenses, such as judicial, attorney, and expert fees. Judicial enforcement typically involves time-consuming procedures and multiple stages, exposing the creditor to other risks, such as delays, debtor insolvency, or the potential rejection of their claim. Furthermore, given the significant volume of economic transactions worldwide, judicial enforcement also burdens the courts.[80]

The solution to these concerns lies in non-judicial enforcement, encompassing self-help and alternative dispute-resolution mechanisms. This approach promises better, faster, and more cost-effective outcomes with less stress and greater participant control.[81] Additionally, non-judicial enforcement can alleviate the courts' burden while ensuring that justice is served.[82]

This phenomenon of 'privatizing' the justice system is not a recent development and is not limited to a specific legal family or jurisdiction. As demonstrated in my previous work,[83] various self-help mechanisms, mainly passive forms,[84] are readily

[80] ibid 73.

[81] Trevor CW Farrow, *Civil Justice, Privatisation and Democracy* (University of Toronto Press 2014) 5.

[82] Tajti (n 71).

[83] Cătălin Gabriel Stănescu, *Self-Help, Private Debt Collection and the Concomitant Risks. A Comparative Law Analysis* (Springer 2015).

[84] The distinction between active and passive forms of self-help belongs to Rizoiu, who stated that despite civilian jurisdictions' wish to eliminate self-help practices, remnants are still found in contract law. He notably mentions the right to withhold performance and the right of retention. Rizoiu called these passive forms of self-help in the sense that the party resorting to them refuses to perform an action, for example, by denying the other party access to an asset or a right under his control. In contrast, historical self-help, from which the right of the secured creditor to take possession of the collateral by private means derives, is an active form of self-help, which implies the active involvement of the party exercising it: 'pulling', 're-possessing' an asset from the breaching debtor. It is this form of self-help that continental systems have tried to ban completely, especially after the appearance of the French Civil Code—until recently. Radu Rizoiu, *Garanții reale mobiliare. O abordare funcțională* (Universul Juridic 2011) 581.

identifiable in European jurisdictions spanning common and civil law countries (with a greater prevalence in the former).[85]

2.5 Summary

This chapter explored the evolution of debt-collection practices from their ancient origins to the sophisticated mechanisms employed in the modern era. By tracing the historical shifts from body-based to asset-based debt enforcement, it illuminated the development of debt-collection agencies and the impact of technological advancements and new business models. The chapter also examined the foundational concepts of money, credit, and security interests, which are essential for understanding the broader financial landscape. This historical and contextual overview sets the stage for a deeper analysis of contemporary debt-collection mechanisms and practices in the next chapter, which explores the complexities of debt assignment and debt commodification.

[85] Stănescu (n 83) 13–99.

III
DEBT TRADING IN THE EUROPEAN UNION

3.1 Debt Assignment

Debt assignment is a crucial process in modern finance. Understanding it is essential for discussing how debts are traded and managed. As mentioned previously, creditors face a choice when it comes to collecting debt: manage it internally (in-house) or outsource the process. Outsourcing may involve hiring a third party, such as a collection agency or a lawyer, to handle the collection (farming out) or entirely disposing of the debt by selling it on secondary markets (debt sale).

Generally, involving a third party in the collection process is referred to as debt assignment, although debt farm-outs are distinguished from debt sales, particularly in terms of debt ownership. With the former, the original creditor retains ownership of the debt; as a result, any debt-collection activities are carried out in their name. Conversely, with the former, debt ownership is transferred to the purchaser, who assumes responsibility for collection.

The voluntary assignment of debt refers to the process by which one creditor (assignor) transfers their contractual rights (claims) to a new one (assignee).[1] Once the assignment is completed, the new creditor is entitled to take legal action against the debtor for performance. Whether the assigned claims are performing or not is not relevant. However, in this book, assignment is assumed to refer to defaulted (non-performing) debts.

Rights to performance by a debtor (claims) are essential in domestic and international trade. Companies often utilize the assignment of claims to secure financing for their regular business operations and projects and to manage credit risks.[2] Consequently, the legal rules on the assignment of rights and claims are of considerable importance for various sectors of the economy, including the supply of goods and services, factoring, banking and finance, and debt-collection, which are interested in the smooth functioning of the assignment system.[3] Debtors are

[1] Marta Requejo Isidro, 'Assignability/Assignment of Claims' in Jürgen Basedow, Giesela Ruhl, Franco Ferrari, and Pedro De Miguel Asensio (eds), *Encyclopedia of Private International Law*, vol 1 (Edward Elgar 2017) 141. See also: Brigitta Lurger, 'Assignment' in Jan M Smits, Jaakko Husa, Catherine Valcke, and Madalena Narciso (eds), *Elgar Encyclopedia of Comparative Law* (Edward Elgar 2023) 152.

[2] Isidro (n 1) 142; Lurger (n 1) 152.

[3] Lurger (n 1) 152.

EU Informal Debt-Collection Regulation. Cătălin-Gabriel Stănescu, Oxford University Press.
 DOI: 10.1093/oso/9780198966159.003.0003

equally concerned with ensuring that their position remains unaffected by the assignment and with being able to prevent the assignment altogether.[4]

Differing national rules on the requirements and effects of assignments present a significant obstacle to cross-border trade.[5] This challenge is exacerbated by discrepancies in regulations concerning the transfer of titles in movable and intangible property, which can influence the validity of assignment transactions.[6] These contentious issues, which pertain to crucial aspects of the assignment process, create uncertainties and risks for parties involved in cross-border assignments, ultimately leading to increased operational costs.[7] Understandably, the European Union (EU) has taken steps to address these problems.[8]

Regulatory efforts, however, have only had partial success. The Rome I Regulation covers the question of applicable law, although not comprehensively and as clearly as stakeholders would have preferred.[9] The Principles of European Contract Law (PECL) on the assignment of claims[10] provide a comprehensive set of rules for contractual claims, including claims for payment of money, without distinguishing between domestic and cross-border transactions.[11] The Draft Common Frame of Reference (DCFR),[12] based in part on the PECL, also deals with contractual assignments of a right to the performance of an obligation.[13] Unlike the Rome I Regulation, the PECL and the DCFR are not formal sources of law. Still, parties can incorporate them into their agreements, and they may serve as model rules for future attempts to unify this area of law at the EU level.[14]

This section is not meant to provide an exhaustive overview of assignments but instead focuses on the relationship between the assignor, assignee, and debtor. In all jurisdictions, rights, including monetary claims, can be effectively assigned without the debtor's consent. However, all legal systems have provisions in place to ensure that the debtors' position, rights, and defences remain unchanged. Essentially, the debt cannot become more onerous than it would have been with

[4] ibid 153.

[5] Wolf-Georg Ringe, 'The Law of Assignment in European Contract Law' in Louise Gullifer and Stefan Vogenauer (eds), *English and European Perspectives on Contract and Commercial Law. Essays in Honour of Hugh Beale* (OUP 2014) 251–52; Lurger (n 1) 153.

[6] Lurger (n 1) 153.

[7] Isidro (n 1) 142.

[8] For a list of EU substantive rules aimed at harmonizing rules on assignments, see Isidro (n 1) 142–43.

[9] Ringe (n 5) 254–57; Isidro (n 1) 150–51; Lurger (n 1) 153.

[10] The Principles of European Contract Law, Chapter 11 <https://www.trans-lex.org/400200/_/pecl/> accessed 22 July 2024.

[11] Ringe (n 5) 258–89; Lurger (n 1) 154.

[12] The Draft Common Frame of Reference, Book III, Chapter 5, Section 1 <https://www.trans-lex.org/400725/_/outline-edition-/> accessed 22 July 2024.

[13] Ringe (n 5) 262–63.

[14] Lurger (n 1) 154.

the original assignor.[15] It is argued that the debtor should not face any disadvantages resulting from a transaction they cannot prevent. Consequently, the debtor can fulfil their obligation by paying the assignor before being notified of the assignment.[16] Furthermore, the debtor retains all defences against the claim that arise from the original legal relationship underlying the claim.[17] The preservation of the debtor's status pervades private international law solutions. It remains a first-rank principle in transnational cases, as the Credit Servicers and Credit Purchasers Directive (CSCPD) shows.[18]

The issue of assignability and its limits are a point of contention.[19] Scholars recognize that certain restrictions can be put in place to safeguard the debtor's interest for personal reasons or to prevent additional costs related to replacing the creditor. Such considerations drive legal limits based on the *intuitu personae* character of the obligation.[20]

English law is clear that a contract's benefit can only be assigned if it makes no difference to the person obligated to fulfil it.[21] It is up to the courts to determine whether an assignment makes any difference to the debtor based on objective grounds related to the contract's nature and subject matter. Nonetheless, it is widely accepted that money payments do not involve personal considerations[22] and can be assigned even if it would make a great deal of difference to a debtor whether his creditor is indulgent or likely to enforce his legal rights ruthlessly.[23] Thus, consumers cannot prevent the change in creditor for their financial obligations stemming from credit or utilities and can experience harsher and even abusive debt-collection from the side of the new creditor because monetary claims are not regarded as *intuitu personae.*

This approach marks a significant departure from the early tradition of assignment (called 'cession' in Roman law). According to early and classical Roman law, a highly personal obligation was not transferable.[24] Claims were closely tied to the specific creditor–debtor relationship, and changes could only be made through novation and procedural representation.[25] However, post-classical developments

[15] Isidro (n 1) 144, 146. For a similar principle in English law and the exceptions to it, see: Ben McFarlane, 'Assignment and Novation' in Hugh Beale (ed), *Chitty on Contracts*, vol 1 (23rd ed, Sweet and Maxwell 2023) 1906–07.

[16] Lurger (n 1) 158.

[17] Isidro (n 1) 144; Lurger (n 1) 158. However, the right to set off tends to be limited to claims that come into existence before the notification of the assignment.

[18] Directive (EU) No 2021/2167 on credit servicers and credit purchasers [2021] OJ L438 (CSCPD) recital 57 and art 28.

[19] Isidro (n 1) 145.

[20] Isidro (n 1) 145.

[21] *Tolhurst v Associated Portland Cement Manufacturers Ltd* [1902] 2 KB 660, 668; aff'd [1903] AC 414 (United Kingdom), cited in McFarlane (n 15) 1896.

[22] Guido Comparato, *The Financialisation of the Citizen: Social and Financial Inclusion through European Private Law* (Hart Publishing 2018) 1–2.

[23] McFarlane (n 15) 1896–97.

[24] Reinhard Zimmermann, *The Law of Obligations. Roman Foundations of the Civilian Tradition* (OUPUP 1990/96) 58–59.

[25] ibid 59–60.

in Roman law recognized that novation and procedural representation were not satisfactory alternatives to assignment. As a result, they increasingly allowed assignees to bring legal action in their name.[26]

In response to commercial interests, the view on transferring assets within a creditor's estate changed, leading to the abandonment of the Roman doctrine of cession.[27] Consequently, the nineteenth-century civil codes allowed, to various extents, the assignment of claims from the assignor to the assignee.[28] This period also saw the development of principles aimed at protecting debtors. With the accommodation of trade and commerce interests, the law began to address the situation of debtors who faced new creditors without having any say in the matter. To address this situation, limitations were imposed on the assignee's position in two key ways: the debtor should not be in a worse position after the claim has been assigned, and payment made to the assignor should discharge the obligation when the debtor was unaware of the assignment.[29]

In post-classical Roman law, there were also provisions to protect against professional claim purchasers who sought to profit from difficult economic circumstances. If they bought a claim for less than its actual value, they could not collect more from the debtor than they had actually paid.[30] This rule was not preserved in modern civil codes or English law, enabling the debt-collection industry to act unencumbered.

Yet, the idea is not entirely extinct, especially in EU jurisdictions that have struggled with the severe social effects of debt. Two proposals were put to the Romanian Parliament to limit the rights of debt purchasers to no more than twice the amount paid—although the proposals were deemed unconstitutional due to violations of parliamentary debate procedures, raising the question of whether they were meant to be adopted at all.[31] Greek experts consulted by the European Commission also suggested that debt purchasers lack the legitimacy to collect the face value of the debt when they have paid only a small fraction of it.[32]

The following section explores the next step in debt's lifecycle: its commodification. The transformation of debt into a tradeable asset impacts the way debt is managed and enforced.

[26] ibid 62–64.
[27] ibid 64–67.
[28] ibid 59.
[29] ibid 59.
[30] ibid 66. The provisions referred to stem from Lex Anastasiana C 4, 35, 22.
[31] Cătălin Gabriel Stănescu and Albert Albanezi, 'Romania's Struggle to Regulate Informal Debt Collection Practices' in Cătălin Gabriel Stănescu (ed), *Regulation of Debt Collection in Europe: Understanding Informal Debt Collection* (Routledge 2023).
[32] European Commission, 'Study on European Consumers' Over-indebtedness, and Its Implications. Final Report' (*European Commission*, June 2023) 251–52.

3.2 The Commodification of Debt

The commodification of debt refers to the transformation of non-performing loans (NPLs) and other forms of debt into marketable assets that can be traded on financial markets. This practice has gained momentum in recent years, providing opportunities and challenges for creditors and debtors alike. To fully convey the significance of debt commodification, the section begins by exploring its basic definition and relevance in today's financial markets.

3.2.1 The mechanisms of commodification

The ability to sell defaulted debts, individually or packed in portfolios, is a crucial aspect of the process referred to as 'propertization',[33] 'commodification', or 'financialization'. This capitalist process is described by Pistor as the shift of old coding techniques from tangible assets, such as land, to what economists call 'legal fictions': assets protected by corporate or trust veils and intangibles created in law.[34]

The concept of debt to which Pistor refers extends beyond the scope of this book, but the insights remain relevant. The path that led us here is also intriguing, and numerous attempts have been made to unravel it. Placing debt commodification in a historical context helps to appreciate the evolution from direct management of debts by original lenders to sophisticated secondary markets.

Ancient Roman law clearly distinguished between property rights (rights *in rem*) and contractual rights (rights *in personam*). According to this view, a debt resulting from a contract between a creditor and a debtor was considered a mere claim, that is, a contractual right (a right *in personam*). However, in the twentieth century this perspective was challenged by Wesley Hohfeld, who proposed a new concept of property rights.[35] Hohfeld suggested that property rights (rights *in rem*) should be seen as a subset of rights *in personam*, with the distinction between the two being primarily quantitative.[36] This led to an understanding of property as a collection of rights encompassing claims, duties, privileges, and liabilities, which could then be traded freely on the market, like any other commodity.[37] The transformation of debts into tradeable property had significant market implications,

[33] Jongchul Kim, 'Propertization: The Process by which Financial Corporate Power Has Risen and Collapsed' (2018) 1(3) Review of Capital as Power 58, 59. By 'propertization', Kim refers to the process by which what is not originally property becomes property. However, he argues that the propertization of contractual claims does not completely transform contracts into property but rather into Janus-faced hybrids of the two legal rights, which constantly change faces to enjoy the benefits and reduce the costs of both rights.

[34] Katharina Pistor, *The Code of Capital* (Princeton UP 2019) 13.

[35] Wesley Newcomb Hohfeld, *Fundamental Legal Conceptions as Applied in Judicial Reasoning and Other Legal Essays* (Yale UP 1923) 12–14.

[36] ibid 113–14.

[37] ibid 112–13.

enhancing liquidity and facilitating transactions while introducing new economic considerations.

3.2.2 Debt as tradeable property

Conceiving contractual claims (debts) as private property benefits the debt-collection system. It allows for the trading of debt, enhancing its liquidity and attractiveness. Viewing debt as property enables the separation of its price or 'market value' from its 'face value', simplifying NPL transactions by eliminating economic barriers. However, various consequences and legal fictions must be considered for such a system to function effectively.

The first fiction posits that financial obligations are inherently neutral rather than based on personal relationships (*intuitu personae*), thereby making the identity of the creditor inconsequential to the debtor. Nevertheless, one may question whether credit (and utility) agreements under EU law are of this nature. For instance, EU consumer credit law assumes that an average consumer has thoroughly evaluated all available offers and picked the best one based on a conscious and informed choice. Similarly, the lender is supposed to have assessed the consumer's creditworthiness, making an informed decision to extend credit. Thus, it could be argued that allowing debt assignments in such cases should not be permitted because they unilaterally alter the *intuitu personae* character of the agreement by substituting the consumer's chosen creditor with another one selected by the original creditor, thereby changing the envisioned relationship and annulling the consumer's informed choice.

The second fiction is that the original creditor can be satisfied with a significantly discounted market price for the debt from anyone but the debtor (see fourth fiction which follows). For instance, selling a debt with a face value of 100 for just 5 would be possible without prompting any concerns about its lack of consideration (legitimacy) or the underlying intent. This contradicts the traditional logic of assignments, whereby creditors received a substantial portion of the debt before the due date, improving their cash flow, whereas they now settle for an insolvency type of deal (cents on a euro).

The third fiction implies that debt buyers and only debt buyers (see fourth fiction) can minimize costs and maximize profits. Since the face value is distinct from the actual 'market value', a debt buyer who paid only a small fraction of the face value can still collect the total amount. The legal fiction here is that the variance between face and market values equals the risk and incentivizes those willing to assume it.

The fourth fiction in treating debt as property is that it can be traded using a contract and, therefore, be subjected to parties' will outside state or judicial control (see subsection 3.3). Consequently, the price can be determined by the market (essentially what the creditor and the purchaser agree on), meaning that the original creditor will be satisfied with accepting a fraction of the face value. However, if the debtors try to negotiate a reduction of the debt or repurchase it at the price offered by the purchaser (either by expressing intent or using protective regulation), they will be prevented from doing so because no one can be compelled to trade against their will. Any attempts to regulate this phenomenon would be seen as interfering with 'party autonomy' in the contract and restricting market freedom. For instance, this would not be allowed for real estate transactions where setting a small price would not enable parties to avoid taxes. Nevertheless, due to this fiction, consumers remain bound by the face value of the debt, and states accept the reduced tax base. Meanwhile, financial speculators can maximize their 'investment' returns by recovering more than the debt's so-called market value and operational costs.

Finally, sellers must receive certain benefits. For credit institutions, the advantage lies in freeing up significant amounts locked in provisions by removing NPLs from their balance sheets, enabling them to resume crediting activities and potentially become more profitable. This is another fiction because they can essentially *create more debt* at face value by discarding the existing debt at market value. To garner societal acceptance of this perpetual debt-creation mechanism, the narrative emphasizes the crucial role of financial institutions in providing credit to the economy and fostering job creation.[38]

These legal fictions raise critical questions about the fairness and regulatory oversight of debt commodification. The next section examines the role of financial institutions and regulatory bodies in shaping these practices.

3.2.3 The regulatory framework and state involvement

Highlighting the fictions that support the idea of debt as tradeable property serves to elucidate why major financial institutions and EU regulators are so deeply invested in promoting the establishment of a secondary debt market and facilitating its operations. When a competent authority grants authorization, it bestows the right to purchase NPL portfolios at market price and collect them at their face value. True to market considerations, the EU hypothesizes that this measure will drive competition, raise the market price closer to the face value, and enhance transparency and professionalism in debt-collection activities.[39] Nevertheless, protective measures for debtors remain scant and undeveloped.

[38] Johnna Montgomerie, *Should We Abolish Household Debts?* (Polity 2019) Section 'The Case against Abolishing Household Debt'; CSCPD (n 18) recitals 2 and 11.

[39] CSCPD (n 18) recitals 10, 11, and 38. See also: European Commission, Tackling non-performing loans in the aftermath of the COVID-19 pandemic, COM(2020)822, 16 December 2020, 7–9 and 11.

Financial investors are strongly motivated to establish effective debt-collection systems in all countries. Notably, they are interested in systems that recognize their ability to purchase debt at market value but recover it at face value and minimize disruptions, duplications, and administrative burdens. Following *Commission v Italy*, which recognized limited instances in which host states could impose additional authorization requirements on debt-collectors,[40] it became essential for debt-collectors to keep regulatory arbitrage and tax optimization options open. Additionally, the CSCPD's formal division between debt-collectors and debt buyers[41] allows the latter to avoid most of the negative reputational consequences of the business.

In *Code of Capital*, Pistor emphasized the pivotal role of states and state law in capital coding. 'Capital and capitalism would not exist without the coercive powers of the states',[42] she argued. However, this does not mean that states ultimately control the legal coding process. When it comes to finance and capital, states take a step back, providing the legal tools used by capitalists and their lawyers and offering their apparatus and sanctions to enforce the newly crafted capital.[43] States' unwavering support for debt commodification and their refusal to alter it perfectly illustrate Pistor's arguments.

In summary, the commodification of debt represents a significant transformation in financial markets, making careful consideration of its regulatory and ethical dimensions essential. States' endorsement of profit-making mechanisms at the expense of debtors underscores the complexity and far-reaching impact of these practices. This complexity is further highlighted when courts endorse these practices and refrain from subjecting them to judicial scrutiny, as demonstrated in the next section.

3.3 The Stance of the Court of Justice of the European Union on Trading Debts: *Banco Santander* and *Banco de Sabadell*

The CJEU addressed issues related to debt assignment under consumer loan agreements in joint cases C-96/16 and C-94/17.[44] The proceedings involved Banco Santander SA against Mahamadou Demba and Mercedes Godoy Bonet (C-96/16) and Rafael Ramón Escobedo Cortés against Banco de Sabadell SA (C-94/17).

[40] Case C-134/05 *Commission of the European Communities v Italian Republic* [2007] ECLI:EU:C:2007:435 para 26–31.

[41] CSCPD (n 18) arts 2 (6) and (8); Cătălin Gabriel Stănescu, 'The Impact of the Credit Servicing Directive on Regulating Abusive Informal Debt Collection in the European Union: A Step Forward or a Missed Opportunity?' (2023) 12(1) Journal of European Consumer and Market Law 4.

[42] Pistor (n 34) 19.

[43] ibid 20.

[44] Cases C-96/16 *Banco Santander SA v Mahamadou Demba, Mercedes Godoy Bonet* and C-94/17, *Rafael Ramón Escobedo Cortés v Banco de Sabadell SA* [2018] ECLI:EU:C:2018:643 (*Banco Santander*).

In Case C-96/16, Mr Demba and Ms Godoy Bonet had ceased payments on their loans, leading Banco Santander to declare the acceleration of the maturity dates, which also attracted penalty interest rates, and assign their debts to a third party for a sum significantly lower than the outstanding amount.

This assignment occurred without their knowledge or consent and without offering them the opportunity to buy back their debts by reimbursing the assignee the price paid plus interest and costs.[45] The referring court raised doubts about the compliance of this practice with EU law, mainly the Unfair Terms in Consumer Contracts (UCTD), in the absence of a specific contractual provision allowing for debt transfer.[46]

3.3.1 The Advocate-General's opinion

Advocate-General (AG) Wahl opined that the UCTD only extends to general business practices such as debt assignment if they are regulated explicitly by consumer contracts. He emphasized that the directive concerns contractual terms rather than overall business practices.[47]

Furthermore, the AG observed that national provisions, such as Article 1535 of the Spanish Civil Code and Articles 17 and 540 of the Spanish Civil Procedure Code, which govern debt assignments and the substitution of the assignee in ongoing proceedings, are beyond the UCTD's scope. These provisions were considered mandatory statutory or regulatory provisions, presumed to be fair, and therefore not subject to the directive.[48]

3.3.2 The ruling of the Court of Justice of the European Union

The CJEU ruled that the UCTD does not prohibit the business practice of assigning or purchasing a consumer's debt without the consumer's prior notice or consent, or the opportunity to extinguish the debt by reimbursing the assignee. The court emphasized that the directive applies to contractual terms, not business practices. Consequently, the national provisions governing debt assignments and the substitution of the assignor by the assignee are not subject to the directive's provisions given that they reflect mandatory statutory or regulatory requirements.[49]

The court further clarified that the UCTD applies exclusively to contractual terms and does not cover mere practices unless these practices are reflected

[45] *Banco Santander* (n 44) Judgment, paras 22–24.
[46] ibid paras 25–27.
[47] *Banco Santander* (n 44) Opinion of Advocate-General Wahl, paras 43–44.
[48] ibid paras 45–46.
[49] *Banco Santander* (n 44) Judgment paras 38–47.

in specific contractual terms.[50] In this case, the loan agreements did not contain terms regarding debt assignment, so the directive did not apply. The CJEU also confirmed that specific provisions of the Spanish Civil Code (Article 1535) and the Spanish Civil Procedure Code (Articles 17 and 540), being mandatory provisions, fall outside the directive's scope.[51]

3.3.3 The cases' implications

These cases highlight the limitations of the UCTD in addressing business practices not explicitly covered by contractual terms. This underscores the importance of national laws in regulating such practices to protect consumer interests. In particular, the question arises of whether these practices can be challenged under the Unfair Commercial Practices Directive (UCPD), given that it is designed to deal with commercial practices arising from or concerning consumer agreements. Providing a definite answer would require a significant amount of speculation. Still, AG Wahl's Opinion suggests that the UCPD may also be of limited assistance in this situation:

> This assignment is neutral from the point of view of the debtor. The fact, mentioned by the referring court that the assignment is made to 'vulture funds', acting for speculative purposes, for a much lower or even negligible price by comparison to the original debt is extraneous to the nature of the consumer's contractual obligation per se.[52]

The footnote[53] that supports this statement offers additional arguments. The AG acknowledges that the purpose of the right of first refusal, outlined in Article 1535 of the Spanish Civil Code in respect of 'disputed' debts, is to address situations where debts are assigned for speculative purposes, as observed by the referring court. However, he overlooks the fact that a transaction in which a creditor relinquishes their claim for a small fraction of its face value inherently involves speculation, regardless of the circumstances. If this were not the case and a fraction of the debt could be fully settled, there would be no logical explanation for the creditor not to propose and accept a partial payment from the debtor. The AG's view stems from his underlying assumption, namely, the legal fiction of *debtor neutrality*, which posits that who the creditor is, is immaterial to the debtor.

[50] ibid para 41.
[51] ibid para 42.
[52] *Banco Santander* (n 44) Opinion of Advocate-General Wahl, para 47.
[53] ibid n 13.

The AG's statement reveals complex intersections between legal theory, ethical principles, moral philosophy, and societal structures. It points to the need to rethink the nature of debt and obligation, the ethics of debt transactions, and the broader implications for human dignity and social justice. Ultimately, it encourages a holistic understanding of the economic system that integrates legal, ethical, moral, and social considerations.

3.3.3.1 The legal perspective: The nature of legal obligations and contracts

The AG's statement highlights the foundational legal principle of *pacta sunt servanda* (agreements must be kept). It maintains that the assignment of a debt does not alter the debtor's legal obligations, which remain anchored in the original contract. This position asserts the immutability of financial and contractual commitments and the complete separation of legal obligations from the moral standing of the parties involved in the assignment.

Nonetheless, broader implications must be considered. A contract supposes that both parties have the right (and a corresponding obligation) to receive what they have bargained for. According to conventional wisdom, a creditor anticipates the return of the principal amount plus interest. In the event of default, additional expenses and costs may be added.[54] However, transferring the nominal debt for a portion of the creditor's right implies that the creditor has relinquished the right to complete satisfaction.

The law treats the debtor's obligations as neutral to the assignee's identity or intent, suggesting a fundamental separation between the legal structure and the moral or ethical dimensions of transactions. This reflects a positivist approach, viewing the law as a set of rules to be applied objectively. One may thus question why a similar rationale should not be extended to the assignor.

By keeping the debtor's obligations unchanged, the legal system emphasizes the autonomy and agency of individuals in forming contracts. This underscores the profound belief in personal accountability and the sanctity of free will in contractual engagements. Nonetheless, the debtor's obligation is invariably tied to the creditor's expectation as the law acknowledges the creditor's right to pardon, reduce, or restructure the debt, thereby altering its extent or even its existence. This indicates that the debtor's obligation is not as sacrosanct and independent from the creditor as positivists may suggest.

3.3.3.2 The ethical perspective: The ethics of financial transactions

The AG's statement also points to the ethics of financial speculation and the role of intent in ethical evaluations. The acquisition of debts by debt purchasers for

[54] ibid Opinion of Advocate-General Wahl, para 48.

speculative purposes raises a pertinent question: can the ethical considerations of a financial transaction be disentangled from its intent and consequences?

The ethical evaluation of debt purchasing practices can be viewed through the lens of deontological ethics (focusing on the intent behind the actions) or consequentialist ethics (focusing on the outcomes of the actions). This duality underscores a fundamental ethical dilemma, which extends to whether it is just to capitalize on financial distress for profit. This raises issues about the moral duties of creditors and the ethical boundaries of profit-seeking in financial markets. At the same time, one may question the legal and ethical ramifications of allowing banks to create nominal debt that they can dispose of at market value to enable the creation of more nominal debt. This situation not only underscores complicit involvement in wealth extraction but also reveals a lack of accountability.

3.3.3.3 The moral perspective: The moral philosophy of debt

Morally, the AG's statement invites reflection on the philosophy of debt and the wide-ranging implications of financial obligations on human dignity and social justice. It prompts us to consider the moral foundations of debt enforcement and the human consequences of economic distress.

The aggressive pursuit of debts by debt purchasers has the potential to erode human dignity, which calls for a moral examination of financial practices that disregard individuals' well-being. It thus urges a re-evaluation of the principles of social justice within the realm of debt, raising the question of whether the economic system fosters a fair distribution of resources and opportunities or perpetuates cycles of exploitation and inequality.

3.3.3.4 The social perspective: Societal structures and financial systems

Finally, from a societal standpoint, the statement implicates the 'structural dynamics of financial systems' and their impact on social cohesion and stability. It encourages a deeper exploration of the role of financial markets in shaping social relations and the power dynamics between economic actors. Selling debts reflects broader systemic inequalities within the financial system, raising questions about the concentration of financial power and the disproportionate influence of particular actors on outcomes. Additionally, aggressive debt-collection practices can undermine trust in financial institutions and erode social cohesion. Thus, regulatory frameworks are needed to balance the interests of creditors and debtors while upholding the financial system's integrity (see Chapter X, Subsection 10.1).

In tackling these issues, a comprehensive approach is essential. First, it is crucial to improve transparency in the debt assignment process. Regulations should require that consumers be informed about debt assignments and the sale price, and they should be given the option to repurchase their debts at the purchase price plus reasonable costs. Second, it would be beneficial to strengthen EU consumer protection laws to encompass contractual terms and business practices related to debt assignments, ensuring robust consumer rights. Lastly, setting limits on the amounts that third-party debt buyers can recover, tied to the purchase price of the debt, can prevent excessive financial demands on consumers. These measures would advance fairness, shield consumers from exploitative practices, and increase social equality while reducing financial speculation.

3.4 Summary

This chapter examined the multifaceted debt assignment and commodification process, illustrating its profound implications on modern financial systems. It explored the intricate dynamics between creditors, assignees, and debtors, highlighting the legal, ethical, and social ramifications of transforming debt into a tradeable asset. The analysis traced the historical evolution from direct debt management to sophisticated secondary markets, revealing opportunities and challenges in this shift. Examining regulatory frameworks and judicial perspectives, particularly through the lens of the CJEU, illuminated the complexities and contentious issues surrounding debt commodification, ultimately questioning the fairness and regulatory oversight of such practices.

In the next chapter, the focus broadens to examine the pivotal role of debt-collection within the financial system. This exploration addresses how debt-collection practices shape financial stability, influence market behaviours, and impact both creditors and debtors on a macroeconomic scale. Understanding these dynamics is crucial for appreciating the broader economic and social implications of informal debt-collection in today's globalized financial landscape and the need to regulate it adequately.

IV
THE ROLE OF DEBT-COLLECTION

4.1 Formal versus Informal Debt-collection

When a debtor defaults, the creditor has two options. One is to litigate and attempt to enforce the debt with the help and force of the state apparatus; this is known as *judicial* or *formal debt-collection*.[1] While a viable option, formal debt-collection suffers from several shortcomings, such as exposing the creditor to additional expenses (judicial and legal fees), lengthy procedures, and the risk of the claim being invalidated by the court.[2]

The other option is for the creditor to try to collect the debt on their own or by employing professional debt-collectors, a phenomenon referred to as *non-judicial* or *informal debt-collection*.[3] Informal debt-collection is faster and less risky than formal debt-collection;[4] however, given the absence of court supervision or due process, it can quickly turn abusive. The next section focuses on the darker side of debt-collection, emphasizing the need for ethical conduct and regulatory protection.

4.2 Abusive Informal Debt-collection

Exploring debt-collection practices naturally leads to the issue of abuse. While debt-collection is considered a legitimate business with a positive contribution to the economy, some for-profit[5] debt-collectors may engage in abusive practices to maximize their recovery and earnings.[6]

[1] Cătălin Gabriel Stănescu, 'Regulation of Informal Debt Collection. An Introduction' in Cătălin Gabriel Stănescu (ed), *Regulation of Debt Collection in Europe: Understanding Informal Debt Collection* (Routledge 2023) 7.

[2] John Spanogle, Ralph Rohner, Dee Pridgen, Jeff Sovern, and Christopher Peterson, *Consumer Law: Cases and Materials* (4th edn, West Academic Publishing 2013) 474.

[3] Stănescu (n 1) 6–7.

[4] Adam J Levitin, *Consumer Finance Law: Markets and Regulation* (Aspen Publishing 2018) 693–96.

[5] Elizabeth Warren, Jay Lawrence Westbrook, Katherine Porter, and John AE Pottow, *The Law of Debtors and Creditors: Text, Cases, and Problems* (Aspen Casebook Series 2014) 24–25.

[6] ibid 26–30; Olivier Jérusalmy, Paul Fox, and Nicolas Hercelin, 'Is the Human Dignity of Individual Debtors at Risk?' (*Finance Watch*, 2020) <https://www.finance-watch.org/wp-content/uploads/2020/01/Report_Human-dignity_final_with-annex.pdf> 33–35.

EU Informal Debt-Collection Regulation. Cătălin-Gabriel Stănescu, Oxford University Press.
 DOI: 10.1093/oso/9780198966159.003.0004

Informal debt-collection practices that involve abuse have wide-ranging adverse effects. First, they threaten the consumers' physical, psychological, and economic well-being.[7] Subjecting consumer-debtors to violence, harassment, and invasion of privacy causes family hardship, public shaming, and increased over-indebtedness.[8] Second, these practices expose law-abiding and ethical debt-collectors to unfair competition as unethical collectors may have a higher recovery rate.[9] Third, such practices can erode consumers' trust in the financial[10] and justice systems due to ineffective remedies.[11] Lastly, abusive informal debt-collection practices may even involve criminal activities, such as money laundering and tax evasion, which negatively impact the economy through diminished tax contributions.[12]

These considerations underscore the significant impact of abusive informal debt-collection practices on both consumers and society, highlighting the crucial need for sufficient consumer financial protection. These issues tend to worsen during times of crisis, such as the COVID-19 pandemic. According to the World Bank, consumers are vulnerable to 'aggressive debt-collection practices and late payment or default fees', which can result in immediate harm during economic downturns.[13] In its recommendations, the World Bank stressed the critical need for 'enhanced monitoring of aggressive and unscrupulous debt-collection activities'[14] during such times.

The European Union (EU) and most of its member states (MS) have been slow to react to this recommendation, which is surprising considering the essential role

[7] Cătălin Gabriel Stănescu, *Self-Help, Private Debt Collection and the Concomitant Risks. A Comparative Law Analysis* (Springer 2015) 209; Cătălin Gabriel Stănescu, 'Regulation of Abusive Debt Collection Practices in the EU Member States: An Empirical Account' (2021) 44(1) Journal of Consumer Policy 179, 195–96.

[8] Udo Reifner, Johanna Niemi-Kiesiläinen, Nik Huls, and Helga Springeneer, *Overindebtedness in European Consumer Law: Principles from 15 European States* (Books on Demand 2012); Warren and others (n 5); Stănescu (n 7); Hans-W Micklitz and Irina Domurath, *Consumer Debt and Social Exclusion in Europe* (Taylor and Francis 2016); Iain Ramsay, 'Changing Policy Paradigms of EU Consumer Credit and Debt Regulation' in Dorota Leczykiewicz and Stephen Weatherill (eds), *The Involvement of EU Law in Private Law Relationships* (Hart Publishing 2013); Federico Ferretti and Daniela Vandone, *Personal Debt in Europe* (CUP 2019); Joseph Spooner, *Bankruptcy: The Case for Relief in an Economy of Debt* (CUP 2019); Jodi Gardner, Mia Gray, and Katharina Moser, *Debt and Austerity: Implications of the Financial Crisis* (Edward Elgar 2020).

[9] Stănescu 2015 (n 7); Jérusalmy, Fox, and Hercelin (n 6); Stănescu 2021 (n 7).

[10] Case C-357/16 *UAB 'Gelvora' v Valstybinė vartotojų teisių apsaugos tarnyba* [2017] ECLI:EU:C:2017:573 (*Gelvora*) para 27.

[11] Ferretti and Vandone (n 8); Remo Caponi and Janek Novak, 'Access to Justice' in Burkhard Hess and Stephanie Law (eds), *Implementing EU Consumer Rights by National Procedural Law. Luxembourg Report on European Procedural Law Volume II* (Beck, Hart, Nomos 2019).

[12] Cătălin Gabriel Stănescu and Camelia Bogdan, 'Regulatory Arbitrage and Non-Judicial Debt Collection in Central and Eastern Europe—Tax Sheltering and Money Laundering' (2021) 11(2) Accounting, Economics and Law: A Convivium 119.

[13] Gian Boeddu, Jenniger Chien, Ivor Istuk, and Ligia Lopes, 'Protecting Financial Consumers during the COVID-19 Crisis' (*World Bank Blogs*, 8 May 2020) <https://blogs.worldbank.org/en/psd/protecting-financial-consumers-during-covid-19-crisis>.

[14] ibid.

of informal debt-collection in the soundness of the EU's financial system. The next sections extensively examine this matter.

4.3 The Role of Debt-collection

Chapter II explained that lending and credit depend on repayment. When voluntary compliance is lacking, collection efforts become necessary to ensure repayment, making debt recovery a legitimate and integral part of the financial sector.[15] This section delves into the multifaceted role of debt-collection and its impact on the financial industry.

4.3.1 The soundness of the financial system

This subsection examines the crucial role of debt-collection in the health of the financial system. Since no one would extend credit without repayment, multiple measures have been put in place to ease debt recovery through expedited enforcement measures against the collateral or other assets belonging to the debtor, swift judicial procedures, and even self-help mechanisms. The availability of informal (extra-judicial) debt-collection is part of the same logic of streamlining recovery.

Among others, banks provide loans that enable companies to invest and create jobs or individuals to purchase assets, such as cars or houses. The banks earn money from the interest received on these loans. A loan is considered 'performing' if the borrowers pay the agreed instalments and interest as scheduled. Nevertheless, there is always a risk that the company or individual will not be able to repay as agreed due to changes in circumstances. Generally, the loan is considered 'non-performing' when more than ninety days have passed since the last payment.[16]

Since banks expose themselves to non-payment risks when they grant loans to their clients, they must prepare to incur losses from those loans. They do so by estimating the future loss on the loan and booking a corresponding provision.[17] The provision only covers part of the face value of the loan because the bank might still receive some payments from their clients or recover part of the loaned amount by selling their clients' assets. Thus, only the expected net loss is covered, and the bank uses its capital for this purpose. There is little other connection between the

[15] International Finance Corporation, 'Responsible Debt Collection in Emerging Markets' (*World Bank Group*, 2012) 3 <https://openknowledge.worldbank.org/server/api/core/bitstreams/69efc8f5-aa78-5e72-889c-5e4045a7f09a/content> accessed 11 April 2023.

[16] European Central Bank, 'What Are Non-Performing Loans (NPLs)?' (*European Central Bank*, 12 September 2016) <https://www.bankingsupervision.europa.eu/about/ssmexplained/html/npl.en.html> accessed 11 April 2023. See also: Maria Balgova, Michel Nies, and Alexander Plekhanov, *The Economic Impact of Reducing Non-Performing Loans* (EBRD Working Paper No 193, 2016) 2 and 9.

[17] Balgova, Nies, and Plekhanov (n 16) 8.

bank's capital and the loaned amounts because banks no longer extend loans from the funds entrusted by their customers, but essentially 'create' the money they lend.[18]

Following the financial crisis, the Capital Requirements Directive[19] and the Capital Requirements Regulation[20] implemented new prudential rules concerning liquidity standards, leverage ratios, and capital buffers. These prudential rules set a minimum coverage ratio that banks must maintain. This, in turn, can put banks with insufficient capital cushions in trouble, especially if they have many un-repaid loans[21] (i.e. non-performing loans).

Given that the banks make provisions for non-performing loans (NPLs) from their capital, NPLs tie up a part of the banks' capital base without providing commensurate returns. Moreover, that capital cannot be used in other crediting activities, reducing profitability[22] and increasing the banks' capital requirement. This generates a systemic risk for the internal financial market because a banking system impacted by the drag of NPLs cannot drive net new lending and fuel the EU economy[23] by providing credit to businesses and consumers. Empirical studies found that, conversely, 'measures to reduce the stock of NPLs ... help to revive the flow of credit, boost economic confidence and thus stimulate economic activity'.[24] However, if the loans go to consumers, economic activity is not stimulated by productivity but by mass consumption, which is at odds with sustainability goals at all levels.

To deleverage, banks have two major solutions to handle NPLs. One is to work them out through specialist work consisting of re-scheduling payments, seizing collateral, or converting debt to equity, among others.[25] The other is to sell them, individually or in portfolios, to companies specialized in debt-collection, which are willing to shoulder the non-repayment risk. These sales are made at a significant discount (covering the buyer's risk) but enable the credit buyer to recover the face value of the debt, which constitutes its profit and incentive to engage in NPL purchases.

Debt-collection is the vital activity that drives profitability in this context. It is a critical aspect of the debt-collectors' role because without effective debt-collection, banks would struggle to offload NPLs and resume their lending activities. In

[18] Johnna Montgomerie, *Should We Abolish Household Debts?* (Polity 2019).

[19] Directive 2013/36/EU on access to the activity of credit institutions and the prudential supervision of credit institutions and investment firms [2013] OJ L176/338, 338–436.

[20] Regulation (EU) No 575/2013 on prudential requirements for credit institutions and investment firms [2013] OJ L176/1, 1–337.

[21] European Central Bank (n 16).

[22] ibid; Balgova, Nies, and Plekhanov (n 16) 6.

[23] KPMG, 'Non-Performing Loans – Setting Expectations to Meet SSM Priorities' (*KPMG*, 9 May 2016) <https://kpmg.com/xx/en/home/insights/2016/05/non-performing-loans-fs.html> accessed 11 April 2023. See also: Balgova, Nies, and Plekhanov (n 16) 6–7.

[24] Balgova, Nies, and Plekhanov (n 16) 20–29.

[25] ibid.

addition, debt purchasers would face challenges in recovering their investments and realizing profits without efficient debt-collection processes. Accordingly, the next section discusses the balance between access to finance, economic growth, and the need to ensure ethical debt-collection practices.

4.3.2 Responsible finance

The International Finance Corporation (IFC) links debt-collection to responsible finance. In their view, access to finance fosters economic growth and helps lift people out of poverty (albeit not singlehandedly). To be responsible, finance must be delivered without exposing or subjecting lenders to excess leverage, costs, or indignity.[26]

The concept of responsible finance is especially significant in emerging economies due to the high credit growth and delinquency rates and the legal recourse mechanisms prevailing in these regions. These challenges generate a regulatory backlash, lead to reputational losses for banks and other crediting institutions, and cause the discontinuation of entire lines of business as well as legal difficulties for some bank staff, negatively impacting investment and finance access.[27] In turn, these affect economic growth and efforts to alleviate poverty.

Recent interdisciplinary literature on consumer credit revealed the inadequacy of consumer credit policies that continue to rely on debt-financed welfare (i.e. providing credit to consumers rather than adequate living means) and the information paradigm (i.e. assuming, wrongly, that a consumer provided with enough information is magically protected and capable of making sound choices about the financial products offered).[28] Access to credit often lures consumers into a spiral of debt, from which many never get out.[29] Information does little to improve the financial products available, especially without real national or intra-EU competition.[30]

[26] International Finance Corporation (n 15) 5.

[27] ibid 3.

[28] Mallory E SoRelle, *Democracy Declined. The Failed Politics of Consumer Financial Protection* (University of Chicago Press 2020); Guido Comparato, *The Financialisation of the Citizen: Social and Financial Inclusion through European Private Law* (Hart Publishing 2018) 84–87.

[29] Mark Horsley, *The Dark Side of Prosperity. Late Capitalism's Culture of Indebtedness* (Routledge 2015); Joe Deville, *Lived Economies of Default* (Routledge 2015).

[30] According to the latest European Commission Study on Possible Impacts of a Revision of the Consumer Credit Directive (CCD), low levels of direct cross-border credit transactions (0.9 per cent) kept consumer credit markets segmented by MS, reducing consumer choice and keeping interest rates higher in specific markets. In this regard, the study observed that differences in the transposition of the CCD concerning information-related requirements in advertising and the pre-contractual stage prevent direct cross-border transactions. This concerns both consumers, who hesitate to use systems that appear different, and financial institutions, which have to adapt their offers to local conditions. This had led to a high concentration of banks in the EU. European Commission, 'Study on Possible Impacts of a Revision of the CCD. Final Report' (*European Commission*, May 2021).

Nonetheless, no fundamental changes have occurred in the regulation of EU financial services and products for consumers. Although responsible finance, through responsible lending, became a mantra in consumer financial regulation following the economic crisis, it manifested more in connection to consumer mortgages.[31] Even there, incentives for responsible lending are weak. The Consumer Mortgage Directive (CMD)[32] contains no provision that could sanction irresponsible lending by a bank in the absence of national rules on the issue. As Mak noted, 'although this [the CMD] could boost the "responsible lending" approaches in national legal systems', many MS chose not to include duties to deny credit in the event of a failed creditworthiness assessment.[33] In essence, the EU and most national legislators allowed creditors to continue as usual, even at the risk of consumer over-indebtedness, which would throw them in the path of debt-collectors.

The consequence is that the current system is designed so that banks and other crediting institutions have no incentive to act responsibly. On the contrary, they can continue to grant credit and, in case of default, easily outsource collection or dispose of the NPLs, clearing provisions and resuming lending activities. Meanwhile, financial investors (debt buyers) and debt-collectors continue to thrive on the repeat credit business. Responsible lending, including debt-collection, remains a mere slogan without sector-specific regulation that is more responsive to consumer needs and truly transforms the current financial system.

Considering these aspects, the next section delves into the necessity of regulating the debt-collection market to prevent abusive practices and ensure the fair treatment of debtors.

4.3.3 The need for regulation and its impact

Since the debt-collection market is mainly driven by profit and profit depends on recovery rates, lenders and debt buyers or collectors may be tempted to employ practices that enable the highest recovery possible, some of which are abusive, rather than focus on the ethical treatment of debtors.[34] Empirical data from the past decade suggests that these are more prevalent in emerging markets.[35] However, this does not mean that more developed ones are preserved; they are simply more controlled.[36]

[31] Vanessa Mak, 'Financial Services and Consumer Protection' in Christian Twigg-Flesner (ed), *Research Handbook on EU Consumer and Contract Law* (Edward Elgar 2016) 321–25.

[32] Directive 2014/17/EU on credit agreements for consumers relating to residential immovable property [2014] OJ L60/34 (CMD).

[33] Mak (n 31) 324.

[34] International Finance Corporation (n 15) 1 and 11.

[35] ibid 1.

[36] ibid 27.

One of the first studies to consider informal debt-collection was the European Financial Management Association's '2011 report on retail banking in the Central and Eastern European area and debt recovery in times of crisis'.[37] Approximately fifty banks active in the region[38] were interviewed regarding their collection activities for distressed retail debt. The starting point was the effect of the financial crisis on the EU's retail lending business and the soaring NPL ratios in the region. With one in five borrowers defaulting in Romania and an expected delinquency rate of 85 per cent in the retail segment, the study noted that 'sound collection practices turned out to be a key lever to maintain the bank's profitability'.[39]

The 2011 report focused on the collection process of the surveyed banks, from the due date to legal execution and write-off. Informal debt-collection was characterized as *pre-legal collection*, taking place in two stages: early and late collection.[40] The former was mostly conducted in-house, while the latter was generally outsourced. The study identified three pillars of successful debt-collection practices (i.e. a well-defined process set, a dedicated collection unit, and measurement and incentivization), all built on a supporting infrastructure consisting of functional, integrated information technology systems and standardized, automated steps.[41]

What is striking about this 2011 report is the quasi-absence of consideration for borrower well-being. Among the critical success factors in retail debt-collection, there is no mention of observance of ethical standards or due consideration of the borrower's economic situation.[42] None of the 'Dos' or 'Don'ts' in retail debt-collection drawn from EU banks' experience considers the interests or rights of consumer-debtors.[43] On the contrary, measures that depersonalize the debtors (such as using automated, non-individualized processes and an industrialized approach) or might expose them to abuse and psychological pressure (by measuring and rewarding staff performance based on recovery rates, following payment promises tightly, or contacting debtors outside business hours or on weekends) were ranked highest.[44]

The 2011 report also considered outsourcing debt-collection activities to specialized third parties, noting that this option is used in the late collection phase due to higher efficiency (cost versus recovery) and internal capacity constraints.[45]

[37] European Financial Management Association, 'Retail Banking in Central and Eastern Europe (CEE)—Debt Collection in Times of Crisis, Summary of Study Findings' (*European Financial Management Association*, 31 May 2011) <https://www.yumpu.com/en/document/read/25832109/debt-collection-in-times-of-crisis-roland-berger> accessed 13 April 2023.

[38] For the study, the CEE region included: Bulgaria, Croatia, Czechia, Hungary, Poland, Romania, Serbia, Slovakia, the Russian Federation, and Ukraine. Among these, only Bulgaria, Czechia, Hungary, Poland, and Romania were EU MS. Croatia joined in 2013.

[39] European Financial Management Association (n 37) 5 and 7.

[40] ibid 11.

[41] ibid 13.

[42] ibid 14.

[43] ibid 15.

[44] ibid 15, 17, 21, and 22.

[45] ibid 24.

Selling debt to external parties was used or planned by 79 per cent of the banks to reduce risk and for balance sheet management (54 per cent), and in cases of no or very low expected recovery (54 per cent). For these reasons, coupled with market insecurity, sale prices were very low (e.g. 10 per cent or less of the face value in Romania and Ukraine).[46]

Similarly to the early collection phase (in-house collection), the methods employed did not rank among the top three selection criteria of collection agencies, being contemplated by only a third (36 per cent) of the surveyed banks.[47] Moreover, the study recommended debt-collection practices that lay at the fringes, if not outside, of the law: using robocalling, predictive diallers, evening and weekend calls, experimental and behavioural analytics, recruiting staff from other industries known for 'strong collection' capabilities, and granting staff incentives linked to recovery rates.[48] These practices were already used in the surveyed countries, taking advantage of the absence of sector-specific legislation and quasi-lack of supervision or control.

The IFC's 2012 study found a strong correlation between the available legal infrastructure for enforcing claims and the sophistication of the controls employed by collectors, noting that 'field collections tend to be the dominant mode of customer contact, while in more developed markets, collectors tend to rely more heavily on voice contact, where oversight options are stronger'.[49] Another finding was that emergent market economies generally lacked external oversight over the debt-collection industry and ethical standards to be observed.[50] None of the twenty countries surveyed was in the EU, but the study mentioned that Central and Eastern European countries (i.e. Kazakhstan, the Russian Federation, and Ukraine) were among the most challenging environments for collectors.[51] Finally, the study found that emergent markets were characterized by limited training of debt-collectors and weak incentives for following a process discipline.

The 2012 study made three recommendations: (1) enacting wide-scale regulations and policies that provide consumers with protections and remedies and enable state agencies to monitor and supervise debt-collectors' activity; (2) implementing responsible practices by financial providers, which would reduce customer conflicts; and (3) enhancing the financial literacy of consumers to not only improve their financial decision-making but also defend themselves against coercive and improper treatment by collectors.[52] The study also listed several guiding principles adapted from collection practices in developed markets to

[46] ibid 26.
[47] ibid 25.
[48] ibid 30–32.
[49] International Finance Corporation (n 15) 1 and 11.
[50] ibid.
[51] ibid 11.
[52] ibid 1.

be used as a foundation for responsible and ethical collection standards. More recent, large-scale surveys conducted in the EU have endorsed many of its findings and suggestions.[53]

However, the 2012 study's concern for the borrower's welfare is subordinated to the efficiency of the collection process. As the IFC puts it, 'more responsible collections processes require being smart about collections, not being soft'.[54] Lenders (creditors) and debt-collectors are encouraged to implement (the suggested) measures that reduce the risk of collection abuses because they will not impair their ability to deliver financial results: 'Fortunately, many of those steps will actually improve collections performance by bringing a more scientific approach to decisions about how to approach each customer and by improving line-of-sight to collections activities.'[55] In other words, by taking the initiative to create standards for responsible collection, assuming a leading role in promoting financial awareness among borrowers, and centralized mechanisms for raising and resolving or publicizing customer complaints,[56] the financial industry can pre-emptively control the process and narrative to avoid more stringent measures and control by public bodies.

The lack of consistent regulatory measures for the debt-collection industry across EU MS is also revealing. In 2020, only nine MS had sector-specific legislation addressing abusive debt-collection practices, but these laws varied widely in their scope and approach.[57] The European Commission recognized this fact in the final version of the Credit Servicers and Credit Purchasers Directive (CSCPD).[58] The remaining eighteen MS, which account for approximately two-thirds of the total EU population (i.e. 281.47 million people), relied on traditional civil and criminal remedies or judicial innovation to balance the rights of creditors seeking repayment with the fair treatment of debtors.[59] As a result, in most EU jurisdictions, debt-collectors have operated discreetly, largely unnoticed and with relative impunity.

This reality stresses the importance of strict regulation and oversight of debt-collection activities given their impact on individuals and the scale of the market. In theory, this should have happened once the CSCPD was transposed into national legislation by the end of 2023. However, by November 2024, only eighteen

[53] Jérusalmy, Fox, and Hercelin (n 6); Stănescu (n 7).
[54] International Finance Corporation (n 15) 24.
[55] ibid 29.
[56] ibid 27.
[57] Stănescu, 'Regulation of Abusive Debt Collection Practices in the EU Member States' (n 7).
[58] Directive (EU) No 2021/2167 on credit servicers and credit purchasers [2021] OJ L438 (CSCPD) recital 10.
[59] Cătălin Gabriel Stănescu (ed), *Regulation of Debt Collection in Europe: Understanding Informal Debt Collection* (Routledge 2023).

out of twenty-seven MS had reported full transposition measures,[60] five of which already had sectoral legislation when the CSCPD was adopted.[61] Infringement proceedings were pending against twenty-one MS.[62]

Moreover, the CSCPD does not provide guidelines for how MS should regulate informal debt-collection practices, focusing on the authorization procedure for debt-collectors ('credit servicers') and their relationship with debt buyers ('credit purchasers').[63] Thus, MS are responsible for developing national regulations for debt-collection activities to the extent they deem necessary, leading to a risk of divergent solutions and protection levels. Such outcomes could hinder harmonization efforts and affect debtors, particularly consumers and small (family) businesses (see Chapters XIV–XVI).

4.4 Summary

This chapter presented an in-depth analysis of the mechanisms and contemporary issues in debt-collection. It distinguished between formal and informal debt recovery, introduced the concept of abusive informal debt-collection practices, and discussed their part in the financial sector, stressing the need for adequate regulation.

At this point, it becomes crucial to understand the broader context in which consumer debts arise. The expansion of consumer credit markets, the significant role of utility bills in household debt, and policy changes over the decades have all shaped the current landscape of consumer indebtedness. The next chapter explores historical and ongoing developments in consumer credit markets and their profound effects on European economies, laying the groundwork for a deeper analysis of consumer over-indebtedness and debt-collection practices.

[60] European Commission, 'Transposition Status—Credit Servicers and Credit Purchasers Directive' (*European Commission, 2024*) <https://finance.ec.europa.eu/credit-servicers-and-credit-purchasers-directive_en> accessed 22 July 2024.

[61] Denmark, Germany, Greece, Latvia, Romania, and Sweden.

[62] European Commission 2024 (f 60).

[63] CSCPD (n 58) arts 4–10.

V
CONSUMER CREDIT AND UTILITY MARKETS

5.1 Household Debt in the EU: Trends, Impacts, and Economic Implications

In the past decade, the total financial liabilities of households in the European Union (EU) have increased yearly. According to Eurostat,[1] although total financial liabilities fell slightly after the financial crisis (2011–14), they steadily grew from 7,648 billion euros in 2011 to 9,090 billion euros in 2021, an overall increase of 18.9 per cent. In 2021, 93 per cent of these were loans, putting the size of the EU household credit market at 8.45 trillion euros. Other accounts receivable/payable (i.e. utilities) accounted for most of the rest (6.4 per cent).[2]

The situation is similar at the member state (MS) level. In 2021, loans were the primary form of household liabilities in every EU country, constituting at least 81 per cent of the total, except in Romania, where their share was 73.3 per cent. This exception does not mean that Romanian households are less exposed but rather that they struggle with other types of liabilities. Notably, Romania has the highest share of obligations stemming from other accounts receivable/payable, at 18.3 per cent, surpassing Bulgaria (17.2 per cent), although the latter has the lowest gross domestic product (GDP) and consumption per capita in the EU.[3]

Household debt affects more than EU states with lower socioeconomic status. Five MS—Germany, France, Italy, the Netherlands, and Spain—collectively account for 71 per cent of the financial liabilities of households in the EU. However, the figure is matched by their share in the total financial assets: 72.3 per cent.[4]

[1] Eurostat is the statistical office of the EU. It produces European statistics in partnership with national statistical institutes and other national authorities in the EU MS. Eurostat does not directly collect data, apart from a small number of exceptions. Data collection is conducted in EU countries by national statistical authorities in compliance with common EU statistical regulations and standards and monitored by Eurostat. These national authorities verify and analyse national data and send them to Eurostat. Eurostat then carries out data validation and quality control checks and produces aggregated figures, particularly at the EU level. For details, see: European Commission, 'Statistics' (*European Commission*) <https://commission.europa.eu/topics/statistics_en> accessed 29 June 2024.

[2] Eurostat, 'Households—statistics on financial assets and liabilities' (*Eurostat*) <https://ec.europa.eu/eurostat/statistics-explained/index.php?title=Households_-_statistics_on_financial_assets_and_liabilities#Structure_of_assets_and_liabilities> accessed 30 February 2023.

[3] ibid.

[4] ibid.

EU Informal Debt-Collection Regulation. Cătălin-Gabriel Stănescu, Oxford University Press.
 DOI: 10.1093/oso/9780198966159.003.0005

Conversely, the remaining twenty-two MS share 29 per cent of the liabilities but 27.7 per cent of the assets. Still, these are not equally distributed among them. In Poland, Portugal, Finland, Greece, Slovakia, and Cyprus, the share of liabilities is significantly higher than that of held assets.[5] Thus, while financial liabilities affect all EU households, it is safe to infer that not all of them are impacted equally.

These are staggering figures considering the added effects of the economic recession caused by the COVID-19 pandemic, the ongoing war in Ukraine, and the most significant increase in consumer prices in decades coupled with anti-inflationary measures (consisting of interest rate increases and diminished purchasing power), all of which exposed EU households to financial distress and debt defaults.[6] Simulations conducted by the European Central Bank in the euro area revealed that households with lower incomes and smaller financial cushions, for which food and energy costs represent a large share of expenditure, face a higher risk of debt default.[7]

Given that households are the largest recipients of lending from the banking system, a substantial deterioration of households' financial positions could translate into loan defaults, impacting banks' asset quality and the economy[8] and triggering debt-collection. In light of the inextricable link between informal debt-collection and the consumer credit and utilities markets, the next sections offer an overview of their development and evolution, particularly in the wake of the financial crisis.

5.2 The Rise of Consumer Credit Markets in Europe (1980–2008)

In the European Credit Research Institute's (ECRI)'s 2002 Consumer Credit in the European Union Report, the starting points are the growth of the volume of outstanding consumer credit since the early 1980s and the wide variations of its use in the surveyed countries. This shift was driven by changes in the regulatory framework governing consumer credit at the EU and national levels. This was primarily due to the liberalization of international capital flows and the deregulation of domestic financial markets, including the deregulation of interest rates, the removal of credit controls, and the reduction of restrictions on bank activities.[9] At the same time, the EU removed restrictions on capital movements, harmonized

[5] ibid, Figure 2.

[6] Daniel Dieckelmann and Julian Metzler, 'Household Inequality and Financial Stability Risks: Exploring the Impact of Changes in Consumer Prices and Interest Rates' (*European Central Bank*, November 2022) <https://www.ecb.europa.eu/pub/financial-stability/fsr/special/html/ecb.fsrart202211_02~8c5b8be620.en.html> accessed 30 March 2023.

[7] ibid.

[8] ibid.

[9] ibid 6–7.

the regulatory framework for financial services, and adopted consumer credit regulations.[10] The combined consequence of these measures was rapid growth in outstanding consumer credit in most countries. Meanwhile, protections remained limited to pre-contractual disclosures and withdrawal rights. Once these were provided, consumers bore full responsibility and remained trapped in unescapable debt peonage.

The effects of this liberalization of credit were so dramatic that some EU countries became debtor pools in just a few decades. In the 1990s, the growth of outstanding consumer credit was slower, with an average rate below 5 per cent. Growth rates were very high in Greece and Italy, which was explained as catching up due to the low initial volume of credit outstanding in the 1980s.[11] The variations also reflect economic growth. During the period 1990–7, the weight of consumer credit in the economy was the highest in Sweden (14.8 per cent), the United Kingdom (UK) (10 per cent), and Germany (11 per cent) among EU countries. In Spain, France, and Finland, the ratio stood at an intermediate level, and it was comparatively the lowest in Greece, Italy, and the Netherlands.

Consumer credit results from the interaction between household decisions on consumption and savings. Despite huge differences between national retail financial markets vis-à-vis household saving patterns and consumption financing, the report observes that, on average, household saving rates have declined since the beginning of the 1980s,[12] which has translated into increased reliance on consumer credit. At the same time, the expected convergence in the price of financial services failed to materialize, with evidence showing price differences of up to 200 per cent for the same service.[13]

The declared objectives of EU legislation at the time were two-fold: to protect consumers against unfair credit terms and promote cross-border credit and the free movement of goods and services financed by credit by harmonizing the information provided to consumers, especially concerning the cost of credit. As the 2002 report notes, the accomplished harmonization was limited because MS were given significant leeway in defining the annualized percentage rate and its calculation method. In any case, the gains for consumers would have been minimal.[14]

Subsequent data shows that in most European countries, consumer credit (in this case, differentiated from consumer mortgage credit) rose substantially before the financial crisis and slowed down afterwards due to soft or no regulations and the business's willingness to sell abundant goods.[15] Consumers were lured into mass consumption with easy access to credit and cheap interest rates, while banks and traders amassed profits from every transaction.

[10] ibid 7, 17–29.
[11] ibid 10.
[12] ibid 8.
[13] ibid 15–16.
[14] ibid 26–27.
[15] Maria Lissowska, *Consumer Credit in Europe* (Palgrave Macmillan 2021) 17.

In 2000–8, Ireland, Greece, Spain, Cyprus, Finland, and the UK saw a significant increase (more than 20 per cent) in final consumption. This points to a notable uptick in the ratio of consumer credit to final consumption in the years leading up to the 2008 crisis. Although this fuelled consumption and GDP growth, it also increased household over-indebtedness, ultimately destabilizing the situation for creditors and the overall economy. As a result, there was a surge in debt-collection cases as creditors facing economic challenges moved quickly to recover their debts.

This section revealed a sizeable market that remains under-regulated but whose expansion is relentlessly pursued at both EU and national levels. The result is an increase in the number of debtors struggling to make ends meet and keep up with repayments and a concentrated number of financiers that profit from the credit or debt-collection industries.

5.3 The Consumer Credit and Utility Markets

Evaluating the sizes and roles of the credit and utility markets is a challenging task. As emphasized in the ECRI 2002 Report, any comparative and integrative attempts are constrained by the availability of statistical data. Statistics on household credit are generally extracted from the reports of commercial banks, deposit-taking institutions, and financial companies and published regularly by national central banks. As of September 2023, the outstanding value of loans to households in the euro area (which is smaller than the EU) stood at 6.63 trillion euros, among which mortgages (5.21 trillion euros) and consumer credit (0.73 trillion euros) were the main categories (See Figure 5.1).

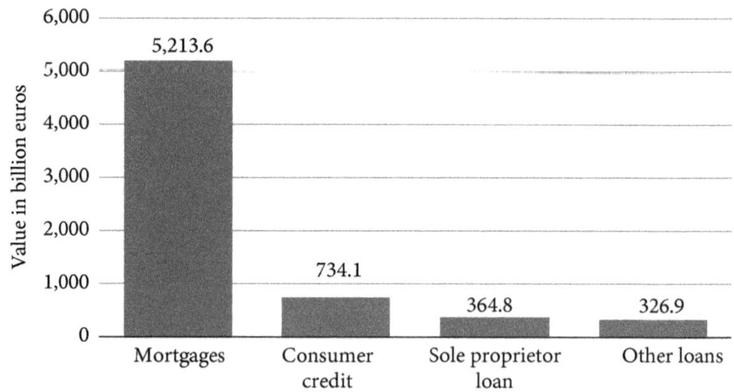

Figure 5.1 Outstanding value of loans to households in the euro area as of September 2023, by type (billion euros).
Source: Statista.

However, these figures only include information from some types of lenders, so the available data tends to be incomplete.[16] Statistical data from international sources are also unharmonized.[17] Besides these, statistical methodologies and conceptual issues, such as what constitutes consumer credit, the level of interest rates, types of lenders, or the definition of households, also differ from one MS to the other, further complicating analyses.[18] Nevertheless, specific trends can be identified within the limits of the available information.

To understand the contemporary landscape of consumer debt, the evolution of consumer credit markets in Europe must first be examined, beginning with their rapid growth in the late twentieth century.

5.4 The Impact of Consumer Credit on European Economies: A Post-Financial Crisis Analysis

According to a 2014 report by the European Commission (EC), in the wake of the financial crisis, outstanding consumer credit debt decreased from 9.1 per cent of GDP in 2009 to 8.2 per cent in 2011. However, the aggregate figures paint a partial picture because the data used cover only banks (monetary financial institutions), leading to an underestimation of the consumer credit market. In addition, there was significant variation in the extent of consumer credit in the EU, with an average outstanding per capita in 2011 ranging from 212 euros in Lithuania to 4,111 euros in Cyprus. Cyprus also had the highest proportion of consumer credit to GDP (19 per cent), followed by Greece (15 per cent), Hungary (14 per cent), the UK (14 per cent), Bulgaria (12 per cent), Romania (11 per cent), Ireland (11 per cent), and Poland (10 per cent). Conversely, Luxembourg and the Baltic States had the lowest proportions, below 5 per cent.[19] Consumer credit denoted in a foreign currency was common in some MS, particularly outside the eurozone.[20]

Notwithstanding, the report also found evidence that from 2000 to 2011, the per capita consumer credit outstanding equalized gradually. That is, it increased more rapidly in MS with historically low levels of consumer credit than in MS where consumer credit levels were already high.[21] This finding supports one of the conclusions of the 2002 ECRI report.

[16] European Credit Research Institute, '2002 Consumer Credit in the European Union Report' (*European Credit Research Institute*, 2002) 4–6.

[17] ibid 6.

[18] ibid 2–5.

[19] European Commission, Report on the implementation of Directive 2008/48/EC on credit agreements for consumers, COM(2014)259 <https://eur-lex.europa.eu/legal-content/EN/TXT/PDF/?uri=CELEX:52014DC0259> accessed 29 January 2024.

[20] ibid 12.

[21] ibid 11.

Following the 2008 financial crisis, mounting unpaid debts led to a reluctance to extend loans among creditors. This was exacerbated by the deteriorating financial positions of banks and calls to reinstate regulatory measures, particularly related to responsible lending. Consequently, more stringent regulations governing banks' lending activities were implemented.[22] Despite this, variations were observed in the extent of reductions in consumer credit. The highest retrenchment was evident in the newer EU MS, such as Bulgaria, Estonia, Lithuania, Hungary, Romania, and Greece, where consumer credit had experienced the most pronounced growth in previous years. Similar reductions were observed in Denmark, Spain, Ireland, and Portugal, despite the slower pace of credit expansion before the crisis.[23]

The available data reveals several traits of the EU states most affected by the crisis and unsustainable levels of consumer credit. All were transitioning from centralized economies to free market economies, affected by severe income inequality and high poverty levels. The populations of these countries displayed a particular willingness to use consumer credit to finance consumption. Consequently, while the proportion of consumer and mortgage credit to GDP was close to 0 in 2000, by 2008 the ratio of consumer credit to GDP had escalated to levels comparable to those of Western European countries.

However, this increase occurred with interest rates much higher than those available in Western Europe and with foreign denominations. This was not solely due to general optimism but also to the accessibility of easy credit and the overall naivete of the local population. The former can largely be attributed to the inflow of foreign capital seeking rapid and substantial profits, along with legal changes designed to safeguard the interests of creditors. The latter mainly stemmed from a lack of comprehensive understanding of financial products and inadequate financial education. Economic hardships and the allure of easy money for the impoverished populations of the East may also have contributed to the debacle.

Consumer credits contributed to the rise of households' consumption between 2000 and 2008, amounting to 78 per cent in Bulgaria, 77 per cent in Estonia, 75 per cent in Latvia, 93 per cent in Lithuania, and 121 per cent in Romania. In contrast, across all EU countries, household consumption only increased by 14 per cent during the same period. While this surge in credit-driven consumption boosted overall GDP growth, it exposed the population to heightened levels of indebtedness.[24] Concurrently, informal debt-collection became more visible in people's daily lives. Building on this post-crisis analysis, the next section explores how consumer credit markets have evolved until today.

22 Lissowska (n 15) 21.
23 ibid.
24 Lissowska (n 15) 23.

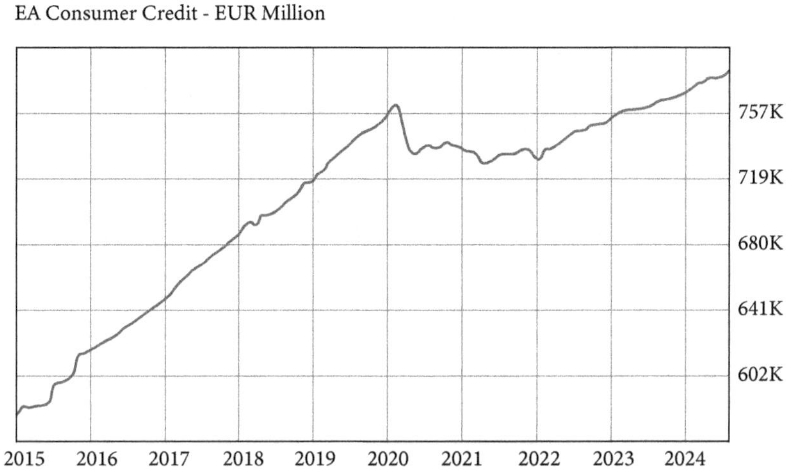

Figure 5.2 Euro area consumer credit (in billion euros).
Source: European Central Bank.

5.5 Consumer Credit Markets from the Financial Crisis to the Present

Following the crisis, from 2009 to 2013, consumer credit in the EU contracted due to unsustainable lending practices. Although the proportion of consumer credits to shrinking final consumption increased numerically, it was insufficient to boost consumption during the deep recession. The rise resumed after 2014 when signs of economic recovery appeared[25] and lasted until the COVID-19 pandemic.

The outstanding consumer credit in the EU28 reached approximately 1.8 trillion euros in 2017. By September 2019, EU banks' exposure to consumer loans had increased to 1.14 trillion euros, a 14 per cent rise from September 2015 (1 trillion euros). This growth in consumer credit outpaced the overall credit growth (+10 per cent) over the same period. The largest consumer credit markets in the EU were Germany, France, Italy, Spain, and Poland. The surge in consumer credit sales (see Figure 5.2) was likely influenced by the historically low interest rates prevalent across Europe.[26]

At the close of 2019 the EU's macroeconomic situation was stable, with a relatively modest proportion of consumer credits to GDP in most MS, ranging between 5 per cent and 8 per cent. Nonetheless, the situation shifted rapidly in March 2020 following the outbreak of the pandemic and the implementation of

[25] ibid 21–23.

[26] Finance Watch, 'Consumer Credit Market Malpractices Uncovered. An In-depth Study of Consumer Credit Markets in Spain, Romania and Ireland and What It Means for the Consumer Credit Directive Review' (*Finance Watch*, February 2021) <https://www.finance-watch.org/wp-content/uploads/2021/04/Consumer-credit-market-study-V13.pdf> accessed 30 January 2024.

lockdowns. This resulted in a contraction of economic activity and a decline in incomes, prompting changes in the attitudes of credit providers and consumers towards household credit[27] and debt servicing.[28] Among other measures, moratoria on household loan obligations were imposed[29] to grant a respite on debt repayments during temporary income declines and increasing uncertainty about employment prospects.[30] By mid-2020, the EC had also agreed on a set of 'best practices' with the financial sector, including the debt-collection industry,[31] to help mitigate the impact of the pandemic.[32]

To illustrate, the Federation of European National Collection Associations endorsed the governmental measures as 'right and necessary to protect the countless people in need' because of the effects of the pandemic. However, it emphasized that the measures should only be temporary and tied to the duration of the crisis, stressing that 'the success and speed of the economic recovery ... depended on the possibility for creditors to reclaim what they are owed'.[33] The World Bank similarly recommended 'an orderly exit from the ... exceptional borrower relief measures and short-term legal measures, aimed at flattening the bankruptcy curve'. It cautioned that extending these could lead to 'hidden costs, *weakening of repayment discipline* ... and a possible adverse impact on banks' liquidity'.[34]

In 2021 the situation in Europe was quite diverse, with some MS imposing no moratoria while others, such as Portugal, had a high number of loans under moratoria. By the end of 2020, the total value of loans under moratoria was 320 billion euros, down from 590 billion euros three months earlier. These figures encompass both business and consumer loans. The European Banking Authority (EBA) underscored that the decrease was less pronounced for household loans, which were also considered riskier.[35] Concerns were raised by financial institutions as

[27] Lissowska (n 15) 24.

[28] Elena Rancoita, Maciej Grodzicki, Hannah Hempell, Christoffer Kok, Julian Metzler, and Algirdas Prapiestis, *Financial stability considerations arising from the interaction of coronavirus-related policy measures* (European Central Bank Financial Stability Review, November 2020) <https://www.ecb.europa.eu/pub/financial-stability/fsr/special/html/ecb.fsrart202011_01~47160f35a4.en.html> accessed 30 January 2024.

[29] For a list of moratoria, see CMS, 'A global overview of coronavirus (COVID-19) related moratorium on corporate and retail loans' (*CMS*, 9 April 2020) <https://cms.law/en/media/local/cms-dsb/files/a-global-overview-of-coronavirus-covid-19-related-moratorium-on-corporate-and-retail-loans> accessed 30 January 2024.

[30] Rancoita and others (n 28).

[31] FENCA, 'FENCA welcomes European Commission announcement of COVID-19 Best Practices' (*FENCA*, 14 July 2020) <https://fenca.eu/news> accessed 30 January 2024.

[32] European Commission, 'Coronavirus Response: Commission welcomes "Best Practices" to provide relief for consumers and businesses' (*European Commission*, 14 July 2020) Press Release <https://ec.europa.eu/commission/presscorner/api/files/document/print/en/ip_20_1281/IP_20_1281_EN.pdf> accessed 30 January 2024.

[33] FENCA, 'Declaration on COVID-19' (*FENCA*, 22 April 2020) <https://fenca.eu/news> accessed 30 January 2024.

[34] World Bank, 'World Development Report 2022: Finance for an Equitable Recovery' (*World Bank Group*, 2022) 109 <https://openknowledge.worldbank.org/server/api/core/bitstreams/4535b6d5-c91c-5e4c-8a8a-559d2ff0bb7a/content> accessed 1 July 2024.

[35] European Banking Authority, 'Risk Dashboard Data as of Q4 2020' (*European Banking Authority*, 2020) 3 <https://eba.europa.eu/sites/default/files/document_library/Risk%20Analysis%20and%20D

loans under moratoria transitioned into bad loans. Their lobby prompted several members of the European Parliament to question the EC's assessment of the status of loans under moratoria in Europe and their impact on the banking sector.[36]

Although incomplete, the available financial data indicates that consumer credit in the euro area surged over the past twenty-five years, climbing from around 420,000 million euros to approximately 733,503 million euros (see Figure 5.3).[37] During the same period, the household debt-to-income ratio in the euro area rose from 71.02 per cent in 1999 to 93.09 per cent in 2023 (see Figure 5.4).[38]

This information highlights the tremendous contribution of consumer credit to the growth of European economies before the 2008 crisis. The period preceding the crisis saw a surge in consumer credit, particularly in the EU region, fuelled by aggressive advertising and easily accessible and low-cost credit. However, this led to consumer over-indebtedness and contributed to an economic slowdown post-crisis. Additionally, the COVID-19 pandemic and the uncertainty it brought further impacted consumer credit as consumers' willingness to take on credit decreased and banks restricted access to it due to rising levels of NPLs.[39]

Notwithstanding the decrease in the demand for consumer credit, the absolute figures remain high and are projected to increase. Banks in the EU are expected to maintain the upward trend in loans and advances supplied to households. It is anticipated that outstanding household lending will exceed 6.9 trillion euros by the end of 2024. In 2022, the total value of household credit held by banks was 6.48 trillion euros; it was expected to reach 7.14 trillion euros by 2025.[40]

The debt-collection market is also expected to grow in size and significance, reinforcing the need to regulate it and keep it within the confines of the law. Data indicates that debt-collection ranked among the top reasons for consumer complaints after the financial crisis, as revealed in the EBA's Consumer Trends reports from 2010–21.[41] The conspicuous absence of such complaints from EBA's 2022–3

ata/Risk%20dashboard/Q4%202020/972092/EBA%20Dashboard%20-%20Q4%202020%20-%20footnote%20%281%29.pdf> accessed 30 January 2024.

36 European Parliament, 'Parliamentary question E-002334/2021—Loans under moratoria and associated risks in Europe' (*European Parliament*, 29 April 2021) <https://www.europarl.europa.eu/doceo/document/E-9-2021-002334_EN.html> accessed 30 January 2024.

37 Trading Economics and European Central Bank, 'Euro Area Consumer Credit' (*Trading Economics*) <https://tradingeconomics.com/euro-area/consumer-credit> accessed 30 January 2024.

38 ibid.

39 Lissowska (n 15) 28–29.

40 Total value of loans and advances to households owned by banks in the European Union from 2020 to 2022, with a forecast until 2025, 15 December 2023, at: https://www.statista.com/statistics/1303513/loans-and-advances-to-households-in-the-eu/> accessed 30 January 2023.

41 European Banking Authority, 'Consumer Trends Reports 2020/2021' (*European Banking Authority*, 10 March 2021) 24; European Banking Authority, 'Consumer Trends Report 2018/2019' (*European Banking Authority*, 20 February 2019) 23; European Banking Authority, 'Consumer Trends Report 2015' (*European Banking Authority*, 18 June 2015) 29; European Banking Authority, 'Consumer Trends Report 2014' (*European Banking Authority*, 28 February 2014) 10; European Banking Authority, 'Report on Consumer Trends. Supervisory Concerns Regarding Consumer Protection Issues in 2012/2013' (*European Banking Authority*, 18 March 2013) 12.

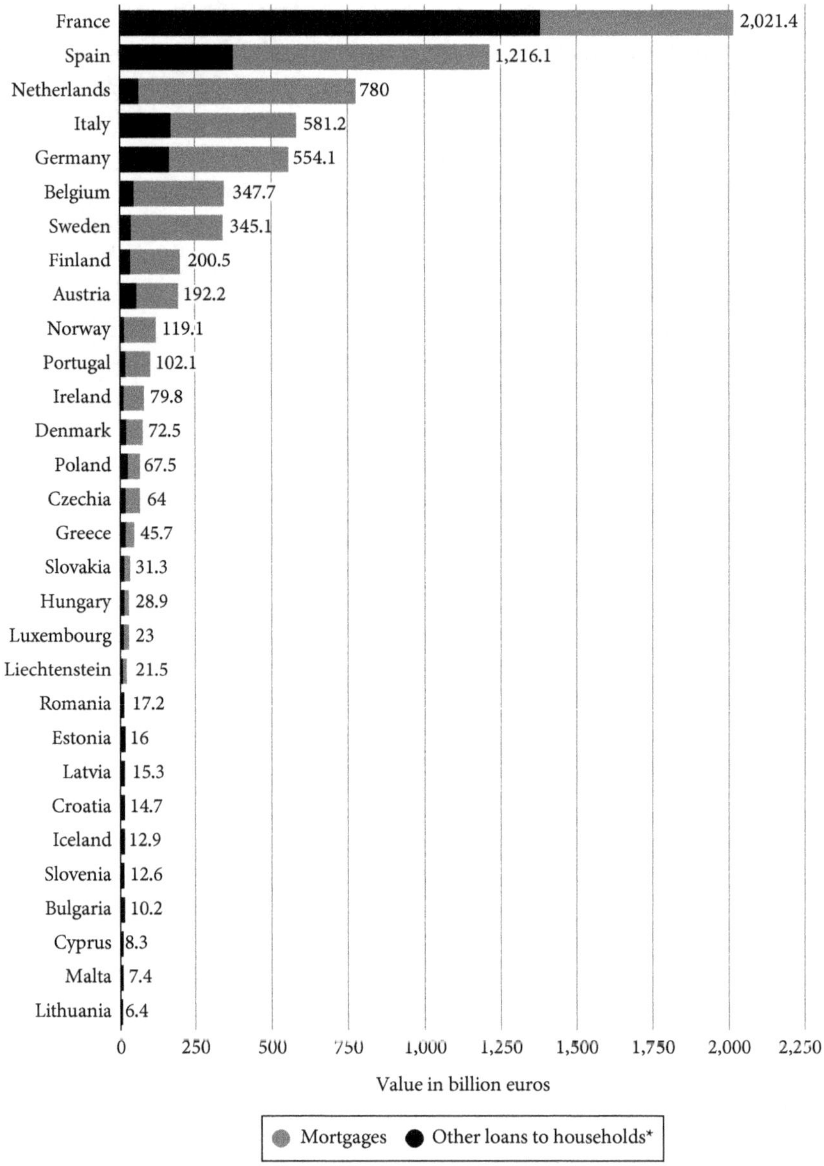

Figure 5.3 Value of loans and advances to households in the European Economic Area as of December 2022, by country and type (billions of euros).
Source: Statista.

report is likely attributable to the moratoria imposed on debt-collection during the pandemic.

Along with traditional consumer credit, utility bills make up a substantial part of household liabilities. The next section will examine their contribution to consumer debt.

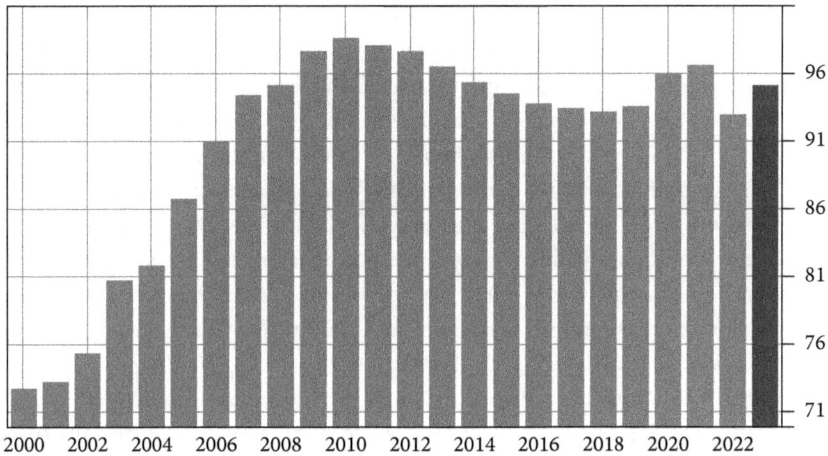

Figure 5.4 Euro area household debt to income.
Source: EUROSTAT.

5.6 Utility Bills and Debt Claims

The issue of consumer debt encompasses more than just credit. Unpaid utility bills also make up a significant portion of legal claims against consumers. According to the World Bank, enforcing these bills is a sensitive policy matter because of the essential nature of these services.[42] However, doing so may also strain the efficiency of the judiciary in some countries due to court congestion[43] and frivolous cases or objections.[44] This is because unpaid utility bills are generally not directly enforceable: utility providers must obtain an enforceable title and then execute it.[45] Although cheaper, swifter, and often non-litigious methods have been introduced,[46] such as the order for payment[47] in the EU, their low value compared to the resources invested in recovery makes judicial enforcement unappealing. As a result, many utility providers resort to self-help mechanisms such as cutting off access to services (where possible) or alternative means of enforcement such as using informal debt-collection or selling debt portfolios.

[42] World Bank and Ministry of Foreign Affairs of the Kingdom of the Netherlands, 'Towards Effective Enforcement of Uncontested Monetary Claims: Lessons from Eastern and Central Europe' (*World Bank Group*, June 2017) 1 <https://documents1.worldbank.org/curated/en/748601499954362710/pdf/117415-P161975-Towards-Effective-Enforcement-of-Uncontested-Claims.pdf> accessed 12 July 2023.

[43] ibid 4–5.

[44] ibid 25.

[45] ibid 8.

[46] As revealed by empirical data, exceptions from the non-litigious rule do exist in MS such as Romania, Slovakia, and Slovenia. World Bank and Ministry of Foreign Affairs of the Kingdom of the Netherlands (n 42) 12.

[47] Regulation (EC) No 1896/2006 creating a European order for payment procedure [2006] OJ L399/1.

Another reason why informal practices are preferred is the safeguards put in place to protect vulnerable debtors, ensuring that enforcement does not deprive them of subsistence or subject them to abusive outcomes.[48] An egregious example is the case of *Vaskrsić v Slovenia*, publicized by the European Court of Human Rights, where the debtor's house was sold at a public auction to cover a low-value debt.[49] These protections generally fall into two categories: (1) prohibitions or restrictions on targeting specific categories of debtors' assets and (2) the implementation of personal insolvency laws. Both categories vary in their effectiveness. Moreover, personal insolvency laws are surrounded by controversy, with claims that they may increase moral hazard and fraudulent behaviour among debtors,[50] despite a lack of supportive empirical evidence.

The EU has actively pursued reforms in monetary claim enforcement mechanisms—which are strongly connected to debt recovery—especially in new MS during the accession process.[51] These attempts to reform were followed by powerful lobbying by international financial institutions to curtail the protections offered to debtors or remove them altogether. In this context, the Credit Servicers and Credit Purchasers Directive represents a natural progression of reform efforts aimed at addressing the demands of business associations for improved enforcement efficiency by reducing administrative burdens, standardizing procedures, and ensuring unimpeded access to relevant national databases.

The aforementioned reforms were met with discontent for several reasons. One significant concern was high enforcement costs because judicial fees for obtaining an enforcement title are added to agents' or attorney's fees, resulting in a total amount that exceeds the original debt. This is particularly burdensome for small claims, such as those related to utility bills. Similar issues are reported in informal debt-collection, where debt-collectors attempt to collect interest or fees on top of the debt and prioritize these additional charges.[52] This practice led to legislative interventions to limit the additional costs that can be applied to the outstanding debt.[53]

[48] World Bank and Ministry of Foreign Affairs of the Kingdom of the Netherlands (n 42) 30–33.

[49] *Vaskrsić v Slovenia* CE:ECHR:2017:0425JUD003137112 (2017) ECHR 375. In the case, a debt in the initial value of 124 euros (increased to 500 euros when interest and enforcement expenses were added) was executed against the debtor's house, which was evaluated at 140,000 euros but sold at a public auction for merely 70,000 euros.

[50] World Bank and Ministry of Foreign Affairs of the Kingdom of the Netherlands (n 42) 32. See also: International Monetary Fund, 'Romania: Letter of Intent, Memorandum of Economic and Financial Policies, and Technical Memorandum of Understanding' (*International Monetary Fund*, 10 June 2013) 17, para 37 <https://www.imf.org/external/np/loi/2014/rou/030514.pdf> accessed 1 July 2024; Joseph Spooner, 'The Quiet-Loud-Quiet Politics of Post-Crisis Consumer Bankruptcy Law: The Case of Ireland and the Troika' (2018) 81(5) Modern Law Review 790.

[51] World Bank and Ministry of Foreign Affairs of the Kingdom of the Netherlands (n 42) 33–38.

[52] Olivier Jérusalmy, Paul Fox, and Nicolas Hercelin, 'Is the Human Dignity of Individual Debtors at Risk?' (*Finance Watch*, 2020) <https://www.finance-watch.org/wp-content/uploads/2020/01/Report_Human-dignity_final_with-annex.pdf> 36–37.

[53] World Bank and Ministry of Foreign Affairs of the Kingdom of the Netherlands (n 42) 41.

Nevertheless, utility companies often do not comply with these limits, as revealed by a market study conducted by the Swedish Data Protection Authority.[54] The study identified several serious deficiencies common to electricity companies involved in collection procedures. Among them, the study noted threats to discontinue service (even though this was not possible), payment requirements for something other than electricity, and additional charges over the amounts allowed by the law or through misleading methods (such as charging debt-collection costs in the consumer's next regular invoice) that lead to double payments.[55] This was not new in Sweden, where an electricity company violated the Swedish Debt Collection Law by charging nearly 3,000 consumers double collection costs in 2012.[56] Such antics artificially inflate the debt and push debtors into deeper over-indebtedness.

5.7 Summary

This chapter has highlighted how the expansion of credit and utility markets led to increased household liabilities and the subsequent rise in debt-collection activities. I now turn to the critical issue of consumer over-indebtedness. The next chapter examines the repercussions of this phenomenon, particularly the growing burden of over-indebtedness on consumers. It explores policy papers and legislative responses (or the lack thereof) aimed at addressing the abusive practices of the debt-collection industry and the additional strain caused by recent global events such as the COVID-19 pandemic.

[54] The Swedish Data Protection Authority was responsible for supervising compliance with the provisions of the Swedish Debt Collection Law until 2024, when the CSCPD was transposed into Swedish law.

[55] Datainspektionen, *Elbolags indrivning av konsumenters obetalda elfordringar* (Datainspektionens rapport 2014:1, 2014) <https://www.imy.se/globalassets/dokument/beslut/rapport-elbolag-indrivning.pdf> accessed 12 July 2023.

[56] IMY, 'Elkunder ersätts för dubbla inkassokostnader' (*IMY*, 12 November 2012) <https://www.imy.se/om-oss/arkiv/nyhetsarkiv/elkunder-ersatts-for-dubbla-inkassokostnader/> accessed 12 July 2023.

VI
CONSUMER INDEBTEDNESS AND DEBT-COLLECTION

6.1 Searching for Legal Remedies to Over-indebtedness in a Credit-driven Society

Consumer indebtedness and its repercussions have become pressing issues. As a result of expanding consumer credit markets, the ratio of consumer indebtedness came to express the volume of outstanding consumer credit relative to households' disposable income. Despite differences in the definition of over-indebtedness, from 1989 to 1993 this ratio remained relatively stable in most European Union (EU) countries. In Belgium, France, Spain, and the UK, the ratios hovered around 10 per cent, while Germany had the highest ratio at 17 per cent and Greece and Italy the lowest at 4 per cent. The subsequent reversal of these ratios in Greece and Italy over just two decades is a stark reminder of the potential risks associated with a credit-driven society. Furthermore, starting in 1993 the UK also experienced a rapid rise in consumer indebtedness, eventually reaching a ratio similar to that of Germany.[1] Addressing over-indebtedness requires exploring the proposed legal remedies and the measures taken by various authorities.

In 2005, the European Ministers of Justice adopted a resolution regarding legal solutions to debt problems in a 'credit society'. They expressed concern about the issues arising, among others, from easy access to credit, which could lead to over-indebtedness for individuals and families. The European Committee on Legal Co-operation was entrusted with preparing an appropriate instrument defining legislative and administrative measures and considering remedies to prevent and solve debt problems.

The Committee of Ministers adopted the resulting recommendation in June 2007. It was published in 2008,[2] making it the first international legal instrument to establish principles to assist legislators in introducing or reinforcing laws and policies in the field. It broadly defined over-indebtedness as 'the situation where the debt burden of an individual or family manifestly and on a long-term basis exceeds

[1] European Credit Research Institute, '2002 Consumer Credit in the European Union Report' (*European Credit Research Institute*, 2002) 13.

[2] Council of Europe, 'Legal Solutions to Debt Problems: Recommendation Rec (2007)8 and Explanatory Memorandum' (*Council of Europe*, September 2008) <https://rm.coe.int/16807096bb> accessed 25 January 2024.

EU Informal Debt-Collection Regulation. Cătălin-Gabriel Stănescu, Oxford University Press.
 DOI: 10.1093/oso/9780198966159.003.0006

the repayment capacity'.[3] With the 2008 financial crisis unfolding, the recommendation could not have come at a better time. Addressing over-indebtedness was justified due to its contribution to social and health issues and the social exclusion of families and because it endangers the fulfilment of children's basic needs.[4] Yet, the recommendation's practical effects are difficult to assess.

The governments of the member states (MS) were encouraged to develop internal legislation and practices regarding solutions to debt problems. They were advised to take appropriate measures to alleviate the impact of debt recovery, in particular by 'respecting the debtor's rights and human dignity at all stages of debt-collection and debt enforcement procedures, without infringing the rights of creditors'[5] and by

> introducing enforcement alleviation procedures, including the protection of the essential assets of the debtor and garnishment of part of his/her revenue, which takes into account the need to strike a balance between the protection of at least the basic living needs of the debtor and his/her family and the efficiency of debt recovery.[6]

The commentary accompanying the recommendation emphasizes that in both judicial and non-judicial debt-collection, 'the debtor rights and human dignity should be duly safeguarded at all stages of debt enforcement'.[7] It also highlights the need to protect the essential assets of the debtor to mitigate any adverse impact on the ability of adult family members to generate income or on the development of their children.[8]

Regrettably, the recommendation failed to materialize. In the aftermath of the financial crisis, a grave social issue unfolded due to widespread repossessions and foreclosures all over Europe. These left many consumers without their homes and saddled with a significant debt burden for deficiency payments (the difference between the face value of their loans and the proceeds from the sale of their properties). A decade later, Croatia (and other EU MS) continued to witness cases in which debtors faced foreclosure on their residences[9] or had their accounts frozen[10] over minor and artificially inflated debts.

[3] ibid 6.
[4] ibid 5.
[5] ibid 6, Recommendation 3(b).
[6] ibid 7, Recommendation 3(c).
[7] ibid para 27.
[8] ibid para 28.
[9] Paula Poretti, 'Debt Collection Practices under Croatian Enforcement Law—Is There a Way Out for Over-indebted Consumers?' (2018) 7(6) Journal of European Consumer and Market Law 233.
[10] Marek Mikuš, 'Making Debt Work: Debating and Devising Debt Collection in Croatia' in Chris Hann and Don Kalb (eds), *Financialization: relational approaches* (Berghahn Books 2020) 241–65.

During the same period, the debt-collection industry witnessed an unprecedented boom and cross-border expansion as specialized recovery agencies followed foreign capital into the most indebted MS. Their expansion into new markets was linked to the increase in banks' sales of bad loans or telecom companies' sales of claims on natural persons. Where ambiguities about the legal recognition of the assignment of debts existed, they were duly removed or clarified.[11] This change altered local debt-collection systems, which became more market-based and profit-oriented.[12] It also led to an increase in complaints and reports about abusive practices.[13]

Concurrently, debt recovery evolved into a thriving industry influenced by interest groups, going well beyond the boundaries of informal practices. Legally sanctioned enforcers[14] also reaped the benefits of newly implemented legal procedures, such as the order for payment procedure, designed for practicality and efficiency.[15] This further facilitated the expansion of consumer credit based on high-interest lending, foreign currency lending, inadequate credit checks, and myriad unfair contract terms and commercial practices. It was a debt-creation bonanza, a well-documented phenomenon in Southern and Eastern European countries.[16] Despite efforts to provide legal solutions, the legislative responses at the MS level had been inadequate, warranting a closer look.

6.2 The Lack of Legislative Response at the EU and Member State Level

This unprecedented development was not countered or balanced by the adoption of fair debt-collection rules or resolution mechanisms. Even though the 2002 Proposal for a Consumer Credit Directive at the EU level included a minimal set of regulations governing debt recovery, none of these made it into the final version adopted in 2008 (see Chapter IX, Section 9.3).[17] At the national level, only four

[11] ibid. See also, regarding Greece, where most bans were lifted by Law 4354/2015 on Servicing of non-performing loans, wage settlements and other urgent provisions implementing the agreement on fiscal targets and structural reforms, Government Gazette, vol A (176/16.12.2015).

[12] Mikuš (n 10) 241–65.

[13] ibid.

[14] Martina Mantovani, 'Notaries and Their Debt-Collection Writs under the Brussels I Regulation. A Difficult Characterisation' (2019) 15(2) Journal of Private International Law 393.

[15] Regulation (EC) No 1896/2006 creating a European order for payment procedure [2006] OJ L399/1, 1–32.

[16] Mikuš (n 10) 241–65. See also: Irina Domurath, Guido Comparato and Hans-W Micklitz (eds), *The Over-indebtedness of European Consumers—a View from Six Countries* (EUI Working Paper LAW 2014/10, ERC-ERPL-08, 2014) <https://papers.ssrn.com/sol3/Delivery.cfm/SSRN_ID2504531_code2171964.pdf?abstractid=2504531&mirid=1> accessed 25 January 2024.

[17] Proposal for a Directive of the European Parliament and of the Council on the harmonization of the laws, regulations and administrative provision of the Member States concerning credit for consumers, Brussels, 11.09.2002, COM (2002) 443 final, 2002/0222(COD).

of the twenty-three EU MS without a sectorial law addressing debt-collection at that time adopted one subsequently (but not necessarily due to the recommendation): Germany (2007), Greece (2009), Latvia (2012), and Romania (2016).

To add insult to injury, many attempts to alleviate debtors' situation in countries such as Ireland or Romania were met with staunch opposition by the financial lobby. Global financial institutions, such as the International Monetary Fund, threatened to cut any financial support to the Irish and Romanian governments if they enacted legislation that could encourage 'moral hazard' and hamper 'payment discipline'.[18] The subsequent austerity measures only deepened the social crisis.[19] Its full impact comes into view through an examination of the profile of over-indebted debtors in the EU following the financial crisis.

6.2.1 Over-indebtedness in the European Union following the financial crisis: A debtor's profile

In February 2008, the European Commission (EC) sought to establish a common operational European definition of over-indebtedness. At the time, there was a lack of comparable statistics regarding the state, extent, and past development of over-indebtedness, hindering the evaluation of policy measures and undermining informed discussions about the effectiveness of prevention measures.[20] Eurobarometer data revealed that 13 per cent of EU households had difficulties meeting credit and other household commitments in 2006, before the financial crisis.

The 2008 EC study revealed that financial difficulties were most prevalent in Eastern and Southern Europe, while they were the lowest in Northern Europe, particularly in Scandinavia and the Benelux countries. Countries with low income and high income inequality were associated with higher levels of financial difficulties.[21] At the micro level, previous research consistently demonstrated that personal characteristics, such as being young, single, and having children, along with economic circumstances such as low income, economic inactivity, and renting a home, were strongly linked to the likelihood of experiencing financial difficulties.

[18] International Monetary Fund, 'Romania: Letter of Intent, Memorandum of Economic and Financial Policies, and Technical Memorandum of Understanding' (*International Monetary Fund*, 10 June 2013) 17, para 37 <https://www.imf.org/external/np/loi/2014/rou/030514.pdf> accessed 1 July 2024; Joseph Spooner, 'The Quiet-Loud-Quiet Politics of Post-Crisis Consumer Bankruptcy Law: The Case of Ireland and the Troika' (2018) 81(5) Modern Law Review 790.

[19] Domurath, Comparato, and Micklitz (n 16).

[20] European Commission, 'Towards a Common Operational European Definition of Over-indebtedness' (*European Commission*, February 2008) <https://www.bristol.ac.uk/media-library/sites/geography/migrated/documents/pfrc0804.pdf> accessed 25 January 2024.

[21] ibid 3.

Additional factors, such as unexpected financial shocks, over-borrowing, and poor money management, compounded the problem.[22]

The authors established five criteria for assessing over-indebted households: (1) high commitment payments that push the household below the poverty threshold; (2) structural arrears on at least one financial commitment (e.g. credit or recurring bills like utilities); (3) a burden of monthly commitment payments, encompassing housing costs and payments for other loans; 4) payment considered 'very difficult' or 'difficult' by the household; and 5) inability to meet unexpected expenses (illiquidity). According to the authors' assessment, households meeting the last four criteria were deemed at risk of over-indebtedness.[23]

6.2.2 Proposed measures for responsible arrears management to prevent over-indebtedness

All the above would earn the households in question a place on a debt-collector's list, making them particularly relevant to the subject of this book. Thus, the EC's study lists 'responsible arrears management' as one step to prevent over-indebtedness. The authors argue that it would be in the creditor's interest to take a proactive approach to managing overdue payments by implementing measures to help prevent them.

Creditors were advised to establish procedures and systems that were adaptable enough to deal with defaulting customers on an *individual* basis. The authors recommended that when customers fall behind on payments, creditors discuss their repayment capabilities, negotiate realistic payment plans, and tolerate a certain degree of forbearance.[24] Court action and debt recovery were considered a last resort that should only be pursued selectively. The text also proposed clear limits on debt-collection agencies' activities based on the Council of Europe's 2007 recommendation and report on legal solutions to debt problems. Lastly, it stressed the need to balance creditors' interests with the protection of the dignity and essential assets of the debtor.[25]

However, during the financial crisis it was evident that creditors, particularly foreign ones, were unwilling to show patience and negotiate with their debtors, especially when their profits or survival were at risk. This worsened the social crisis. Moreover, with stricter prudential regulations looming, disposing of bad debt portfolios became widespread. While policies were proposed, their implementation often fell short, leading to further challenges.

[22] ibid 4.
[23] ibid 6.
[24] ibid 8.
[25] ibid.

6.2.3 Policies on over-indebtedness: Lip service

In the 2013 study conducted in the EU, over-indebtedness was defined as ongoing difficulty in meeting financial commitments, whether related to servicing secured or unsecured borrowing or the payment of rent, utility, or other household debts.[26] Due to the enduring effects of the financial crisis, the issue continued to be severe. According to Eurostat, approximately 10 per cent of European households were over-indebted due to credit activities. Low-income families were found to be particularly vulnerable to economic shocks when in debt as lower earnings or higher interest rates could rapidly lead to an unsustainable debt burden and financial distress.[27]

According to the EU-SILC survey data, in 2011, on average, 11.4 per cent of those surveyed had experienced arrears with payments for rent/mortgage, utility bills, and hire-purchase/loan agreements due to financial difficulties. However, this average masked significant variation in the levels and nature of economic challenges across individual MS. For example, in Bulgaria, Greece, and Romania, more than 30 per cent of respondents had been in arrears in the previous 12 months, while in Sweden, Germany, the Netherlands, and Luxembourg, the percentage was 6 per cent or lower.[28]

When breaking down the overall arrears into specific categories, the 2013 study found the proportion of people in arrears on utility bills in the EU to be the highest (at 8.8 per cent) among overall arrears on critical commitments. Notably, the frequency of overdue utility bills was highest in the twelve MS that acceded to the EU in 2004 and 2007. Data on debt write-offs by creditors was only available for a few MS concerning mortgage default rates.[29]

The study also sought to ascertain whether using unsecured credit increases the likelihood of falling behind on payments. While macroeconomic data did not directly show a link between mortgage borrowing and payment arrears, a more straightforward relationship was observed with consumer credit. The study revealed a significant positive correlation between the level of consumer debt outstanding and the frequency of arrears on hire purchases or other loans. A stronger correlation was also identified between consumer debt levels and the frequency of arrears on utility bills.[30] These findings and previous research suggested that

[26] Civic Consulting, 'The Over-indebtedness of European Households: Updated Mapping of the Situation, Nature and Causes, Effects, and Initiatives for Alleviating Its Impact. Final Report, Part 1: Synthesis of findings' (*European Commission*, 2013) 19 <https://commission.europa.eu/system/files/2018-06/final-report-on-over-indebtedness-of-european-households-synthesis-of-findings_december2013_en.pdf> accessed 25 January 2024.

[27] European Central Bank, 'The Eurosystem Household Finance and Consumption Survey' (*European Central Bank*, 2013) 71 https://www.ecb.europa.eu/pub/pdf/other/ecbsp2en.pdf?2180f869d12ccc366869c9419b3da32e> cited by European Commission, Consumer Financial Services Action Plan: Better Products, More Choice, COM(2017)139, 9.

[28] Civic Consulting (n 26) 5.

[29] ibid.

[30] ibid 9.

lower-income individuals were more inclined to take out loans to cover overdue utility bills or housing costs. Still, the study lacked sufficient data to verify this hypothesis.

At the stakeholder level, an interesting finding of the 2013 study was that most respondents attributed household financial difficulties to high interest-rate credit from regulated lenders.[31] This trend was particularly noticeable in the twelve new EU MS, where foreign-owned banks capitalized on lenient regulations to offer expensive credit products, prioritizing profit over consumer well-being. Their complete disregard for the systemic danger they created for consumers and themselves placed the entire financial sector at risk. Central bank interventions were either insufficient or too late to address these issues effectively.[32] The widespread use of abusive practices in the debt-collection industry significantly worsened the situation for consumers struggling with debt.

6.3 Exacerbating Abusive Industry Practices

The collective impact of reduced living standards, available income, and welfare as well as austerity measures made it challenging for debtors to fulfil their financial commitments. Consequently, the surge in non-performing loans (NPLs) weakened bank balance sheets and diminished credit availability, leading to a significant increase in debt-collection activities.[33]

In the 2013 study, 57 per cent of respondents reported experiencing increased aggressiveness in debt-collection in the previous five years. Some felt that aggressive practices lingered on the edge of the law: repeated calls at inappropriate times, SMS messages, calls at the workplace, and threats of court action and seizure. More severe methods included parking a van from the debt-collection agency in front of a person's house to shame them publicly (Portugal) or threatening older people with repossession of and eviction from their homes despite a governmental moratorium or with jail time, even though that was not possible for civil debt (Greece).

Such practices were observed in countries with diverse economic backgrounds, regardless of whether debt-collection regulations existed. These countries included Austria, Belgium, Bulgaria, Germany, Hungary, Latvia, the Netherlands, Sweden, and the UK.[34] However, aggressive practices were more prevalent in the twelve new MS (52 per cent of all stakeholders) than in the fifteen old MS (43 per cent).[35] Furthermore, the perception of these practices was stronger among civil

[31] ibid.
[32] See the case of Romania.
[33] Civic Consulting (n 26) 11–12.
[34] ibid 200–02.
[35] ibid 202.

society stakeholders (more than 59 per cent) than among financial industry stakeholders (32 per cent).

One explanation was the lack of sectorial regulation in this area.[36] The 2013 study recommended, among others, introducing best practices for responsible debt-collection that consider the individual debtor's circumstances and respect their dignity. It also suggested licensing debt-collection and debt-management companies as well as regulatory monitoring and enforcement.[37] Importantly, no references were made to EU legislation, such as the Unfair Commercial Practices Directive, possibly because it could not tackle the problem effectively.[38] Despite these recommendations, the MS did not act quickly to implement the necessary sector-specific legislation. Following the financial crisis, only four MS implemented debt-collection laws, and one did so after the study (Romania in 2016[39]). Additionally, the UK updated its debt-collection Act in 2014.

The 2013 study also noted that creditors were increasingly outsourcing debt-collection to third-party agencies in several MS, such as Austria, Bulgaria, Ireland, Portugal, and Romania.[40] This made it more difficult for consumers and debt advisors to manage debt repayments as it was often unclear which agency was responsible for what debt. Furthermore, in countries such as Austria, Greece, and Germany, creditors were reluctant to engage in discussions towards a settlement agreement.[41] The COVID-19 pandemic then further complicated the landscape, impacting consumers and creditors alike.

6.4 The Impact of the Pandemic and Projections for the Future

The latest EC report mapping the over-indebtedness of households in the EU, released in 2023, reflects the impact of the COVID-19 pandemic, increasing interest rates, and inflation caused by the onset of the war in Ukraine. It uses the same definition as the 2013 report. The report states that in 2020, 8.8 per cent of households were in arrears with their essential financial commitments, representing 17.2 million households and approximately 40 million people across the Union.[42]

36 ibid 202–03.

37 ibid 237.

38 Cătălin Gabriel Stănescu, 'Is the Unfair Commercial Practices Directive Fit to Effectively Tackle Abusive Debt Collection? A Critical Evaluation' (2020) 9(6) Journal of European Consumer and Market Law 235, 235–47.

39 However, Romania first attempted to adopt a debt-collection act in 2012, predating the study.

40 Civic Consulting (n 26) 202.

41 ibid 223.

42 European Commission, 'Study on European Consumers' Over-indebtedness, and its Implications. Final Report' (*European Commission*, June 2023), 17, 24–29 <https://commission.europa.eu/document/download/5002ff16-a502-4b98-91cd-4536b5cd70ec_en?filename=Study%20of%20consumer%20over-indebtedness_Main%20report_9.18.pdf> accessed 1 July 2024.

The report highlights the minimal progress in reducing the significant variations in the prevalence of over-indebtedness across the EU over the past decade. In 2020, Greece and Bulgaria continued to exhibit the highest levels of over-indebtedness, while Luxembourg, the Netherlands, and Sweden maintained the lowest levels. Furthermore, the report notes no significant changes in the complex nexus of factors influencing over-indebtedness.[43]

Minor fluctuations were observed in the trends between 2013 and 2020. Over this period, there was an overall 32 per cent decrease in the share of the population in arrears (from 12.9 per cent to 8.8 per cent).[44] This decline was likely due to the economic recovery post financial crisis. The lowest percentage (8.2 per cent) was recorded at the EU level in 2019. However, considerable variations among MS persisted, indicating that countries with a high share of households in arrears in 2013 did not necessarily experience the most significant decrease during the surveyed period. Additionally, the decline in over-indebtedness levels was reversed after 2019 due to the COVID-19 pandemic.[45]

The study estimates that in 2020, around 1.17 million households (approximately 2.7 million people) throughout Europe fell into over-indebtedness due to the pandemic.[46] Nearly one in three Europeans could not cover unforeseen financial expenses, and one in five struggled to make ends meet. Although the percentage of people feeling unable to make ends meet had decreased to 18.5 per cent between 2013 and 2020, it rose to 25.5 per cent between 2019 and 2020.[47] Despite the implementation of countermeasures by MS, such as mortgage and consumer loan repayment moratoria or the EC's list of best practices agreed on with the financial sector, the expected outcomes failed to materialize. Households in Ireland and Spain were significantly impacted in their ability to manage housing costs, experiencing the most dramatic increase in arrears on hire purchase or loan payments since 2019.

The 2023 study reaffirmed previous findings that consumer loans and credit card debt are the main contributors to consumer over-indebtedness in the EU.[48] Furthermore, it noted an increase in the number of EU households in arrears on utility bills, a trend expected to continue due to factors such as higher energy prices, the lingering effects of the pandemic, the war in Ukraine,[49] and rising inflation and interest rates.[50]

The EC 2023 report provides projections regarding over-indebtedness from 2020 to 2032. It anticipates that the share of affected households will rise from

[43] ibid 17, 30–39.
[44] ibid 40.
[45] ibid 41–42.
[46] ibid 18.
[47] ibid 19, 58–64.
[48] ibid 51–53.
[49] ibid 18–19, 45–46.
[50] ibid 140–41.

8.8 per cent in 2020 (17.2 million households) to 11.3 per cent in 2032 (22.1 million), representing a 28 per cent increase over the entire period.[51] Nonetheless, the growth and trajectory would vary significantly between MS. For instance, countries with high household indebtedness in 2020 may experience a 50 per cent increase in 2027, with notable implications for individual MS, such as Greece and Bulgaria.[52] While such projections pose concerns for households, they signify a positive trend for the debt-collection industry, which has already enjoyed several years of growth and expansion and can expect a further increase in business and revenue. Concomitantly, these projections highlight the need for adequate regulation of informal debt-collection. In light of these challenges, updated recommendations for handling over-indebtedness and arrears management are essential.

6.5 Over-indebtedness and Arrears Management: The 2023 Recommendations for Handling Debtors

Finally, the 2023 report dedicates attention to preventive and remedial measures addressing the impact of over-indebtedness. Additionally, it includes a legal analysis of EU and national rules governing consumer credit, mortgages, and personal bankruptcy in twelve selected MS. The report briefly touches upon the issue of abusive debt-collection regulation, but only in the context of the newly adopted NPL directive—the Credit Servicers and Credit Purchasers Directive (CSCPD).

The report notes that the CSCPD may significantly impact the economy and consumer over-indebtedness. Although the material scope of the CSCPD does not directly cover borrowers and consumers, they may still be affected in various ways once it is transposed into national systems. One such impact is the change in creditor experienced by the consumer when the defaulting loan is transferred to a debt buyer or another third party. The report's authors believe that the risks associated with the change are mitigated by the certification process of credit servicers, who must obtain authorization to carry out their activities.[53] However, crucially, the process does not affect the change in creditor because credit purchasers only undergo the same certification requirements if they plan to recover the debt themselves. Furthermore, the certification process cannot fully account for the loss of the original agreement's *intuitu personae* character once the debt is transferred.

On the positive side, the report highlights the presence of provisions that establish an obligation for lenders and credit servicers to treat their borrowers in good faith, safeguard their privacy, and communicate without engaging in harassment, coercion, or undue influence. Additionally, the CSCPD imposes a duty on

[51] ibid 166–67.
[52] ibid 167–68.
[53] ibid 245–46.

creditors to try 'reasonable forbearance measures' before initiating debt-collection actions and requires consumers to be notified of any change in creditor for it to be binding on them.[54] Moreover, the directive's wording could be interpreted as preventing creditors from imposing excessive or abusive charges on consumers (including vulnerable consumers) due to default.[55]

However, the positive observations stop here. The report recognizes that notification of transfer does not imply consent and that consumers cannot object to or resist the transfer of their loan to a different party.[56] Additionally, creditors are not required to implement forbearance measures, leaving the decision mainly to their discretion. Furthermore, the CSCPD allows MS to offer fewer measures than those outlined in the directive and determine the extent of the cap on additional charges.[57]

The national experts raised additional concerns. Variations in national legislation, such as the ten-year prescription period for civil obligations in Bulgaria, could result in consumers being required to pay exorbitantly high amounts, exceeding 100 per cent of the initial debt. This has created an appealing environment for debt purchasers and collectors who were already acquiring debt portfolios.[58] The Italian respondent expressed concerns regarding the unintended consequences of consumer privacy in driving NPL transactions and enabling debt-collectors' activities by providing them with access to a significant amount of sensitive data across the Union.[59] Both the Italian and Greek respondents also had reservations about the legitimacy of NPL transactions that occur without the consumers' consent.

The report neither rejects nor supports the national experts' criticisms, leaving this task to future assessments.[60] It stresses the importance of carefully balancing efforts to increase banks' profitability by creating a secondary market for NPLs and facilitating debt-collection with measures to protect consumers' interests and prevent harm.[61] Yet, it does not propose specific measures or clarify how this balance could be achieved. Due to the relative novelty of the report, it is also challenging to assess its impact on EU policy or predict the measures the EC will adopt in response.

The aforementioned reports consistently indicate that consumer loans and credit card debt are the primary contributors to consumer over-indebtedness in the EU. Therefore, it is not surprising that in 2017 the EC adopted a plan of action to deal with NPLs, of which consumer credit constitutes a significant portion. Facilitating a secondary market for NPL transactions by standardizing

54 ibid 247–48.
55 ibid 249.
56 ibid 248.
57 ibid 249.
58 ibid 250–51.
59 ibid 251.
60 ibid 252.
61 ibid 252, 268.

authorization requirements and easing debt-collection activities is a natural step in helping banks manage their bad debts and resume credit operations (new debt creation).

However, the externalization of debt and debt-collection has led creditors across the EU to completely disregard the EC's recommendations to address each struggling debtor individually and offer them personalized solutions. Subsequent calls from consumer non-governmental organizations[62] and academia to establish rules for debt-collection were also ignored. The adoption of the CSCPD may imply that the EC has succumbed to financial interests. As a result, debts will be bundled into large portfolios and discarded on secondary markets for cents on a euro, making debtors someone else's problem.

6.6 Summary

The preceding chapters analysed the empirical background of consumer debt markets and over-indebtedness. They delved into the evolution of consumer credit in Europe, its implications for economies following the financial crisis, and the exacerbation of debt challenges during the pandemic. The discussion centred on the increase in consumer credit, the enduring nature of over-indebtedness, and the aggressive tactics employed in debt-collection, highlighting the need for responsible arrears management and comprehensive policy reform to protect consumer interests. Addressing these issues is crucial for mitigating the negative impact of debt-collection and ensuring a fair and balanced approach to consumer debt.

With a thorough understanding of consumer indebtedness and the challenges posed by aggressive debt-collection practices, it is essential to broaden the perspective to the larger debt market landscape. The complexities of informal debt-collection regulation can only be fully grasped by analysing the key actors and structures within the debt markets. The following chapters examine the size and scope of these markets across the EU and scrutinize the roles of industry associations at the EU and national levels as well as multinational debt-collection agencies. These insights will further illuminate the challenges posed by the debt-collection sector.

[62] Olivier Jérusalmy, Paul Fox, and Nicolas Hercelin, 'Is the Human Dignity of Individual Debtors at Risk?' (*Finance Watch*, 2020) 40 <https://www.finance-watch.org/wp-content/uploads/2020/01/Report_Human-dignity_final_with-annex.pdf>; Finance Watch, 'From Debtor Prisons to Being Prisoners of Debt. Making the Case for Harmonised EU Consumer Insolvency Rules' (*Finance Watch*, January 2022) 16 <https://www.finance-watch.org/wp-content/uploads/2022/01/Personal-insolvency-paper-january-2022.pdf> accessed 30 January 2024.

VII
THE DEBT MARKET IN THE EUROPEAN UNION

7.1 The Non-performing Loan Market

In the European Central Bank's (ECB) view, the fact that uncollateralized consumer debt is historically characterized by higher default rates than mortgages is especially problematic because lower-income households hold a large share of it. The risk increases in member states (MS) where lower-income households with high debt-servicing costs but limited savings hold a relatively large percentage of the banking system's debt.[1] Although the ECB does not envision significant changes in the short term, other scenarios suggest that unless the current economic circumstances improve, many countries will see a considerable increase in their NPL ratio.[2]

The ECB's conclusions are troublesome because following the financial crisis, the NPL ratio in the EU peaked at 1.2 trillion euros in June 2015, including both consumer and business loans. The figure shrank by more than half in September 2022, primarily due to NPL sales on secondary markets and securitization. A record sale was held in 2018 when European NPL trade hit 208.2 billion euros, whereas it fell to 67.7 billion euros during the pandemic (see Figure 1).[3]

NPL ratios continued to decline (see Figure 7.2), reaching a record low in 2022,[4] although the ECB feared a reversal due to changing economic and political realities.[5]

[1] Daniel Dieckelmann and Julian Metzler, 'Household Inequality and Financial Stability Risks: Exploring the Impact of Changes in Consumer Prices and Interest Rates' (*European Central Bank*, November 2022) <https://www.ecb.europa.eu/pub/financial-stability/fsr/special/html/ecb.fsrart202211_02~8c5b8be620.en.html> accessed 30 March 2023.

[2] ibid.

[3] Debashis Dey, Dennis Heuer, Victoria Landsbert, Jeffrey Rubinoff, and Lisa Seifman, 'Covid-19 and the State of the European NPL Market' (*White & Case*, April 2021) <https://www.whitecase.com/insight-our-thinking/covid-19-and-state-european-npl-market> accessed 31 January 2023; Romina Tsouni, 'The NPL Situation in Europe for Q3 2022 and Beyond' (*Exus*) <https://www.exus.co.uk/blog/the-npl-situation-in-europe-for-q3-2022-and-beyond> accessed 31 January 2023; Sarah Caldwell, Jason Richardson, and Richard Hakes, 'EU Directive for NPLs Sets New Standards for Investors and Servicers' (*Reed Smith*, 7 February 2022) <https://www.reedsmith.com/en/perspectives/2022/02/eu-directive-for-npls-sets-new-standards-for-investors-and-servicers> accessed 31 January 2023.

[4] Romina Tsouni, 'The NPL Situation in Europe for Q3 2022 and Beyond' (*Exus*) <https://www.exus.co.uk/blog/the-npl-situation-in-europe-for-q3-2022-and-beyond> accessed 31 January 2023.

[5] Eric Cloutier, 'Non-Performing Loans: Early Signs Point Towards an Increase Next Year' (*KPMG*, November 2022) <https://kpmg.com/xx/en/home/insights/2022/11/non-performing-loans-early-signs-point-towards-an-increase-in-2023.html> accessed 31 January 2023.

EU Informal Debt-Collection Regulation. Cătălin-Gabriel Stănescu, Oxford University Press.
 DOI: 10.1093/oso/9780198966159.003.0007

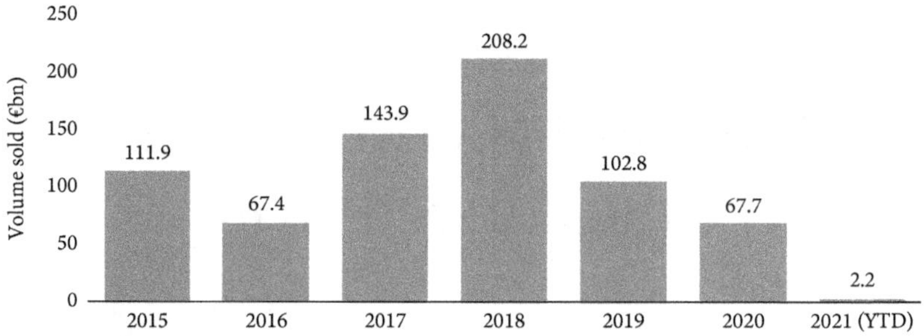

Figure 7.1 Non-performing loans and non-core loan deals in Europe by year.
Source: White & Case.

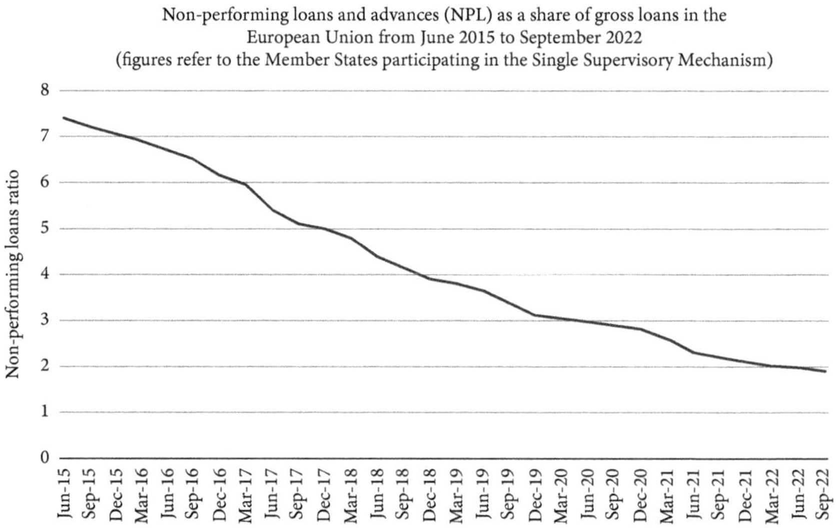

Figure 7.2 Non-performing loan ratio in the EU, 2015–2022.
Source: European Central Bank. Compiled by Statista.

By 2024,[6] EU banks, particularly in the South, had largely completed the clean-ups that fed the bad loan bonanza and pulled in overseas investment firms. In Italy, the biggest market for bad debts, sales in 2023 totalled 31 billion euros, a third of the 2018 peak. However, if in 2018 nearly all disposals came from banks, more than half were re-sales in 2023.

6 Valentina Za, 'Europe's Debt Collectors Face Reckoning as Bad Loans Vanish' (*Reuters*, 20 March 2023) <https://www.reuters.com/markets/europe/europes-debt-collectors-face-reckoning-bad-loans-vanish-2024-03-20/> accessed 9 July 2024.

Even so, the significance of NPL transactions should not be ignored. Although they are removed from balance sheets, they must still be collected, and the debt-collection industry plays a key role. For example, consumer credit represented 5.6 per cent (35.6 billion euros) of the total remaining NPL figures in 2019 (636 billion euros), and small and medium enterprises (SMEs) amounted to 8.5 per cent (54 billion euros).[7] Applying the exact percentage to written-off NPLs suggests that between 2015 and 2019, 31.5 billion euros worth of defaulted credits to consumers and 47.9 billion euros of defaulted credits to SMEs were discarded, many of them on the secondary NPL market to entities specializing in debt purchasing and debt-collection.[8] This hints at an EU debt-purchasing and debt-collection market's average annual size of at least 20 billion euros. The figures are much higher because serviced consumer debt stems not only from bank loans but also from unpaid utility bills.

Another relevant factor is that NPLs are generally sold at significant discounts while debt buyers retain the right to collect the face value of the defaulted loans. This means a substantial profit margin,[9] which explains the investors' increased appetite for NPLs and the development of a secondary market for NPLs.[10]

Adding to this the risk posed by NPL ratios to the overall economy and the financial system, it should be no surprise that the EU has taken a keen interest in the matter. De-risking the banking sector has been a high political and supervisory priority because some view it as a prerequisite to completing the European banking union.[11]

7.2 The Debt-collection Market

To provide an accurate background to the discussion, I gathered empirical data concerning the debt-collection markets in each MS. To that end, I contacted the central banks of all twenty-seven EU MS. My efforts were only partially successful: only eleven addressees responded to my solicitation for public

7 European Banking Authority, 'Report on NPLs. Progress Made and Challenges Ahead' (*European Banking Authority*, 2019) 8 <https://www.eba.europa.eu/sites/default/documents/files/document_library/Risk%20Analysis%20and%20Data/Risk%20Assessment%20Reports/2019//Final%20EBA%20Report%20on%20NPLs-for%20publication_final.pdf> accessed 30 March 2023.

8 ibid 16. According to the consulted banks, the decrease in NPL volumes was due to internal workouts and more efficient NPL strategies that focused not only on cures but also on sales, write-offs, cash collections, and foreclosures.

9 According to the available data, in 2017, the purchase price for NPLs averaged between 3% and 10%. See: John Murray Brown and Robert Smith, 'Europe's Debt Collectors Face Own Loan Concerns' (*Financial Times*, 22 November 2017) <https://archive.is/20220322074448/https://www.ft.com/content/1bc35d86-c9e9-11e7-aa33-c63fdc9b8c6c> accessed 10 July 2024.

10 European Banking Authority (n 7) 16.

11 ibid 60.

information. Moreover, only two of these (Greece[12] and Romania[13]) provided me with information regarding the size of their debt-collection markets. The Spanish Central Bank informed me that it does not disclose this information, while the remaining respondents stated that they do not have such data.

Obtaining similar records from the Federation of European National Collection Associations (FENCA) or the affiliated national debt-collection associations proved equally challenging. Currently, on its webpage and in all press releases, FENCA informs that the

> European credit management, debt-collection and debt purchase sector re-inject between 45 and 55 billion EUR of valid claims back into the EU-economy each year, thereby securing above all the liquidity of micro, small and medium enterprises within the EU, while helping to keep the cost of credit at a reasonable level for all consumers.[14]

The amalgamation of consumer and business debt figures may be accurate, although I could not verify it. In its early years, FENCA collected data about debts referred to member associations. A survey from August 1999 attempted to ascertain the number of members of each national agency, the total number of debts sent to agencies, the face value of the debts in euros, and the actual amount collected in euros. The survey covered ten member associations, but only four provided responses (Austria, Belgium, Norway, and Switzerland), two from outside the EU.[15] According to their responses, the four members acquired debts of a face value of more than 2 billion euros, of which they recovered around 984 million euros. The survey does not contain information about the market price, so it is impossible to assess the profitability of the assignments.

After contacting the national associations, I received only one answer—from the Danish one, which stated that because it is a 'small industry federation,' it does not have the requested information. The inquiry could have been quickly addressed with an internal request to its members, but the association was not interested in extending help that could bring their activity further into the spotlight.

However, where the law requires, debt-collection associations publish information about their yearly activities and results. Here a different issue presents itself, namely, a mismatch between the self-reported figures of the industry and those communicated to the supervisory agency. In the case of Romania, for instance, the numbers published on the debt-collection association's website are at least

[12] As of May 2024, the debt-collection market for consumer debt in Greece amounted to 37.6 billion euros.

[13] As of December 2020, the debt-collection market in Romania amounted to 244.8 million euros.

[14] European Banking Authority (n 7) 60. See also: FENCA, 'FENCA welcomes European Commission announcement of COVID-19 Best Practices' (FENCA, 14 July 2020) <https://fenca.eu/news> accessed 30 January 2024.

[15] FENCA, 'Survey no 6: Debts referred to member associations' (*FENCA*, August 1999 <https://www.fenca.org/images/pdf/surveys/6.debts_referred.pdf> accessed 19 January 2024.

50–60 per cent higher than those reported to the National Authority for Consumer Protection.[16] This discrepancy can have significant consequences in establishing the tax base for the industry, efforts to combat the grey economy, and ensuring compliance with the disclosure rules set by the debt-collection legislation. The matter is further complicated by the fact that the Romanian Debt-collection Association gathers only 12 of the 102 registered entities,[17] even if the former are the most prominent actors.[18] Thus, the discrepancy might be greater, but the exact figures from other unaffiliated debt-collectors are missing.

As it turns out, most EU economies have yet to learn about the size of their NPL and debt-collection markets. In the World Bank's view this is troublesome because 'effective NPL resolution requires the availability of economically meaningful data about banks' exposure to problem assets', and 'regulators and supervisors need this information to gauge the magnitude of the problem, inform their NPL resolution strategies, ensure that banks provision appropriately for credit losses, and follow up with banks with a high NPL exposure'.[19] As the World Bank argues, 'softening regulatory definitions and supervision only increases *opacity* without addressing the underlying problem'; therefore, 'regulatory definitions need to be underpinned by robust supervisory enforcement, particularly in an environment where pressures on asset quality *may incentivise banks to disguise the true extent of their difficulties to banking supervisors* ... These *challenges may be exacerbated by industry and political pressures on the operational independence of regulators*' (emphasis added).[20] The interest of banks and other players in the industry, such as debt buyers and collectors, in maintaining secrecy over NPL operations and refusing cooperation by opposing and lobbying against mandatory disclosures to supervisory agencies cannot be more evident.

Yet, the ECB opines that increased awareness via reporting requirements imposed on credit servicers, credit purchasers, and credit institutions would amount to a 'significant ... burden' that would 'impede the efficient functioning of the secondary market for NPLs' and 'deter new entrants to the market'.[21] Thus, the ECB seems to believe that the debt-collection market can only develop and function adequately if secrecy is maintained.

[16] Cătălin Gabriel Stănescu, 'The Enforcement of Consumer Financial Protection in Romania. Thirty Years Later—An Empirical Evaluation' (2023) 12(3) Journal of European Consumer and Market Law 102, Tables 2 and 3.

[17] The list of registered debt-collection entities is available at <https://anpc.ro/wp-content/uploads/2024/06/LISTA-ENTITATILOR-CARE-DESFASOARA-ACTIVITATEA-DE-RECUPERARE-CREANTE-12.06.2024.pdf> accessed 9 July 2024.

[18] The list of ACDM's members is available at <https://www.amcc.ro/en/about-amcc/> accessed 9 July 2024.

[19] World Bank Financial Sector Advisory Center, *COVID-19 and non-performing loan resolution in the Europe and Central Asia region. Lessons learned from the global financial crisis for the pandemic* (World Bank Policy Note, December 2020) 8.

[20] ibid.

[21] European Central Bank, 'Opinion of 20 November 2018 on a proposal for a directive on credit servicers, credit purchasers and the recovery of collateral', CON/2018/54, OJ C444, 10 December 2018, 15, Section 2.1.

The ECB's stance is surprising considering that the institution must gather and centralize this data under the Credit Servicers and Credit Purchasers Directive. Instead of aligning with its duties, the ECB's position closely resembles those of national debt-collector associations. For instance, in response to the European Commission's (EC) targeted consultation on improving transparency and efficiency in secondary markets for NPLs,[22] the German Association of Debt-collection Companies (BDIU), the largest professional association at the MS level and one of the most active lobbyists for the industry's interests, adamantly opposed any proposals that would enhance transparency regarding NPL portfolios, such as information about sales and realization data, valuation, performance, or data on costs and workout strategies.[23]

BDIU acknowledges that post-trade information provided by NPL buyers on recovery cash flow for their purchased assets could yield crucial insights into the NPL market. However, the association believes that mandatory disclosure of this data would compel NPL purchasers to disclose trade secrets.[24] In its words, 'full transparency ... would cause lasting damage for established and successful credit purchasers/servicers and ... reduce competition on the purchaser side to a minimum'.[25] It recommends that the EC revisit the idea so that any disclosure meets three conditions: (1) trade secrets are respected and protected, (2) the scope of the data is limited, and (3) post-sale data are excluded.[26] In essence, the German association prefers not to disclose anything that might reveal the market amounts it pays for face-value debt and the actual profit margin of the business.

Given financiers' reluctance to gather or share data, it is difficult to get a clear overview of the figures involved in the debt-collection market. Still, based on combined data from eleven MS, the amount of debt managed by the members of the surveyed debt-collection associations was above 505 billion euros in 2022, nearly triple the EU budget for that year.[27] Furthermore, by compiling data on the revenue generated by debt-collection agencies and credit bureaus in eighteen EU MS, using figures and projections provided by Statista Industrial Market Insights based on information from Eurostat, a combined revenue of more than 76.2 billion US dollars (53.3 billion euros) can be confirmed for the period 2012–24 (see Table 7.1).

[22] European Commission, 'Targeted consultation on improving transparency and efficiency in secondary markets for non-performing loans—Summary Report' (*European Commission*, December 2021) <https://commission.europa.eu/system/files/2021-12/2021-non-performing-loans-summary-of-responses_en.pdf> accessed 22 July 2024.

[23] Bundesverband Deutscher Inkasso-Unternehmen (BDIU), 'Targeted consultation on improving transparency and efficiency in secondary markets for non-performing loans (NPLs)' (*BDIU*, 8 September 2021) <https://www.inkasso.de/fileadmin/user_upload/stellungnahmen/2021_09_08_BDIU_Targeted_Consultation_Data_Hub.pdf> accessed 19 January 2024.

[24] ibid 3.

[25] ibid 4.

[26] ibid.

[27] The EU budget for 2022 amounted to 167.7 billion euros. European Council and Council of the European Union, 'EU budget for 2022' (*European Council and Council of the EU*) <https://www.consilium.europa.eu/en/policies/eu-annual-budget/2022-budget/> accessed 8 July 2024.

Table 7.1 Industry revenue of activities of debt-collection agencies and credit bureaus from 2012 to 2025 (in millions of US dollars). Compiled by the author.

	Industry revenue of activities of collection agencies and credit bureaus from 2012 to 2025 (in millions of US dollars)																		
	Austria	**Belgium**	**Bulgaria**	**Denmark**	**France**	**Germany**	**Italy**	**Portugal**	**Romania**	**Slovenia**	**Sweden**	**Estonia**	**Greece**	**Croatia**	**Cyprus**	**Finland**	**Latvia**	**Slovakia**	**Total**
2012	268.43	216.5	12.47	123.55	1,053.17	4,212.38	1,745.85	44.35	50.14	10.80	538.41	12.18	72.64	2.31	3.73	386.32	13.16	51.55	8,817.94
2013	270.01	174.38	13.81	123.65	1,035.81	4,230.99	1,590.84	46.62	64.95	10.89	590.36	14.56	68.66	2.13	1.33	455.29	13.05	41.04	8,748.37
2014	307.36	237.73	14.22	143.65	1,071.05	5,641.43	1,889.48	49.30	62.06	10.90	582.30	18.80	76.81	2.92	2.26	444.76	12.69	43.45	10,611.17
2015	274.97	167	11.76	129.83	906.67	3,297.06	1,528.06	40.39	57.37	9.65	484.13	19.31	68.57	2	2.89	420.88	13.76	34.95	7,469.25
2016	229.40	149.72	14.83	142.75	989.85	3,411.65	1,605.67	35.52	63.74	7.30	491.11	23.57	70.38	1.88	2.66	426.04	13.64	80.56	7,760.27
2017	239.86	168.38	14.57	160.25	718.90	3,759.73	1,683.76	34.33	93.84	7.68	557.41	22.59	90.79	10.05	2.82	468.65	13.98	30.60	8,078.19
2018	264.30	172.73	16.30	180.41	803.77	4,969.26	1,816.19	49.74	107.28	10.28	521.39	24.72	62.38	11.46	3.43	551.28	14.25	59.78	9,638.95
2019*	251.33	164.07	15.72	176.63	735.85	3,344.02	1,752.80	47.24	109.34	9.86	493.10	24.32	55.95	12.16	3.21	539.56	14.50	53.89	7,803.55
2020*	236.46	153.36	16.18	173.21	716.19	3,034.83	1,662.61	39.95	127.03	7.89	452.89	23.48	50.63	12.78	3.05	560.26	14.74	54.43	7,339.97
2021*	240.30	154.92	16.23	178.39	698.89	2,965.40	1,699.31	42.30	132.10	8.31	449.64	24.39	50.31	13.76	3.12	564.61	14.97	55.19	7,312.14
2022*	246.14	157.82	16.07	183.58	688.80	2,924.10	1,747.26	46.34	132.58	9.14	450.44	25.47	50.81	14.64	3.20	560.27	15.18	55.46	7,327.30
2023*	254.97	162.69	15.78	189.69	681.15	2,919.59	1,814.41	52.40	128.84	10.45	456.83	26.84	52.15	15.49	3.32	550.58	15.39	55.53	7,406.10
2024*	257.21	163.39	15.85	192.55	677.40	2,842.17	1,833.02	53.55	132.77	10.55	451.82	27.48	52.26	16.13	3.34	553.44		55.94	7,338.87
2025*	258.21	163.38	15.85	194.16	671.97	2,756.41	1,841.44	54.32	135.62	10.58	445.15	27.95	52.20	16.61	3.35	553.60		56.05	7,256.85
TOTAL REVENUE 2012–2024																			76,267.66

Source: Statista Industrial Market Insights and Eurostat. Figures for 2019–24 are projections.

One thing is clear: incomplete as they are, these are not 'marginal' numbers, and large figures correlate with large players, as will be revealed in the next chapter.

7.3 Summary

This chapter critically examined the EU debt-collection market, highlighting its vital role in maintaining financial stability amid the challenges posed by high default rates on unsecured consumer debt and NPLs. Despite reductions in NPL ratios through sales and securitization, the market remains substantial and profitable, with debt buyers benefiting from significant discounts and retaining the right to collect full loan values. The chapter underscored a pervasive lack of transparency, with industry players and the ECB resisting mandatory disclosures that could reveal the true extent and profitability of debt-collection activities. Given this opacity and the significant financial influence of debt-collection agencies, a presentation of the key actors of the debt market is necessary to explore why the EU has struggled to regulate informal debt-collection practices effectively.

VIII
KEY MARKET ACTORS

8.1 The Regional Association: The Federation of European National Collection Associations

The Federation of European National Collection Associations (FENCA) was founded in 1993 and comprises twenty-three national member associations from the European Union (EU), the European Economic Area, and other European states.[1] According to its first president, Kurt Obermaier, the crucial drivers for establishing a European forum were to (1) *unify* the fragmented European debt-collection industry, (2) *influence* the growing list of EU legislation, (3) present a *united front* of the debt-collection industry to the European Commission (EC), (4) help and advise smaller national associations in developing common standards and best practices for their associations, and (5) *develop the collection industry* in these countries.[2] FENCA is a powerful lobbying group.

The Federation established immediate contacts at the EU level after its foundation. According to Obermaier, 'that was very easy'[3] due to 'a total lack of knowledge of our industry at the EC'.[4] However, the knowledge gap could not have been 'total' because Obermeier admits that 'Dun and Bradstreet and Intrum Justitia … companies with a large international collection portfolio at the time' had already been in contact with the EC. FENCA, with its 500 member European agencies, 'got the ear of Brussels' through the large individual agencies.[5]

Collective lobbying efforts outpaced and proved more effective than individual endeavours, with FENCA soon playing a pivotal role in shaping legislation on prompt payment in commercial transactions.[6] This led to 'much less prejudice to our industry by the EC officials than still exists in many national governments today'.[7] In other words, the lobbying efforts of the Federation found a more receptive partner in the EC than in certain member states (MS), owing to the EC's pronounced neoliberal position regarding markets.

[1] FENCA, 'Associations' (*FENCA*) <https://fenca.eu/members/associations> accessed 27 June 2023.
[2] FENCA, '25 years of FENCA—How this all started' (*FENCA*) <https://fenca.eu/news/25-years-of-fenca-how-this-all-started> accessed 27 June 2023.
[3] ibid.
[4] ibid.
[5] ibid.
[6] ibid.
[7] ibid.

EU Informal Debt-Collection Regulation. Cătălin-Gabriel Stănescu, Oxford University Press.
 DOI: 10.1093/oso/9780198966159.003.0008

FENCA's lobbying[8] prowess relies on its extended representativeness. Member associations represent 75 per cent of all credit management, debt-collection, and debt purchasers in Europe, holding an 80 per cent market share in the EU. Their combined workforce of more than 80,000 serves more than five million businesses.[9] This level of representation makes the Federation an influential voice as these market shares directly translate into a substantial financial impact. As a result, the Federation coordinates exchanges with EU institutions, stakeholders in the European financial services industry, consumer groups, and the European public.

According to FENCA's website, one of its main activities consists in establishing and improving business standards and best practices in the sector across the EU.[10] The Federation introduced a Code of Conduct on Debt Collection Practices for its members in 1999, which was last updated in 2014.[11] Despite this, there has been little harmonization, and the approaches followed by national associations have varied significantly.

In response to data protection rules, namely the General Data Protection Regulation (GDPR) and the ePrivacy Regulation, which were deemed an existential threat to the industry's business model, FENCA swiftly adopted a Code of Conduct for GDPR in 2018 and consistently opposed any restrictions on personal data management, transfer, or use, as well as unsolicited digital communications that may have negatively impacted the debt-collection sector.[12] The Federation also took an active stance in the drafting and implementation of various directives, such as the Credit Servicers and Credit Purchasers Directive (CSCPD),[13] or the

[8] ibid.

[9] FENCA, 'About FENCA' (*FENCA*) <https://fenca.eu/#> accessed 27 June 2023.

[10] ibid. See also: FENCA, 'FENCA is working on a pan-European Code of Conduct' (*FENCA*) <https://fenca.eu/news/federation/fenca-is-working-on-a-pan-european-code-of-conduct> accessed 27 June 2023.

[11] FENCA, 'Code of Conduct' (*FENCA*) <https://fenca.eu/images/pdf/FENCA_Code_of_Conduct.pdf> accessed 9 May 2024.

[12] See: FENCA, 'Congress 2018. FENCA adopts Code of Conduct for GDPR and elects new Board' (*FENCA*, 2018) <https://fenca.eu/news/fenca-congress-2018> accessed 27 June 2023. See also: FENCA, 'EU General Data Protection Regulation threatens work of collection companies' (*FENCA*) <https://fenca.eu/news/eu-general-data-protection-regulation-threatens-work-of-collection-companies> accessed 27 June 2023; FENCA, 'Position paper on the Data Protection—Recast' (*FENCA*, 11 April 2013) <https://fenca.eu/images/pdf/2013/position-paper-on-data-protection.pdf> accessed 27 June 2023; FENCA, 'Comments on the European Commission draft Regulation on Data Protection COM(2012) 11 final' (*FENCA*, 2015) <https://fenca.eu/images/pdf/2015/fenca_data_protection_com.pdf> accessed 27 June 2023; FENCA, 'Comments of Fenca (Federation of European Collection Associations) on the ePrivacy Regulation concerning the respect of private life and the protection of personal data in electronic communications' (*FENCA*) <https://fenca.eu/images/pdf/FENCA-Position-on-ePrivacy.pdf> accessed 27 June 2023.

[13] FENCA, 'Response to European Commission Consultation' (*FENCA*, 20 October 2017) <https://fenca.eu/images/pdf/Publications/20171020_FENCA_Response_NPL_Consultation.pdf> accessed 27 June 2023; FENCA, 'Feedback on the European Commission's Proposal for a Directive on credit servicers, credit purchasers and the recovery of collateral' (*FENCA*, 8 June 2018) <https://fenca.eu/images/pdf/Publications/20180608_FENCA_Response_COM_Directive_Proposal_Credit_Servicers_and_Purchasers.pdf> accessed 27 June 2023.

Directive on Representative Actions for the Protection of the Collective Interests of Consumers.[14]

As the representative body for most European debt-collectors and purchasers, FENCA is a staunch defender of the status quo regarding secondary non-performing loan (NPL) markets in the EU. It thus contended that these markets were functioning well and that the existing tools could address potential issues. FENCA instead emphasized the need for improved industry access to adequate, detailed, and standardized information about the debtor and the removal of existing barriers for cross-border investments, such as authorization requirements. The organization encouraged the EC to maintain its 'current light-touch approach' and avoid over-regulating the markets,[15] stating that self-regulation was sufficient. The lack of any provisions for protecting consumer-debtors in the 2018 CSCPD Proposal suggests that FENCA's lobbying efforts were successful (see Chapter IX, Subsection 9.5).

In response to the EC's initiative to develop secondary markets for NPLs, the Federation claimed that its members had collectively raised 300 billion euros.[16] As shown previously (see Chapter VIII, Subsection 8.1), these assertions lack empirical substantiation and regular updates. FENCA is not keen on enhancing transparency regarding the amounts levied by its members at the European level. On the contrary, in its feedback on the CSCPD Proposal, the Federation criticized the notification regime of debt sales across the EU as being 'of dubious value' to the MS because it would only provide a partial record.[17] According to FENCA, the industry should be allowed to continue operating in the shadows.

8.2 National Associations

Based on data from FENCA, national debt-collection associations are found in at least eighteen of the twenty-seven EU MS, namely, Austria, Belgium, Bulgaria, Croatia, Czechia, Denmark, Finland, France, Germany, Greece, Italy, Poland, Portugal, Romania, Slovakia, Spain, Sweden, and the Netherlands.[18] It is unclear whether similar associations exist in the remaining nine EU MS, but if so, they are not affiliated with FENCA. However, debt-collection agencies are present in those

[14] FENCA, 'Feedback on the European Commission's Proposal for a Directive on representative actions for the protection of the collective interests of consumers, and repealing Directive 2009/22/EC' (*FENCA*, 21 June 2018) <https://fenca.eu/images/pdf/Publications/20180620_FENCA_Response_COM_Directive_Representative_Action.pdf> accessed 27 June 2023.

[15] FENCA, 'Response' (n 13).

[16] ibid.

[17] FENCA, 'Feedback' (n 13).

[18] For the full membership list, see: FENCA, 'Associations' (*FENCA*) <https://fenca.eu/members/associations> accessed 27 June 2024.

markets. For instance, individual debt-collectors from Cyprus or Luxembourg are among FENCA's affiliate members.[19]

Lobbying efforts are not solely aimed at EU authorities. National associations primarily seek to engage with local lawmakers and defend industry interests by monitoring and influencing the regulatory process and supporting self-regulation.[20] At least at the declarative level, all are committed to promoting ethical debt-collection standards among their members via codes of conduct. National associations vary in size and transparency, with the vast majority having a purely national focus (see Table 8.1).

The information available on national debt-collection associations' websites is generic, but it still gives an idea of the scale and significance of the sector. For example, in Spain, the members of ANGECO, the national association, handled a total of 426 billion euros in 2022 (of which 46 per cent was attributed to consumer debt) and 463 billion euros in 2023. They also recovered 10.1 billion euros in 2022 and 12.4 billion euros in 2023,[21] equivalent to 1 per cent of the country's gross domestic product. The association's president acknowledged that 'the sector is completely unregulated and generates amounts larger than the country's entire public expenditure', highlighting the startling nature of the Spanish situation.[22] Given the substantial amounts of money at stake, it is not surprising that the Spanish debt-collection industry has thus far managed to avoid sectorial regulation.

Another point to consider is the absence of data on the resolution of complaints related to members' adherence to the associations' ethical codes. Additionally, there is a lack of a genuinely impartial and transparent mechanism for handling these complaints. A few instances that stand out positively are the practices of the Italian and Dutch associations. The Italian association has established a dispute-resolution mechanism in collaboration with several consumer organizations.[23] Although the results are not publicly disclosed, the involvement of consumer

[19] For the complete list of affiliates, see: FENCA, 'Affiliate members' (*FENCA*) <https://fenca.eu/members/affiliate-members> accessed 27 June 2024.

[20] Examples can be found on the national organizations' webpages. Austria: <https://www.inkassoverband.at/vereinsstatuten.html>; Czechia: <https://www.aiacz.cz/o-nas/o-asociaci>; Denmark: <https://www.inkassobranchen.dk/om-dib/>; France: <https://www.lesyndicatdurecouvrement.fr>; Poland: <https://pzzw.pl/polski-zwiazek-zarzadzania-wierzytelnosciami/cele-zwiazku/>; Portugal: <https://www.aperc.pt/acerca-da-associacao/missao-e-objectivos/>; Romania: <https://www.amcc.ro/wp-content/uploads/2021/06/CODE-OF-CONDUCT-1.pdf>; Sweden: <https://svenskinkasso.se/vad-vi-gor/> all accessed 27 June 2024.

[21] ANGECO, 'Estudio anual sobre el Sector de la Gestión de Crédito y la Morosidad' (*ANGECO*, 2023) <https://www.angeco.com/presentacion-de-los-resultados-del-estudio-de-mercado-sobre-el-sector-de-la-gestion-del-credito-y-la-morosidad-2023/> accessed 9 July 2024; ANGECO, 'Estudio de mercado sobre el sector de la gestión del crédito y la morosidad en España' (*ANGECO*, 2022) <https://www.angeco.com/la-recuperacion-de-deuda-llego-a-los-10-116-millones-de-euros-en-el-ano-2022/> accessed 9 July 2024.

[22] ANGECO, 'Estudio de mercado sobre el sector de la gestión del crédito y la morosidad en España' (*ANGECO*, 2022) <https://www.angeco.com/la-recuperacion-de-deuda-llego-a-los-10-116-millones-de-euros-en-el-ano-2022/> accessed 9 July 2024.

[23] UNIREC, 'Buone Prassi' (*UNIREC*) <https://unirec.it/buone-prassi> accessed 10 July 2024.

Table 8.1 Characteristics of EU national debt-collection associations.

No	Organization	Founding year	Number of members	Market share	Country	Year of code of conduct adoption	Consumer associations' involvement (Yes/No)	Sector-specific legislation as of 20201 (Yes/No)	Number of employees
1	Federal Association of Austrian Collection Agencies (IVO) inkassoverband.at	1990	58	70%	Austria	2012	N/A	No	N/A
2	Belgian Association of Debt-collection Companies (ABR-BVI) abrbvi.be	1993	12	NA	Belgium	2018	N/A	Yes	N/A
3	Receivables Management Association (RMA) Rma.bg	2011	14	80%	Bulgaria	2011	N/A	No	1,200
4	Croatian Association of Debt-collection Agencies (HUAN) Huan.hr	2008	8	NA	Croatia	2011	N/A	No	N/A
5	Association of Collection Agencies (AIA) Aiacz.cz	2002	30	NA	Czechia	2011 (revised 2018)	N/A	No	N/A
6	Danish Debt-collection Branch Association (DIB) inkassobranchen.dk	1992	12	NA	Denmark	N/A	N/A	Yes	N/A
7	The Association of Finnish Debt-collection Agencies suomenperimistoimistojenliitto.fi	1981	15	NA	Finland	2019	N/A	Yes	N/A

(*continued*)

Table 8.1 Continued

No	Organization	Founding year	Number of members	Market share	Country	Year of code of conduct adoption	Consumer associations' involvement (Yes/No)	Sector-specific legislation as of 20201 (Yes/No)	Number of employees
8	National Federation of Business Information and Debt Management (FIGEC) Figec.com	1936	NA	NA	France	2010 (debt acquisition) 2015 (civil investigation) 2004 (principles of debt recovery)	Yes	No	N/A
9	The Union of Recovery Actors (SAR) lesyndicatdurecouvrement.fr	1980	60	N/A	France	2015 (revised 2021)	N/A	No	N/A
10	Federal Association of German Collection Agencies (BDIU) Inkasso.de	1956	450	90%	Germany	2020	N/A	Yes	20,000
11	Hellenic Association of Debt Notification and Negotiation Companies (ESEDA) Eseda.gr	2005	9	N/A	Greece	2010	N/A	Yes	2,500
12	National Union of Credit Protection Companies (UNIREC) Unirec.it	1998	194	80%	Italy	2017 (revised 2023)	Yes	No	14,800
13	Netherlands's Association of Certified Debt-collection Firms (NVI) Nvi.nl	1989	23	65%	Netherlands	2019	N/A	Yes	N/A

14	Polish Association of Credit Management (PZZW) Pzzw.pl	2003	47	N/A	Poland	2015	N/A	No	N/A
15	Portuguese Association of Credit Management and Recovery Companies (APERC) Aperc.pt	2003	23	N/A	Portugal	2003	N/A	No	1,790
16	Trade Credit Management Association (AMCC) amcc.ro	2007	12	75%	Romania	N/A	N/A	Yes	1,700
17	Association of Slovak Debt-collection Companies (ASINS) Asins.sk	X	15	90%	Slovakia	2019	N/A	No	N/A
18	National Association of Collection Management Entities (ANGECO) Angeco.com	1994	88	N/A	Spain	1996 (revised 2022)	N/A	No	21,000
19	Swedish Debt-collection Association (SI) svenskinkasso.se	X	43	N/A	Sweden	N/A	N/A	Yes	1,575

Source: Websites of national debt-collection association; compiled by the author.

organizations adds balance and credibility to the conciliation procedure. For its part, the Dutch association publishes all complaint outcomes on a publicly accessible webpage, available for consultation at no cost in the original language.[24]

Still, empirical data from specific national associations evidences the notable lack of deterrent sanctions. Typically, sanctions are confined to written warnings, fines paid to the association, and occasional exclusions from the association.[25] Given the enduring negative public perception of the industry, any resulting reputational damage is unlikely to have a detrimental impact. Major EU players are seemingly unaffected by negative publicity. This includes multinational corporations, which play a significant role in the debt-collection landscape alongside associations, with major players such as Intrum and EOS leading the industry.

8.3 Multinational Corporations

Importantly, not all national associations have the same number of members or degree of power. Generally, a relatively small number of agencies dominate the debt-collection industries in MS (see Table 8.1 above). This indicates significant market concentration, which is expected to increase as competition drives prices up and profits down.[26] The number of collection agencies seems to correlate with the size of the population but also with the amounts to be recovered. The exception is Germany, which has more than 2,000 debt-collection agencies (450 of which are affiliated to the German debt-collection association, BDIU). This may be due mainly to the country's historical internal fragmentation and preference for small, local players. However, even in Germany, there are dominant national champions,[27] following the general trend in the industry (see Subsection 8.3.2).

As shown previously (Chapter II, Subsection 2.1.4), the debt-collection sector is consolidating as a matter of necessity due to the combined effect of expanding markets, digitalization, and regulatory efforts. Intrum, the leading market player in the EU, asserts that 'a certain size is required to be able to make the necessary investments and to achieve economies of scale and cost efficiency'.[28] As a result, former local operators are evolving into regional or global entities, leading to a less

[24] The cases until 2023 are available in Dutch at: NVI, 'Uitspraken klachten voor Wki' (*NVI*) <https://nvi.nl/uitspraken-inzake-klachten> accessed 16 May 2024.

[25] Cătălin Gabriel Stănescu and Jakub Kepinski, 'Regulating Abusive Informal Debt Collection via Codes of Conduct. Evidence from FENCA Members' (forthcoming) Journal of Consumer Policy.

[26] Valentina Za, 'Europe's debt collectors face reckoning as bad loans vanish' (*Reuters*, 20 March 2023) <https://www.reuters.com/markets/europe/europes-debt-collectors-face-reckoning-bad-loans-vanish-2024-03-20/> accessed 9 July 2024.

[27] Carsten Dierig, 'Säumige Kunden sind ein Warnsignal für Konjunkturprobleme' (*Die Welt*, 22 June 2016) <https://www.welt.de/print/die_welt/wirtschaft/article156438246/Saeumige-Kunden-sind-ein-Warnsignal-fuer-Konjunkturprobleme.html> accessed 9 July 2024.

[28] Intrum, 'Annual and Sustainability Report 2021' (*Intrum*, 2022) 18 <https://www.intrum.com/media/pc5p3qnq/intrum-asr-2021_eng.pdf> accessed 26 June 2023.

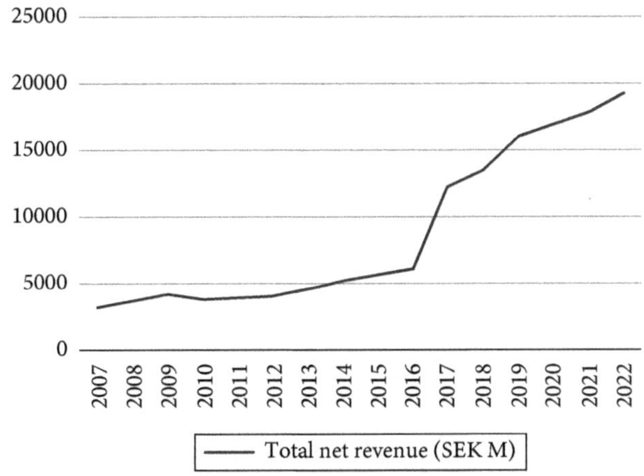

Figure 8.1 Intrum's Yearly Net Revenue from 2007 to 2023.
Source: Intrum's Annual Reports. Compiled by author

fragmented market. This book also underscores that the EU's efforts to establish an internal, secondary single market for NPLs will drive further consolidation, reducing the relevance of national markets.

Financial data from some of the most prominent companies in the EU market confirms that debt purchase and collection are highly lucrative, amounting to billions of euros. It also reveals the patterns and business models that have evolved over the past fifteen years. For instance, following the 2008 financial crisis, Intrum's net revenue surged nearly sixfold, from 3.2 billion Swedish kronor (276 million euros) to 19.85 billion Swedish kronor (1.73 billion euros) in 2023 (see Figure 8.1).[29] In the same year, EOS reported total revenue of 977.1 million euros,[30] with its most substantial increase coming from Eastern Europe (414 million euros, a 47.8 per cent increase from the previous year) and Western Europe (302 million euros, a 34.4 per cent increase).[31]

Intrum's financial data points to a shift in net collections. While collection fees, commissions, and debtor fees were the primary sources of collections from 2007 to 2012, there has been a notable reversal over the past decade, with collections from portfolio investments taking the lead. Both revenue categories increased significantly, particularly in 2019–24 (see Figure 8.2). In 2022, collection fees, commissions, and debtor fees amounted to 8.3 billion Swedish kronor (718 million euros).

[29] Intrum, 'Annual and Sustainability Report 2023' (*Intrum*, 2024) 39 <https://www.intrum.com/media/mq1nvhm0/intrum-asr23_1a.pdf> accessed 9 July 2024.

[30] EOS, 'Our Financial Year 2022/2023' (*EOS*, August 2024) 3 <https://eos-solutions.com/en/dam/jcr:2c37ca87-b8a6-41cf-b280-854a4fba05dd/EOS_Annual%20Report%202023_EN.pdf> accessed 9 July 2024.

[31] ibid 5.

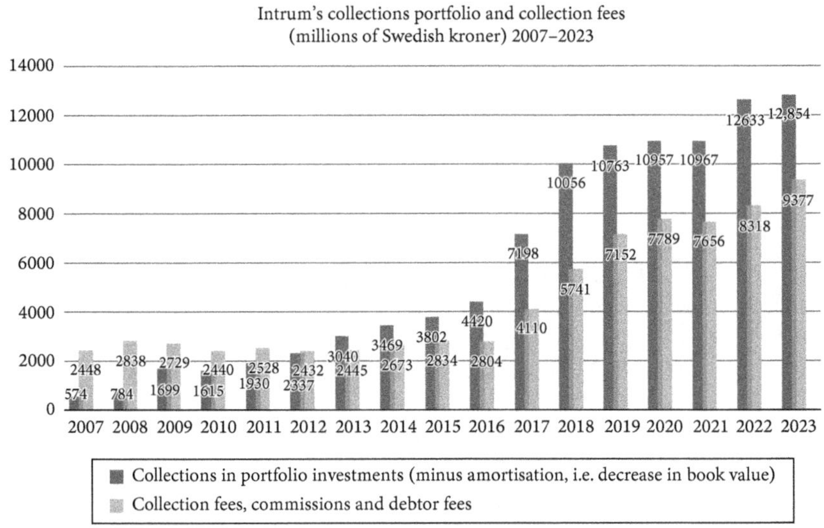

Figure 8.2 Intrum's collections revenue streams from portfolio investments versus collection fees and other charges (in millions of Swedish kroner) from 2007 to 2023.
Source: Intrum's Annual Reports. Compiled by author.

It is unclear whether this shift is an effect of the EU's plan to create an NPL market or vice versa.

The next subsections explore two prominent entities in the European market: Intrum, from Sweden, and EOS, from Germany.

8.3.1 Intrum

With 80,000 clients in twenty-five countries and approximately 10,000 employees, the Swedish group Intrum is undoubtedly the largest debt-collection multinational in the EU. It offers a wide range of services centred on two main categories: credit-management services—ensuring that companies receive payment from their customers for the goods and services they provide—and portfolio investments—taking overdue receivables, paying the client, and seeking a solution with the customer.[32]

[32] Intrum, 'European Consumer Payment Report 2022' (*Intrum*, 2023) 2 <https://www.intrum.com/media/50bjgmow/epr-2022-mainreport.pdf> accessed 23 June 2023. See also: Intrum, 'European Consumer Payment Report 2021' (*Intrum*, 2022) 2 <https://www.intrum.com/media/d5kbq1nf/intrum-ecpr-2021.pdf> accessed 23 June 2023.

According to the *Financial Times*, in 2017, Intrum held around 20 per cent of the European market in terms of debt portfolios purchased.[33] The group's strength lies in its diversification across twenty-five countries and considerable fee-based servicing revenue, which complements its balance sheet-intensive investment activities.[34] An overview of Intrum's market power can be drawn from its yearly financial reports, as highlighted in Table 8.2 below.

Intrum's stated purpose in 2022 and 2023 was to lead the way to 'a sound economy'.[35] In its view, its market-leading position allows it to drive the development of the entire industry in a more ethical direction. However, this is subordinated to creating value and meaning for its employees,[36] not debtor protection.

According to Intrum's 2022 European Consumer Payment Report (ECPR), the start of the war in Ukraine following the COVID-19 pandemic increased economic unpredictability and the risk of late or non-payment for economic operators. Thus, most respondents stated that improving debt management was a strategic priority (81 per cent)—an increase of 10 per cent compared to before the invasion. When questioned about the steps they took to improve debt management, 26 per cent reported working with debt-collection agencies.[37] On the other end of the spectrum, the 2022 report noted that consumers faced acute financial anxiety due to inflation, rising interest rates, and uncertainty regarding the impact of these on household finances, with countries such as Greece, Latvia, and Romania at the forefront.[38]

Intrum's 2021–3 ECPRs suggest that late or non-payment might become the norm or a form of penalizing unethical firms. The latest study (2023) reveals that approximately three in ten respondents (31 per cent) would not feel as guilty about skipping payment of a bill as they did a few years previously.[39] The figure increased to 68 per cent in the case of companies perceived as acting unethically or practising greedflation.[40] Nevertheless, the real issue remained inadequate income. According to Intrum's 2021 survey, more than one consumer in four borrowed or reached their credit card limit to pay their bills. The figure increased to 40 per cent among consumers under 37 years old.[41] This information unmistakably reflects

[33] John Murray Brown and Robert Smith, 'Europe's Debt Collectors Face Own Loan Concerns' (*Financial Times*, 22 November 2017) <https://archive.is/20220322074448/https://www.ft.com/content/1bc35d86-c9e9-11e7-aa33-c63fdc9b8c6c> accessed 10 July 2024.

[34] Fitch Ratings, 'Rating Action Commentary: Fitch Affirms Intrum at BB/Stable', 11 July 2022 (*Fitch Ratings*) <https://www.fitchratings.com/research/non-bank-financial-institutions/fitch-affirms-intrum-at-bb-stable-11-07-2022> accessed 23 June 2023.

[35] Intrum, 'European Consumer Payment Report 2023' (*Intrum*, 2024) 3 <https://www.intrum.com/publications/european-consumer-payment-report/european-consumer-payment-report-2023/> accessed 9 July 2024.

[36] ibid.

[37] Intrum, 'ECPR 2022' (n 32) 14.

[38] Intrum, 'ECPR 2021' (n 32) 7.

[39] Intrum (n 35) 12.

[40] ibid 13.

[41] Intrum, 'ECPR 2021' (n 32) 25.

Table 8.2 Intrum's key financial metrics for the past 15 years, 2007–2023 (in millions of Swedish kronor).

	2007	2008	2009	2010	2011	2012	2013	2014	2015	2016	2017	2018	2019	2020	2021	2022	2023
Total net revenue (SEK M)	3.225,2	3.678	4.128	3.766	3.950	4.056	4.566	5.184	5.628	6.088	12.219	13.442	15.985	16.848	17. 879	19.131	19,853
Collections in Portfolio Investments (minus amortization, i.e. decrease in book value)	573,7	783,6	1.699,4	1.614,9	1.929,7	2.337	3.040	3.469	3.802	4.420	7.198	10.056	10.763	10.957	10. 967	12.633	12,854
Collection fees, commissions and debtor fees	2.447,8	2.838,1	2.728,8	2.439,8	2.528,1	2.432	2.445	2.673	2.834	2.804	4.110	5.741	7.152	7.789	7.656	8.318	9.377

Notes: Due to changes in the reporting methodology, yearly figures were adjusted based on the report for the following year: 2023 and 2022 figures are from the 2023 report, figures from 2021 are from the 2022 report, and so on.

Source: Intrum annual reports 2007–2023; compiled by the author.

the downward trend in consumer financial well-being following the economic crisis. For instance, in 2014, Intrum's first market study into consumer payment revealed that less than one in five consumers had to borrow money to settle bills.[42] This chronic inability to repay obligations leads to unsustainable lending coupled with defaults, contributing to the lucrativeness of the debt-collection business.

The 2022 report highlighted the increasing commitment of businesses to eradicating unethical practices, such as racial or social profiling of customers. This focus may lead them to consider organizations with a strong track record on late-payment issues and the expertise to manage debt-collection in a socially responsible manner.[43] The 2023 ECPR no longer mentions ethical standards towards debtors, but the concern remains in the 2023 Annual and Sustainability Report.[44]

Given the current socioeconomic landscape, which values sustainability and respect for the individual, it is no surprise that Intrum's marketing strategy dedicates so much attention to 'ethical debt-collection'.[45] Nonetheless, social media sentiment paints a different picture, indicating a considerable disparity between the company's marketing assertions and reality. On Trustpilot, a platform dedicated to measuring business trustworthiness through verified reviews,[46] Intrum scores 1.2 out of five stars based on 587 reviews. A staggering 96 per cent of reviewers gave the company the lowest rating, citing unethical and unlawful conduct.[47] Similarly unfavourable ratings on Google[48] suggest that the company is far from winning any popularity contests (see Table 8.3).

One could argue that biased and disgruntled debtors wrote the overwhelmingly negative reviews. Still, the consistent complaints and outcomes across EU jurisdictions point to a potential pattern of behaviour by the company that contradicts its public relations statements.

Intrum proactively leverages its market position to influence credit-management regulation. As per the 2022 Annual Sustainability Report, the company actively engages in dialogue at both the EU and local levels to shape the development of future legal requirements that impact the industry.[49] According to FENCA, this

[42] Intrum, ''European Consumer Payment Report 2014' (*Intrum*, 2015)' 2, 4 <https://www.intrum.com/media/6937/consumerreport_2014.pdf> accessed 9 July 2024.

[43] Intrum, 'ECPR 2022' (n 32) 17.

[44] Intrum (n 28) 25–26.

[45] ibid 25 and 117.

[46] Trustpilot, 'Transparency Report 2022' (*Trustpilot*) <https://cdn.trustpilot.net/trustsite-consumersite/trustpilot-transparency-report-2022.pdf> accessed 23 June 2023.

[47] Trustpilot, 'Intrum' (*Truustpilot*) <https://www.trustpilot.com/review/intrum.com> accessed 9 July 2023.

[48] <https://www.google.com/search?tbs=lf:1,lf_ui:4&tbm=lcl&q=intrum&rflfq=1&num=10&ved=2ahUKEwi6j_LRs9n_AhVE3aQKHWIuDDoQtgN6BAgcEAg#rlfi=hd:;si:;mv:[[50.438506259499874,4.0250492710937555],[46.86375720055971,0.7291508335937548> accessed 23 June 2023.

[49] Intrum (n 28) 34.

Table 8.3 Intrum's and EOS's social scoring based on data from Trust Pilot and Google reviews as of July 2024.

Office	Intrum		EOS	
	Number of reviewers	Score	Number of reviewers	Score
Hungary	344	1.4	83	1.3
Slovakia	32	1.7	147	3.9
Italy (Milan)	98	2.4	NA	NA
Italy (Rome)	31	1.9	NA	NA
France (Saint-Priest)	299	1.4	NA	NA
France (Paris)	12	1.0	414	1.6
France (Rueil-Malmaison)	89	1.3	NA	NA
Spain (Madrid)	116	1.3	1577	4.4
Spain (Sevilla)	22	1.6	NA	NA
Spain (Barcelona)	17	1.4	NA	NA
Portugal (Lisbon)	365	1.4	NA	NA
Portugal (Porto)	70	1.3	NA	NA
Germany	186	1.3	1052	1.5
Netherlands	241	1.3	NA	NA
Belgium	115	1.4	182	2.0
Ireland	33	1.1	NA	NA
Austria	29	1.5	49	1.6
Poland	144	1.2	541	4.5
Denmark	50	1.6	2	1.0
Latvia	23	1.0	NA	NA
Estonia	6	2.3	NA	NA
Finland	91	1.5	NA	NA
Sweden	272	2.1	NA	NA
Romania	274	1.3	88	2.8
Greece	196	1.8	175	1.2
Czechia	35	2.5	55	1.8
Croatia	NA	NA	278	1.2

dialogue has been going on for at least thirty years, suggesting that the group's influence in Brussels is substantial.

The company has been involved in the NPL Advisory Panel since 2021, advising the EC and its departments. In 2022 the group completed the steering document to clarify the processes for selling debt portfolios for banks and NPL investors, the Best Execution NPL Sales Guideline. Another focus was the development of a steering document on the key differences between EU markets in terms of legal requirements and practical NPL management. Because of its geographic presence, the group was at the forefront of the production of the first draft of the document for the EC.[50] Thus, it would appear that Intrum can write its own legislation and then use EU institutions to carry it through.

Intrum's role is backed by its cooperation with FENCA in 'interpreting new NPL rules' and pursuing 'a common agenda'. The group's local offices were involved in dialogues with trade associations and decision-makers at the national level. It also participated in the revision of the 2023 Consumer Credit Directive (CCD), meeting with rapporteurs from the EU Parliament and Finance Watch to promote the harmonization between the CCD and the NPL Directive from the point of view of debt-collection processes and the protection of consumers.[51] Ultimately, it has been pushing for the development of a European Code of Conduct for Data Protection in the Debt-collection Industry, which awaits certification by the European Data Protection Board. All these reveal the group's leading position in advancing industry interests and influencing and controlling the regulatory agenda alongside top EU and national legislators, including on consumer-related matters.[52]

8.3.2 EOS

In 2023, the German EOS Group counted 6,411 employees in twenty-four countries.[53] The group's cross-border centre handled more than 81,000 cases from 1,519 clients in 189 countries in 2021–2, with 98 per cent settled non-judicially.[54] According to its latest financial report, the fiscal year 2022–3 witnessed an over-positive performance despite adverse conditions such as the war in Ukraine, inflation, and the energy crisis.[55]

[50] Intrum, 'Annual and Sustainability Report 2022' (*Intrum*, 2023), 34–35 <https://www.intrum.com/media/x5mbcdc3/intrum-asr-22.pdf> accessed 9 July 2024.
[51] ibid 35.
[52] ibid 35–36.
[53] EOS (n 30) 2; EOS, 'Our Responsibility 2022/23' (*EOS*, July 2023) 8 <https://eos-solutions.com/en/dam/jcr:40ca1401-7c57-4d18-8e4f-734b10853cc1/EOS%20Our%20Responsibility%202022-23.pdf> accessed 9 July 2024.
[54] Intrum, 'Annual and Sustainability Report 2022' (n 50) 47.
[55] EOS (n 30) 2.

Regarding debt purchase, 2023 was a record year for EOS, with an investment of 1.2 billion euros in NPLs and real estate—nearly double the amount spent during the previous fiscal year (665 million euros), which was another record at the time.[56] The face value of purchased portfolios at the end of the financial year was 2.7 billion euros, a 34 per cent (approximately 680 million euros) increase from the previous year.[57] Of this, 934.4 million euros came from Eastern Europe, 1.02 billion from Western Europe (one portfolio with a face value of 753 million euros came from Spain), 640.8 million from Germany, and 66.8 million from Central Europe.[58] The investments were facilitated by the company's overall increase in revenue of 21.5 per cent (172.2 million euros) globally.

In 2022, EOS stood out as a data-driven debt-collection company, offering algorithmic instalment plan models to assist consumers in finding feasible ways out of debt. These customized solutions used historical data to devise models that proposed an individual payment plan tailored to each person's specific situation. An algorithm analysed the likelihood of success and then proposed the most effective strategy to the consumer. The company's primary aim in profiling debtors was to maximize recovery, stating that 'the better the plan fits the consumer's situation, the greater its likelihood of payment'.[59] This approach confirmed the industry trend of adopting technological advancements in daily operations (see Chapter II, Subsections 2.1.3 and 2.1.4).[60]

Technological innovations are also mentioned in EOS's fair debt-collection reports. As of 2023, the group has undertaken to implement a policy that ensures consistent and ethical treatment of defaulting consumers—which is rather late for a company founded more than seventy years ago. This internal policy will require it to communicate clearly and tactfully and take responsibility for its words and actions.[61] Technology will streamline the payment process, depersonalizing the experience (e.g. no contact with EOS employees unless requested) and profiling consumers (e.g. suggesting preferred payment methods based on data analysis).[62] Whether these new collection practices align with the GDPR and the Court of Justice of the EU's decision in *Schufa* (see Chapter XIII, Subsection 13.2) remains to be seen.

Numbers support the shift in EOS's approach. In 2022–3, EOS successfully resolved more than five million consumer debt cases. Eight countries where EOS operates have fully implemented digital tools to find solutions for consumer debts,

56 ibid 4.

57 EOS, 'Our Annual and Sustainability Report 2022/2023' (*EOS*, August 2024) <https://eos-solutions.com/annual-report?utm_campaign=annualreport_2022_23&utm_medium=pdf&utm_source=qr&utm_content=financepdf#download> accessed 10 July 2024.

58 ibid.

59 ibid 36.

60 Joe Deville, *Lived Economies of Default* (Routledge 2015).

61 EOS (n 57).

62 ibid.

and five more are planning to do so. During the reporting period, 61 per cent of defaulting consumers managed their debts independently through online service portals, and there was an 83 per cent increase in the number of payment plans generated via digital channels compared to the previous financial year.[63]

This reality reveals the significant international dimension of informal debt-collection and the relevance and necessity of strict, binding industry standards. Like Intrum, EOS can shape and influence them. Its Chief Compliance Officer and Head of Public Affairs is the President of BDIU, a highly persuasive lobby group at the national level. In 2023, BDIU successfully lobbied German legislators to change the national supervisory agency during the CSCPD's transposition.[64]

Despite EOS's public commitment to promoting ethical debt-collection practices, its social media score is on par with Intrum's. Trustpilot rates it at 1.3 out of five stars based on 314 reviews, 96 per cent of which are negative.[65] While Google reviews paint a slightly better picture, they also indicate a general dissatisfaction with the company's treatment of debtors (see Table 8.3). Surprisingly, these reviews do not seem to impact the company's standing in the German and international markets, suggesting that creditors value a fierce reputation among debtors.

8.4 Summary

This chapter presented a comprehensive examination of the main entities in the debt-collection market, including regional associations such as FENCA, national associations, and major multinational corporations like Intrum and EOS. This is essential for grasping the power dynamics and regulatory challenges that characterize the sector. The chapter shed light on the extensive influence of the debt-collection market, which is shaped by a variety of stakeholders who impact its operations and policies. Having provided the reader with a more precise understanding of the industry's power and influence, the next chapter delves into the reasons behind the EU's failure to address informal debt-collection.

[63] ibid.

[64] BDIU, 'Stellungnahme zum Referentenentwurf eines Kreditzweitmarkt-gesetzes (KrZwMG)' (*BDIU*, 9 August 2023) https://www.inkasso.de/fileadmin/user_upload/Stellungnahme_BDIU_RefE_KrZwMG_9.8.23.pdf> accessed 10 July 2024.

[65] Trustpilot, 'EOS Solutions' (*Trustpilot*) <https://www.trustpilot.com/review/de.eos-solutions.com> accessed 9 July 2024.

IX
FAILURE TO REGULATE: FINANCIAL LOBBYING AND REGULATORY CAPTURE AT THE EUROPEAN UNION LEVEL

9.1 Regulatory Capture in the Financial Sector

Regulatory capture is broadly defined in this chapter as financial institutions influencing regulatory agencies and legislatures to weaken or avoid regulation.[1] This can occur at the individual, national, and global levels,[2] driven by the financial sector's organized and concentrated power,[3] unlike the dispersed influence of consumer-debtors.[4]

A related concept is rent seeking, in which industries manipulate the regulatory process to gain economic rents, that is, extra profits from limited competition. Regulations that control market access or establish particular criteria often facilitate this, allowing companies to demand higher prices. Stigler explained that such regulations predominantly cartelize industries, enhancing their market power at consumers' expense.[5] A notable illustration of rent creation occurs through occupational licensing. Industries can advocate for strict licensing standards, limiting the number of individuals entering their fields and leading to decreased

[1] Daniel C Hardy, *Regulatory Capture in Banking* (IMF Working Paper WP/06/34, 2006); Richard A Posner, 'The Concept of Regulatory Capture. A Short, Inglorious History' in Daniel Carpenter and David A Moss (eds), *Preventing Regulatory Capture: Special Interest Influence and How to Limit It* (CUP 2014); Theodore H Cohn, 'The Effects of Regulatory Capture on Banking Regulations: A Level-of-Analysis Approach' in Anil Hira, Norbert Gaillard, and Theodore H Cohn (eds), *The Failure of Financial Regulation. Why A Major Crisis Could Happen Again* (Springer 2019); George J. Stiegler, 'The Theory of Economic Regulation' (1971) 2(1) The Bell Journal of Economics and Management Science 3; Tony Porter, 'Risk Models and Transnational Governance in the Global Financial Crisis: The Cases of Basel II and Credit Rating Agencies' in Eric Helleiner, Stefano Pagliari, and Hubert Zimmermann (eds), *Global Finance in Crisis: The Politics of International Regulatory Change* (Taylor and Francis 2010).

[2] Cohn (n 1).

[3] Daniel W Drezner, *The System Worked. How the World Stopped Another Great Depression* (OUP 2014).

[4] Joseph Spooner, 'The Quiet-Loud-Quiet Politics of Post-Crisis Consumer Bankruptcy Law: The Case of Ireland and the Troika' (2018) 81(5) Modern Law Review 790.

[5] Stiegler (n 1).

EU Informal Debt-Collection Regulation. Cătălin-Gabriel Stănescu, Oxford University Press.
 DOI: 10.1093/oso/9780198966159.003.0009

competition. As a result, licensed professionals can command higher earnings and be shielded from potential newcomers who could otherwise lower prices.[6]

The next sections demonstrate that, in the realm of debt-collection, lobbying endeavours have transitioned from thwarting legislative initiatives (the 2002 CCD proposal) to influencing the substance of legislation and reducing consumer safeguards (the 2021 CSCPD).

There is ample evidence that as the financial industry's power and influence increased, it was able to shape or even block the adoption of legal and regulatory norms governing consumer debt, debt-collection, and personal bankruptcy.[7] Even after the 2008 economic crisis, which resulted in a tougher stance towards the sector, national governments adopted pro-creditor policies to attract non-performing loan (NPL) investors.[8] Governments may also have limited regulatory freedom in consumer financial protection due to concerted pressure from global financial institutions.[9]

The following excerpt from a Letter of Intent and Memorandum of Understanding from Romania to the International Monetary Fund makes for a telling example:

> Because preserving credit discipline among debtors contributes significantly towards enhancing financial stability, we will take all efforts to *avoid the adoption of legislative initiatives* dealing with personal insolvency *that create a moral hazard and are open to widespread abuse by debtors* as this *would undermine credit discipline*. Furthermore, in order to avoid threats to financial stability from the new provisions on abusive clauses ... we will ... take all necessary measures to ensure a harmonised application of these provisions, such as training of judges. If the new institutional arrangement of this specialised court does not succeed in avoiding financial stability threats, we will consult extensively with all relevant stakeholders as well as with the IMF [International Monetary Fund] and EC [European Commission] to come up with alternative solutions. Given the substantial NPL overhang, the authorities will remove, where possible, impediments to ... household out-of-court debt restructuring and NPL resolution.[10] (emphasis added)

Ample empirical evidence shows that private banking interests would find it challenging to influence regulatory decisions without the backing of politicians.[11] This

[6] ibid.
[7] Spooner (n 4).
[8] ibid.
[9] International Monetary Fund, 'Romania: Letter of Intent, Memorandum of Economic and Financial Policies, and Technical Memorandum of Understanding' (*International Monetary Fund*, 10 June 2013) para 37 <https://www.imf.org/external/np/loi/2013/rou/061013.pdf> accessed 22 July 2024; Spooner (n 4).
[10] International Monetary Fund (n 9) para 37.
[11] Cohn (n 1); Spooner (n 4); Simon Johnson and James Kwak, *13 Bankers* (Pantheon Books 2010); Lucia Quaglia, 'Setting the Pace? Private Financial Interests and European Financial Market Integration'

is especially evident when politicians or their close associates have ties with financiers and their interests. For instance, in 2010 Romania, some of the largest debt-collection agencies were owned by Members of Parliament or the government, including a former Minister of Finance.[12] However, although multiple studies agree that the financial sector wields significant political influence, there is ongoing debate concerning the extent of and factors determining its impact.[13] Nevertheless, it is well documented that opposition from various financial industry groups has frequently hindered the implementation and effectiveness of sectoral reforms devised in response to the financial crisis.[14] Extensive research on the subject has identified two primary sources of influence that define the financial sector: instrumental and structural power.

9.1.1 Instrumental power

The first of these, instrumental power,[15] may partly result from the considerable financial resources available for lobbying regulators and policymakers to align the European Union (EU) agenda with their objectives.[16] Yet, the crux of the matter is the technical complexity and dynamism that give financial companies a persistent edge over other stakeholders in terms of knowledge and information. This informational imbalance empowers the industry to entrench its domination and capture the regulatory process.[17]

Another significant source of direct influence that allows the industry to shape regulations, as previously highlighted in Chapter VIII, is its direct access to policymakers.[18] Their special position as crucial market players gives financiers a unique role within domestic and international policy networks.[19] This interaction is further enhanced by the 'revolving doors' phenomenon, which refers to regulators

(2008) 10 British Journal of Politics and International Relations 46; Daniel Mügge, 'Reordering the Marketplace: Competition Politics in European Finance' (2006) 44(5) Journal of Common Market Studies 991.

[12] Klaudia Fabian, Alexandra Andhov, and Cătălin Gabriel Stănescu, 'Is Self-Help Repossession Possible in Central Europe?' (2011) 4(1) The Journal of Eurasian Law 83.

[13] Stefano Pagliari, 'Financial Industry Power and Regulatory Policies: What Lessons from the Global Financial Crisis' (2015) 2 Rivista Italiana di Politiche Pubbliche 209.

[14] Ranjit Lall, 'From Failure to Failure: The Politics of International Banking Regulation' (2012) 19(4) Review of International Political Economy 609.

[15] Michael Barnett and Raymond Duval, 'Power in International Politics' (2005) 59(1) International Organization 39; Steven Lukes, *Power: A Radical View* (Macmillan 1974).

[16] David Lowery and Virginia Gray, 'A Neopluralist Perspective on Research on Organized Interests' (2004) 57(1) Political Research Quarterly163; Pagliari (n 13).

[17] Lall (n 14) 3.

[18] Hardy (n 1) 4.

[19] Éric Monnet, Stefano Pagliari, and Shahin Vallée, *Europe Between Financial Repression and Regulatory Capture* (Bruegel Working Paper No 8, 2014) 5–7. For a similar position, see: Cornelia Woll, *The Power of Banks* (Speri, University of Sheffield 2013).

seeking career opportunities within the regulated sectors and, conversely, regulatory agencies employing individuals from the financial industry.[20]

Instrumental power is also wielded based on the understanding that other stakeholders, such as consumers or consumer-debtors, are not only constrained by the intricate nature of financial regulations but also rarely unite and mobilize with enough collective strength to effectively counter the industry's voice.[21]

9.1.2 Structural power

Beyond lobbying, the financial industry uses structural power to constrain regulatory options[22] due to its pivotal economic role,[23] particularly in credit access.[24] Governments must consider financial sector demands because bank lending impacts investment and economic performance.[25] This structural power, heightened by global financialization,[26] has allowed the industry to weaken many reforms even post-crisis.

Structural power is also reinforced by the institutional environment and national or regional policies that affect the sector's ability to exert its influence. The completion of the European banking union has given the EU increased authority over the regulation and oversight of financial institutions, making the sector a key player in regulatory design at the union level. The adoption of the CSCPD, which includes provisions favourable to the industry and overly complex but lax consumer-protection mechanisms, is seen as necessary for completing the banking union.[27] This strategic objective has provided the industry with tremendous leverage and influence in the regulatory process.[28]

Another aspect that must be considered is the widespread concern that regulatory jurisdictions will compete to attract companies by introducing less stringent

[20] Toni Makkai and John Braithwaite, 'In and Out of the Revolving Door: Making Sense of Regulatory Capture' (1992) 12(1) Journal of Public Policy 61, 61–62.

[21] Andrew Baker, 'Restraining Regulatory Capture? Anglo-America, Crisis Politics and Trajectories of Change in Global Financial Governance' (2010) 86(3) International Affairs 647; Jan Aart Scholte, 'Civil Society and Financial Markets: What Is Not Happening and Why' (2013) 9(2) Journal of Civil Society 129.

[22] Doris Fuchs, *Business Power and Global Governance* (Lynne Rienner 2007).

[23] Monnet, Pagliari, and Vallée (n 19) 9.

[24] Baker (n 21); Monnet, Pagliari, and Vallée (n 19) 6.

[25] Stephen Bell and Andrew Hindmoor, 'Taming the City? Ideas, Structural Power and the Evolution of British Banking Policy Amidst the Great Financial Meltdown' (2014) 20(3) New Political Economy 454.

[26] Ewald Engelen, 'The Case for Financialization' (2008) 12(2) Competition & Change 111; Guido Comparato, *The Financialisation of the Citizen: Social and Financial Inclusion through European Private Law* (Hart Publishing 2018).

[27] Directive (EU) No 2021/2167 on credit servicers and credit purchasers [2021] OJ L438 (CSCPD) recital 2.

[28] Influence over societal narratives and approaches to debts and debtors; societal stigma may also contribute to the legislators' reluctance to adopt debtor-friendly policies.

regulations. This is referred to as a regulatory 'race to the bottom' and may also lead to undue influence over regulators, who may become concerned that the national actors of very lucrative sectors, such as finance, might move to friendlier jurisdictions.[29] This risk is even more prominent in the EU, where the passport rule allows any company registered in one of the member states (MS) to pursue activities across the entire Union. The next section explores how these dynamics unfold within the EU.

9.2 The Financial Lobby in the European Union

Much empirical evidence shows that the financial lobby consistently shapes the EU agenda.

9.2.1 The industry's lobbying dominance

In 2009, a report by ALTER-EU revealed that the vast majority of financial expert groups advising the European Commission (EC) were overwhelmingly dominated by representatives of the industry (229), with scarcely any representatives from academia, consumer groups, or unions (58 combined). Consequently, the report called on the Commission to 'break free from this stranglehold of partial advice'.[30] In 2010, the pattern of the EC's new initiatives to regulate financial markets that were based on unbalanced advisory groups dominated by financial service lobbyists was again brought to the forefront by a report published by the Corporate Europe Observatory (CEO).[31]

As the initial outrage caused by the financial crisis faded, the financial lobby in Brussels continued to consolidate. According to the CEO, in 2014 the financial industry employed more than 1,700 lobbyists and spent at least 120 million euros a year to influence the EU.[32] Representatives of the financial sector also outnumbered the consumer advocacy groups during reform debates. The CEO's 2014 report revealed that the financial industry had seven times more encounters with

[29] Hardy (n 1) 17.

[30] ALTER EU, 'A Captive Commission—The Role of the Financial Industry in Shaping EU Regulation' (*ALTER EU*, 5 November 2009) 9 <https://corporateeurope.org/sites/default/files/sites/default/files/files/resource/a-captive-commission-5-11-09.pdf> accessed 28 February 2024.

[31] CEO, 'EU Financial Lobby Power Must Be Curbed' (*CEO*, 14 April 2010).

[32] CEO, 'The financial industry employs 1.700 lobbyists and spends €120 million a year to influence the EU—at least' (*CEO*, 9 April 2014) <https://corporateeurope.org/en/pressreleases/2014/04/financial-industry-employs-1700-lobbyists-and-spends-120-million-year> accessed 28 February 2024.

EU institutions than non-governmental organizations (NGOs), trade unions, and consumer organizations taken together.[33]

9.2.2 Challenges to reform

In 2016 the issue triggered the attention of the European Parliament, which voted in favour of the recommendations of a report seeking to tighten the rules on the EC's advisory groups. Corporate interests had long dominated these groups, and they were able to shape the early stages of legislation. One year later, CEO research proved that claims of increased transparency, avoiding conflicts of interest, and ensuring a balanced representation of interests had not materialized.[34]

According to data from 2017, corporate lobbying influence also remained strong over the Council of the European Union, another key player in regulatory efforts at the EU level. As reported by the CEO, 'the Council adopts far more business-friendly positions than the Parliament, while MS are often keen to promote the lobby positions of major domestic companies and adopt them as their own'. Moreover, corporate lobbyists could influence EU decision-making through MS governments.[35] In 2018 the CEO stated that, ten years after the 2008 financial crisis, its research showed that the financial sector had successfully avoided significant reform and won almost all major battles on the matter, leaving new legislation full of loopholes and conditions similar to those that created the crash in the first place.[36]

9.2.3 Advocacy efforts

Notwithstanding, other voices have claimed that in some cases, newly mobilized groups were able to translate key advocacy goals into policy by deploying counter-expertise and cooperating with policymakers, which they take as evidence that financial industry groups' influence was curtailed after the economic crisis, thereby

[33] CEO, 'The fire power of the financial lobby. A Survey of the size of the financial lobby at the EU level' (*CEO* and *ÖGB*, April 2014) 11 <https://corporateeurope.org/sites/default/files/attachments/financial_lobby_report.pdf> accessed 28 February 2024.

[34] CEO, 'Corporate interests continue to dominate key expert groups. New rules, little progress' (*CEO*, 14 February 2017) <https://corporateeurope.org/en/expert-groups/2017/02/corporate-interests-continue-dominate-key-expert-groups> accessed 28 February 2024.

[35] CEO, 'Corporate lobbying influence over the Council of the European Union' (*CEO*, 6 December 2017) <https://corporateeurope.org/en/power-lobbies/2017/12/corporate-lobbying-influence-over-council-eu> accessed 28 February 2024.

[36] CEO, 'How the financial lobby won the battle in Brussels' (*CEO*, 13 September 2018) <https://corporateeurope.org/en/financial-lobby/2018/09/how-financial-lobby-won-battle-brussels> accessed 28 February 2024.

reducing the sector's overall political influence.[37] If that was indeed the case, it was short-lived and selective, and Kastner acknowledges that after 2016 'the European Institution's engagement with civil society has started to fade' and that 'civil society mobilisation ... only temporarily curtailed regulatory capture'.[38]

9.2.4 Member states as industry proxies

A relevant aspect stemming from this critical approach is the role played by MS in watering down reform proposals. While evidence shows that consumer advocates found some support in the European Parliament and the Commission, the industry groups reoriented their lobbying efforts towards their MS at the Council of the European Union and national members of the European Parliament (MEPs) to tone down the proposals.[39] The outcome was presented as a settlement, a compromise between groups; a pattern which was revealed once more in the adoption of the CSCPD.

9.3 Regulatory Capture and the Revision of the Consumer Credit Directive

The revision of the CCD makes for a compelling case study of regulatory capture. This section outlines how well-organized financial stakeholders[40] leveraged their influence to shape the directive at the expense of consumer protection.[41] Additionally, because conflicting policies at the EU and national levels can lead to divergent views, compromise in regulatory scope may be necessary. Ultimately, political will and institutional power determine the outcomes of regulatory efforts, with all these factors working together.

9.3.1 Early attempts at regulating consumer credit and debt-collection

EU regulation of consumer credit was part of its ground rules concerning a 'competitive social market economy'. Ramsey suggests that in formulating consumer

[37] Lisa Kastner, 'From Outsiders to Insiders: A Civil Society Perspective on EU Financial Reforms' (2019) 57(2) Journal of Common Market Studies 223, 230.
[38] ibid 237.
[39] ibid 232, 235.
[40] See the example of FENCA below.
[41] Iain Ramsay, 'Changing Policy Paradigms of EU Consumer Credit and Debt Regulation' in Dorota Leczykiewicz and Stephen Weatherill (eds), *The Involvement of EU Law in Private Law Relationships* (Hart Publishing 2013) 165.

credit policy, the EU has fluctuated between two opposing ideas: viewing consumer credit as a 'lubricant' that requires increased and non-discriminatory access to financial resources, and recognizing it as a potentially dangerous product that can lead to 'over-indebtedness' and systemic risks,[42] thus requiring protective measures.

9.4.1.1 The 1987 Consumer Credit Directive

Harmonizing efforts for consumer credit began in the 1960s and 1970s with a series of proposals that were constantly criticized by the banking lobby. Yet, the first CCD was only enacted in 1987 (1987 CCD).[43] Due to the requirement for unanimity at the time, the adopted directive provided minimal protection against potentially unfair terms and enforcement processes. Specifically, it restricted repossessions of goods acquired on credit without the consumers' consent.[44] This self-help mechanism allowed secured creditors to enforce their claims without involving state agents but did not address informal debt-collection.

9.4.1.2 Specific concerns regarding debt-collection measures

The 1995 EC report on the implementation of the 1987 CCD concluded that the provision in question had little regulatory value and was more akin to a code of conduct. This resulted in varying levels of consumer protection in different states.[45] However, the report also noted that certain recovery practices might violate the debtor's privacy, a concern addressed by some MS.

Specifically, the 1995 report mentions measures such as banning debt-recovery agencies that organize debt payments at the debtor's expense (a method of loan sharking) and proscribing or restricting recovery charges.[46] It also discussed regulations governing communication with the debtor, including bans on making threats or indicating overdue status on envelopes.[47] Given the sensitivity of the matter for consumers, the Commission explored the potential establishment of guidelines, such as a code of conduct, which would have regulated not only the actions of creditors but also those of specialized recovery agencies.[48]

[42] Ramsay (n 41) 162.

[43] Directive 87/102/EEC of 22 December 1986 for the approximation of the laws, regulations and administrative provisions of the Member States concerning consumer credit [1986] OJ L42/48, 48–53.

[44] ibid art 7.

[45] European Commission, Report on the operation of Directive 87/102/EEC for the approximation of the laws, regulations and administrative provisions of the Member States concerning consumer credit, COM(95)117, para 185–86.

[46] ibid para 269.

[47] ibid.

[48] ibid para 270.

9.3.2 The 2002 Proposal for revising the Consumer Credit Regulation

The 2002 proposal for a revised CCD marked the first and most significant effort to regulate informal debt-collection at the EU level. The drafting of the proposal was entrusted to the Directorate-General (DG) for Health and Consumer Protection (SANCO).

The choice of DG spelled trouble for the financial industry. As Ramsay pointed out, DG Market usually addressed financial services. It had greater expertise and was closer to the financial industry. Entrusting a consumer DG with the new CCD proposal meant that little consultation occurred with the financial sector before the initial draft, which was primarily based on input from consumer lawyers.[49] Moreover, the official responsible for drafting was Belgian,[50] and Belgium's implementation of a debt-collection law may have inspired the insertion of such rules in the proposal.[51]

The initial 2002 draft suggested the complete harmonization of community rules based on the principle of country of origin. It also contained provisions for all phases of consumer credit transactions, aiming to strike a balance between market growth, improved credit access, and consumer protection. This was particularly important considering that the total amount of credit circulating in the fifteen MS at the time exceeded 500 billion euros (equivalent to more than 7 per cent of their combined gross domestic product), with an annual growth rate of approximately 7 per cent.[52]

9.3.2.1 Proposed measures against abusive debt-collection practices

The 2002 CCD proposal acknowledged widespread dissatisfaction with national consumer-protection legislation concerning financial services and the need to harmonize consumer financial protection at the EU level. This called for a realignment of rights and obligations between consumers and credit providers, along with an improvement in how professionals handled payment defaults.[53]

As a result, Article 27 of the proposal, which dealt with recovery, aimed to encompass anyone responsible for the informal enforcement of a credit agreement, including creditors, credit insurers, and recovery agencies, while excluding those involved in judicial processes or repossession procedures, such as bailiffs. The clear intention of the European legislator was 'not to regulate the profession of the

[49] Ramsay (n 41) 167.
[50] ibid 167, n 47.
[51] European Commission (n 45) para 242.
[52] Proposal for a Directive of the European Parliament and of the Council on the harmonisation of the laws, regulations and administrative provisions of the Member States concerning credit for consumers, COM(2002)443, 11 September 2002 (2002 CCD Proposal) 3.
[53] ibid 4–5.

"collection agencies" or "debt counsellors" but to prohibit certain practices in connection with the non-performance of credit agreements'.[54]

The proposed measures would have banned a set of practices in informal debt-collection,[55] including but not limited to:

1) charging default-related costs exceeding those specified in the credit agreement;[56]
2) using deceptive methods to create the impression that a correspondence originates from an authoritative entity;[57]
3) sending written communications containing inaccurate information regarding the repercussions of payment default,[58] such as repossession or legal action where such measures were not applicable;
4) seizing goods without judicial proceedings or explicit consumer consent;[59]
5) engaging in actions that could be construed as an invasion of the consumer's or guarantor's privacy, such as contacting their neighbours, relatives, or employers;[60]
6) subjecting a consumer or guarantor to physical or psychological harassment;[61]
7) pursuing a time-barred debt.[62]

In addition to the specific rules on debt-collection, the 2002 CCD proposal included provisions concerning their mandatory and non-negotiable nature, making it impossible to circumvent the CCD's application through conflicting terms or choice-of-law clauses in credit agreements.[63]

Penalties for infringements were required to be effective, proportionate, and deterrent, such as the loss of interest and charges by the creditor or withdrawal of the licence.[64] MS were also mandated to ensure appropriate and effective out-of-court redress mechanisms for consumer disputes.[65] These were designed to encourage aggrieved consumers to act against abusive debt-collectors.

54 ibid 25.
55 ibid 25, recital 24, and art 27.
56 2002 CCD Proposal (n 52) arts 27(1) and (2)(e).
57 ibid art 27(2)(a).
58 ibid art 27(2)(b).
59 ibid art 27(2)(c).
60 ibid art 27(2)(f).
61 ibid art 27(2)(g).
62 ibid art 27(2)(h).
63 ibid art 30.
64 ibid art 31.
65 ibid art 32.

9.3.2.2 Personal data protection and state-controlled credit bureaus

Finally, the proposal included provisions for collecting and processing personal data acquired from consumers and guarantors regarding the conclusion and management of consumer credit agreements. MS were required to establish a central database for registering defaulting consumers and guarantors, which creditors had to consult before concluding a contract.

The proposal restricted access to personal data to an initial creditworthiness assessment,[66] ensuring that all data was promptly destroyed after the conclusion of the credit or surety agreement or in the event of credit refusal.[67] Ultimately, access to this data was limited to the original creditors and could not be shared with debt-collectors.

9.3.3 The financial industry's opposition and lobbying against the proposal

The implications of these measures for the debt-collection industry would have been dire. At that time, only a few MS had regulations concerning informal debt-collection. The directive would have established a minimal yet sufficient set of rules to harmonize debt-collection practices throughout the Union. This would have compelled even reluctant MS to adopt measures they may not have wanted to adopt. As Ramsay points out, countries with major financial industries, such as the UK, Germany, and the Netherlands, were sceptical of the entire revision of the CCD.[68]

Additionally, the measures would have dealt a significant blow to the debt-collection industry by reducing its capacity to collect fees and extra charges, limiting access to the debtor's personal data, and prohibiting the collection of debts that have surpassed the statute of limitations. It is important to note that while the time limits for debt-collection varied among EU MS, many still allowed informal collection attempts after the statute of limitations had expired and no judicial action could be pursued. The prohibition of time-barred debt would have considerably affected the debt-collection business and shifted national approaches. However, due to the reluctance of many MS and opposition from the financial industry, concerted action was taken against the proposal.

In the ensuing discussions, the financial sector exhibited its significant instrumental and structural power. The European Parliament (EP) received input from twenty national and European financial lobbyists but only one consumer group.[69]

66 2002 CCD Proposal (n 52) 15.
67 ibid art 8.
68 Ramsay (n 41) 167.
69 Ramsay (n 41) 167, n 49.

Surprisingly, the overly protective stance adopted by the proposal made it challenging for the EC to garner support from consumer organizations. As Ramsay aptly notes:

> The legislative history of the 2008 Directive reads like a case study in public choice analysis of consumer policy. Financial interests operating through the European Parliament, their national governments (particularly in the UK and Germany), and the Commission (particularly DG Market, which did not agree with Sanco) succeeded in gutting most of the provisions of the original Directive.[70]

9.3.4 Rejection by the European Parliament

The EP's Committee on Legal Affairs and the Internal Market rejected the draft proposal in 2003 in a vote of nineteen to zero and four abstentions.[71] Not a single vote in favour of the consumer-friendly legislation was cast in this committee of the EP, which is the only EU institution directly representing the EU citizenry.

The Committee's 2003 First Draft Report is concise and critical, suggesting that the proposal needed significant revisions to avoid harming the European consumer credit business. The EP even threatened the EC with Rule 67, which would have enabled the EP to call on the EC to withdraw its proposal over the latter's refusal to submit an updated version.[72] How far the EP was willing to take the institutional conflict perfectly illustrates the financial industry's structural power at the EU level.

In its 2004 Second Report, the Committee on Legal Affairs and the Internal Market, supported by the Committee on Economic and Monetary Affairs, proposed eliminating all personal data-protection measures[73] and prohibited practices in debt-collection, including repossession.[74] The rationale for these proposals was that the Data Protection Directive in force at the time was sufficient to address personal data protection and that recovery measures resulting from defaulted credit agreements were less common than those resulting from purchasing agreements or other contracts. In other words, since the CCD would only regulate some debt-collection, it was better to refrain from regulating it at all. The committees

70 Ramsay (n 41) 167.

71 European Parliament, I Draft Report on the proposal for a European Parliament and Council directive on the harmonisation of the laws, regulations and administrative provisions of the Member States concerning credit for consumers, COM(2002)443, C5-0420/2002, 2002/0222 (COD) Committee on Legal Affairs and the Internal Market, Provisional A5-0310/2003 Rev1, 23 September 2003, 4.

72 ibid 7.

73 European Parliament, II Second Report on the proposal for a European Parliament and Council directive on the harmonisation of the laws, regulations and administrative provisions of the Member States concerning credit for consumers, COM(2002)0443, C5-0420/2002, 2002/0222(COD) Amendments 13, 68, and 5.

74 European Parliament (n 73) Amendments 132–35, 90–91, and 93.

concluded that creating a special arrangement for the recovery of debts arising from credit agreements would be inappropriate and contrary to the principle of subsidiarity and would conflict with efforts to establish better and more cohesive legislation.[75]

Furthermore, the committees asserted that the EC had not justified the necessity of any specific regulation for recovery measures related to credit agreements.[76] The Council of the European Union also agreed with this viewpoint.[77] Consequently, when the EC presented its amended proposal in 2005, it no longer included data-protection and debt-collection measures.[78] Facing pressure from all sides, the EU caved in and lost a momentous opportunity to regulate a burgeoning industry, which could have bolstered consumers' confidence in the face of the impending crisis.

9.3.5 Aftermath

In the aftermath, minor references to the fair treatment of the rights of consumer-debtors and debt stakeholders appeared in the EC's Amnesty of Debts: Amicable Agreement and Statutory Solution, Minutes (2006). The document emphasized the 'importance of considering the "good faith" of the creditor as well as the debtor, as a way of balancing creditors' and debtors' rights'.[79]

However, the 2007 Council of Europe's Final Activity Report of the Group of Specialists for Legal Solutions to Debt Problems took a different stance, concluding that 'debtors should fulfil their obligations as far as possible' and that no 'good faith test should be implemented as it is impossible to define good faith'.[80] Ultimately, the adopted version of the 2008 CCD did not mention debt-collection and debtor data protection.

This concluded the first defining attempt to regulate informal debt-collection at the EU level. That EU consumer law and implementation leaned towards the interests of finance capital was not unexpected given that households were becoming a significant profit centre for financial institutions in the EU,[81] much like in the US.

75 ibid 126.
76 ibid 126.
77 Council of the European Union, 'Statement of the Council's Reasons: Modified proposal for a Directive of the European Parliament and of the Council on credit agreements for consumers and repealing Council Directive 87/102/EEC', 9948/2/07 REV 2 ADD 1, 20 September 2007.
78 Amended Proposal for a Directive of the European Parliament and of the Council on credit agreements for consumers amending Council Directive 93/12/EC, COM (2005) 483, 23 November 2005.
79 Richard Heys, Karen Hope, Rohit Ladher, Marguerita Lane, Katarzyna Pasik, Paula Ramada, Miriam Sinn, and James Suter, 'Study on Means to Protect Consumers in Financial Difficulty: Personal Bankruptcy, *Datio in Solutum* of Mortgages, and Restrictions on Debt Collection Abusive Practices' (*London Economics*, 2012) 188.
80 ibid 189.
81 Consumer loans (excluding mortgages) represented on average almost 18% of the gross income of retail banks in the EU in 2007. European Commission, 'Consumer Commissioner Kuneva

Ramsay points out that the intricate nature of credit law, where the devil is often in the detail, favoured the ability of financial interests to influence policy[82] and law-making at both the EU and national levels.

This case study demonstrated the mechanisms of regulatory capture, offering concrete evidence of how financial lobbying shaped an EU directive. Despite the initial consumer-friendly stance, intense lobbying led to the removal of consumer-protection measures against abusive informal debt-collection.

9.4 The Revolving Door in the European Union

The previous section highlighted that depending on the directorate-general responsible for drafting legislative proposals at the EC, the outcomes may exhibit a more consumer-friendly or business-friendly orientation. It also demonstrated that different directorates are associated with distinct policy priorities. One possible explanation is the 'revolving door' phenomenon, which fosters a complex web of interconnected interests between lobbyists and the entities they lobby as individuals seamlessly transition between these roles.

9.4.1 A threat to decision-making in the public interest

The 'revolving door' is a considerable threat to decision-making in the public interest, especially when former EU staff members leverage their knowledge and contacts to lobby for their new employers.[83] This phenomenon involving EU institutions and the financial sector is not recent, dating back to the late 1980s when neoliberal policies and calls for industry deregulation became the norm.[84] The overall outcome, whether at the EU or national level, is that such close connections between public institutions and private interests undermine the adoption of proper financial sector regulation. The European Central Bank (ECB) and the Directorate-General for Financial Stability, Financial Services, and Capital Markets Union (DG FISMA) stand out for reasons that will become clearer in the following sections.

welcomes Member States decision to back new rules on consumer loans' (*European Commission*, 22 May 2007) Press Release.

[82] Ramsay (n 41) 165.

[83] CEO, 'Banking on the revolving door: rules full of loopholes for former finance officials' (*CEO*, 23 January 2013) <https://corporateeurope.org/en/news/banking-revolving-door-rules-full-loopholes-former-finance-officials> accessed 29 February 2024.

[84] For a list of prominent examples between 1986 and 2012, see ibid.

9.4.2 Example 1: The European Central Bank

In 2017, a CEO report noted that the financial industry used the ECB's advisory groups as lobby platforms.[85] Like other EU institutions, the ECB relies on external expertise to inform its policies. At the time, twenty-two advisory groups provided the ECB with recommendations, all of which were predominantly composed of representatives of the most influential financial corporations.

According to the report, more than 98 per cent (508 seats) of the 517 available seats across all advisory groups were assigned to representatives of private financial institutions.[86] Sixteen financial groups, including Deutsche Bank, BNP Paribas, Société Générale, Citigroup, and Unicredit, occupied 208 seats. Notably, financial institutions supervised by the ECB held most posts as 'advisers', accounting for 346 seats, or two-thirds of the total. These statistics raise concerns about whether membership in the ECB's advisory groups is an asset for the financial industry, potentially granting them undue influence over decisions with multibillion-euro stakes.[87] As detailed in Chapter VII, Subsection 7.2, the ECB has demonstrated a willingness to endorse the financial industry's opposition to mandatory disclosures regarding traded debts and NPL portfolios, undermining the legislative measure it is responsible for implementing and monitoring.

9.4.3 Example 2: The Directorate-General for Financial Stability, Services, and Capital Markets Union

A similar problem affected FISMA, the EC directorate responsible for banking and financial regulation. Between 2008 and 2017, one-third of its senior personnel either came from the financial sector or transitioned there following their tenure at the Commission.[88] Additionally, contemporary research by ALTER-EU revealed that 92 per cent of FISMA's interactions involved representatives of corporate interests, predominantly from financial institutions.[89]

[85] CEO, 'Open Door for Forces of Finance at the ECB' (*CEO*, 3 October 2017) <https://corporateeurope.org/sites/default/files/attachments/open_door_for_forces_of_finance_report.pdf> accessed 29 February 2024.

[86] For a list of participants in the ECB advisory groups and their affiliations in 2017, see: CEO, 'Participants in the ECB advisory groups' (*CEO*) <https://corporateeurope.org/sites/default/files/attachments/table_of_ecb_advisory_groups_and_its_members.pdf> accessed 29 February 2024.

[87] CEO (n 85).

[88] Yiorgos Vassalos, 'Le pantouflage financier à la Commission européenne' (2017) 41 Savoir/Agir 49 <https://www.cairn.info/revue-savoir-agir-2017-3-page-49.htm?contenu=article> accessed 29 February 2024.

[89] ALTER-EU, 'Corporate interests dominate EU lobbying on financial services' (*ALTER EU*, 20 February 2017) <https://www.alter-eu.org/corporate-interests-dominate-eu-lobbying-on-financial-services> accessed 29 February 2024.

Furthermore, like the ECB, FISMA's expert groups heavily relied on industry expertise, with 57 per cent of non-governmental members representing corporate interests.[90] Notably, contributions from the financial lobby overwhelmingly dominated public consultations organized by the Commission on financial regulation proposals, accounting for nearly two-thirds of all responses.

This indicates that FISMA failed to strike a balance in consulting with all types of interests when drafting financial regulations for the public interest. Moreover, the structural revolving door points to regulators' dependence on those they regulated or exposed to conflicts of interest and loss of independence. These issues came to light in 2018, prompting questions about whether FISMA maintained the necessary neutrality from the industry it was supposed to regulate or leaned too much towards the vested interests of the financial sector. The fact that the CSCPD Proposal the EC tasked FISMA with drafting (at the behest of the Council of the European Union) that same year included no consumer-protection measures suggests the latter.

9.5 Regulatory Capture and the Adoption of the Credit Servicers and Credit Purchasers Directive

Spearheaded by the banking system and the ancillary debt-collection industry, the financial sector aims to maximize profits within the confines of government regulations and liquidity constraints set by central banks. Consequently, it consistently seeks to ease regulatory burdens (deregulation) by pressuring or lobbying governments and to influence central banks to maximize available liquidity (by reducing prudential measures).[91]

9.5.1 Overlapping interests: Non-performing loan regulation at the European Union level

Sometimes, their interests overlap, as in the case of NPL regulation at the EU level. NPL accumulation on a bank's balance sheet ties up significant resources due to the provisioning and write-offs required to cover expected credit losses. This diminishes the bank's capacity to lend,[92] reduces its profitability,[93] and can even

[90] CEO, 'Financial regulators and the private sector: permanent revolving door at DG FISMA' (*CEO*, 11 April 2018) <https://corporateeurope.org/en/power-lobbies-revolving-doors/2018/04/financial-regulators-and-private-sector-permanent-revolving> accessed 29 February 2024.

[91] Éric Monnet, Stefano Pagliari, and Shahin Vallée, *Beyond Financial Repression and Regulatory Capture: the Recomposition of European Financial Ecosystem after the Crisis* (LEQS Paper No 147, 2019) 3.

[92] Council of the European Union, 'Report of the FSC Subgroup on Non-Performing Loans', 9854/17 EF 113 ECOFIN 481, 31 May 2017, paras 67–69 <https://data.consilium.europa.eu/doc/document/ST-9854-2017-INIT/en/pdf> accessed 28 February 2024.

[93] ibid paras 54–59.

jeopardize its viability, with potential implications for the stability of the entire financial system.[94] It is a situation perfectly suited for structural influence, stemming from the financial institutions' key role in granting credit.

Recognizing that tackling high NPL levels is primarily the responsibility of the affected banks, interest in establishing legal frameworks that would allow them to efficiently and promptly discard NPLs from their balance sheets has been growing. This would enable banks to free up liquidity, resume lending, and seek profits. While existing frameworks at the national level were deemed inadequate due to fragmentation and administrative barriers,[95] a standardized EU solution was considered preferable for the financial sector to harmonize NPL transfers throughout the Union.[96]

9.5.2 The Credit Servicers and Credit Purchasers Directive Proposal: Harmonizing non-performing loan transfers and improving debt recovery

In addition, the financial industry continued to express interest in streamlining, enhancing, and standardizing the overall debt-recovery process by designing and implementing legal mechanisms to facilitate swift contract enforcement and asset foreclosure. These initiatives were considered essential for 'strengthening debtor discipline'.[97]

The Council of the European Union was receptive to the industry's needs. Toomas Tõniste, the Minister for Finance of Estonia, which held the Council presidency, stressed that 'non-performing loans are a problem for the banking industry for which solutions have until now been mainly defined at the national level', concluding: 'we need to free up these resources, make our financial system more resilient and prevent the re-emergence of NPL issues in the future.'[98]

The Council readily agreed to an action plan to tackle the NPL problem in the banking sector. It urged the EC to

> develop, by summer 2018, a European approach to foster the development of secondary markets for NPLs, in particular, to remove impediments to the transfer of

[94] ibid paras 60–65. See also: European Commission Second Progress Report on the Reduction of Non-Performing Loans in Europe, COM(2018)133, 14 March 2018 <https://eur-lex.europa.eu/legal-content/EN/TXT/?uri=CELEX:52018DC0133> accessed 28 February 2024.

[95] Proposal for a Directive on credit servicers, credit purchasers and the recovery of collateral, COM(2018)135, 14 March 2018 (CSCPD Proposal).

[96] Council of the European Union (n 92) paras 270–74.

[97] ibid paras 218–19.

[98] Council of the European Union, Press release, Banking: Council sets out action plan for non-performing loans, 11 July 2017, at https://www.consilium.europa.eu/en/press/press-releases/2017/07/11/banking-action-plan-non-performing-loans/> accessed 28 February 2024.

> NPLs by banks to non-banks and to their ownership by non-banks ... as well as to simplify and potentially harmonise the licensing requirements for third-party loan servicers and to take legislative initiative in this respect, as appropriate.[99]

Nine months later the EC presented its CSCPD Proposal,[100] acknowledging the need to reduce NPL stocks and prevent excessive NPL build-up due to the interconnected nature of the EU's banking system, particularly in the euro area.

9.5.3 The shift from consumer protection to financial stability

DG FISMA was responsible for drafting the directive. Given DG FISMA's mandate to safeguard financial stability and facilitate access to capital across the EU, it is unsurprising that the initial version did not include any provisions concerning the regulation of informal debt-collection practices, which could turn abusive.

Unlike the CCD, the 2021 CSCPD is not a consumer-protection instrument (see Chapter XIV). Instead, it appears to regulate the debt-collection profession by establishing rules for licensing, staff selection, governance mechanisms, and the content of industry-specific contracts. Responsibilities towards consumers are viewed as secondary to the aforementioned objectives. As a result, the 2021 CSCPD ensures that the narrative and the process are aligned with and subservient to financial interests, all under the guise of fostering the banking union and protecting the financial system's stability.

9.5.4 The European Parliament's amendments and the push for debt-collection regulation

Subsequent events represented a reversal of the situation at the time of the 2002 CCD proposal, making it the second defining moment in the EU's attempts to regulate informal debt-collection. This time EU advisory bodies backed the concerns raised by consumer NGOs,[101] such as the Financial Services User Group[102]

[99] Council of the European Union, 'Banking: Council sets out action plan for non-performing loans' (11 July 2017) Press Release <https://www.consilium.europa.eu/en/press/press-releases/2017/07/11/conclusions-non-performing-loans/> accessed 28 February 2024.

[100] CSCPD Proposal (n 95).

[101] Financial Services User Group, 'Nonperforming Loans (NPLs)—Letter to the European Commission' (*Financial Services User Group*, 2018) <https://ec.europa.eu/info/sites/info/files/fsug-opinions-180227-npls_en.pdf> accessed 20 December 2020; European Economic and Social Committee, 'Opinion on Proposal for a Directive of the European Parliament and the Council on credit servicers, credit purchasers and the recovery of collateral' 2018/C 367/09, 2018.

[102] Financial Services User Group (n 101).

and Finance Watch.[103] These organizations advocated for the inclusion of high levels of consumer protection from abusive informal debt-collection in the proposal, a position later supported by several MEPs.

In January 2020, multiple MEPs proposed amendments that directly and extensively addressed the issue of abusive informal debt-collection practices.[104] These amendments aimed to introduce detailed provisions concerning common *de minimis* standards in debt-collection, including the requirement for evidence of the debt before any collection; transparency conditions and mandatory disclosures;[105] the prohibition of misleading information, harassment, debtor stigmatization, and threats;[106] the protection of privacy and intimacy; the regulation of debt-collection costs;[107] and buy-back rights.[108]

Ironically, the proposed amendments would have incorporated into the 2021 CSCPD most of the provisions that the EP had removed from the 2002 CCD proposal because of the financial industry's lobbying. The change in the EP's attitude between the 2002 CCD proposal and the 2021 proposed amendments may be attributed to shifts following the economic crisis. Previous research has suggested that the EC and the EP, rather than the Council, play a key role in advocating for consumer-friendly outputs, with MEPs supporting consumer protection to depict the EP as an institution representing citizens' interests and an ally of the public.[109]

9.5.5 Industry resistance and renewed regulatory efforts

While the package made its way through the procedural labyrinth, NPL levels declined steadily, dropping to 636 billion euros in June 2019.[110] By the first half of 2020, NPLs decreased even further to 588 billion euros, as reported by the ECB. The market was functioning, requiring no additional help, as the industry repeatedly stated in its attempts to stall the adoption of the CSCPD, which brought the industry into the spotlight.

Despite the industry's claims, the defaulted debt in 2020 in the EU27 exceeded the entire consumer credit market in the EU15 twenty years earlier. The

103 Finance Watch, 'Non-performing loans plan: EU must protect taxpayers and vulnerable borrowers' (*Finance Watch*, 7 June 2018) <https://www.finance-watch.org/press-release/non-performing-loans-plan-eu-must-protect-taxpayers-and-vulnerable-borrowers/> accessed 23 May 2022.

104 European Parliament Committee on Economic and Monetary Affairs, Amendments 204–468 (Draft Report), 2018/0063A (COD), 7 January 2020.

105 ibid Amendments 336, 337, and 350.

106 ibid Amendments 336, 337, and 350.

107 ibid Amendment 350.

108 ibid Amendment 338.

109 Kastner (n 37) 232, 236–37.

110 Alessia Pirolo, 'Decade ends with lowest NPL levels on European bank balance sheets since 2010' (*Debtwire*, 13 January 2021) <https://events.debtwire.com/decade-ends-with-lowest-npl-levels-on-european-bank-balance-sheets-since-2010> accessed 22 November 2021.

uncertain impact of the COVID-19 pandemic and concerning economic forecasts[111] prompted the EC to intensify its efforts, fearing another systemic meltdown.[112] In December 2020, the EC reasserted its commitment to build on the measures presented by the Council of the European Union in 2017 and urged the swift adoption of the CSCPD Proposal.[113] Following the Commission's statement, the process gained momentum.

9.5.6 The rejection of the European Parliament's amendments and the final compromise

Similar to the 2002 CCD proposal, the EP's amendments were criticized for lacking justification.[114] By 28 June 2021 most had vanished, and a compromise text was agreed on.

In October 2021, a second round of amendments was proposed during the EP's discussion of the compromise text, but without much effect. The Council adopted the CSCPD[115] on 5 November 2021.[116] The final version became the first EU act to harmonize the licensing of credit servicers and, to some extent, the regulation of informal debt-collection at the Union level. Nevertheless, all measures concerning the latter are purely derivates and minimal.

9.5.7 Inquiries into the rejection of the European Parliament's amendments

The rejection of the EP's amendments seems illogical from a legislative standpoint. These amendments would have provided clear guidelines for lawful and fair behaviour for all stakeholders, including national policymakers, legislators, creditors, credit servicers, debt purchasers, legal practitioners, and courts. They would have furthered the directive's goal of harmonizing and ensuring a high level of consumer protection.

111 Sam Fleming and Jim Brunsden, 'EU banks urged to prepare for bad loans as pandemic hits economy' (*Financial Times*, 1 November 2020) <https://www.ft.com/content/3c6b4eb0-5b3d-4a37-87e5-d83da8de217d> accessed 22 November 2021.

112 Council of the European Union, 'Strengthening the Banking Union—presidency progress report' 14354/1/19 REV 1, para 16.

113 European Commission, Tackling non-performing loans in the aftermath of the COVID-19 pandemic, COM(2020)822, 16 December 2020.

114 Michael Huertas and Holger Schelling, 'European Union: The EU's new credit servicers directive—where are we now' (*Mondaq*, 19 March 2020) <https://www.mondaq.com/germany/dodd-frank-consumerprotection-act/904974/the-eu39s-new-credit-servicers-directive-where-are-we-now> accessed 20 December 2020.

115 CSCPD (n 27) 1–37.

116 Council of the European Union, 'Voting result, Brussels' 13688/21, 9 November 2021.

Ultimately, these amendments would have facilitated the proper functioning of the secondary NPL market by regulating the *activity*, not just the *profession*, of debt-collectors. The failure to adopt these changes appears to be another triumph for the financial industry in the game of interests shaping financial regulation. Furthermore, the regulation of the profession rather than the activity enabled it to establish entry barriers to retain control over the permissible level of interference.

9.5.7.1 Reasons provided by the Directorate-General for Financial Stability, Financial Services, and Capital Markets Union

Further inquiries revealed more. In 2023, I reached out to DG FISMA and the offices of the MEPs who had proposed the amendments to the directive. I wanted to understand why the amendments were not adopted despite their conspicuous benefits. DG FISMA invited me to a discussion about the perceived shortcomings of the directive. Conversely, most MEPs declined my meeting invitation, citing either a busy political agenda or limited recollection of an 'old' proposal. Still, I managed to secure an informal interview with one person closely involved in drafting and proposing the amendments.

According to DG FISMA, two reasons led to the rejection of the EP's amendments. First, there was no impact assessment for the proposed amendments. Second, some MS opposed the amendments, believing that they would interfere with their private laws and expand the EC's regulatory intervention. Therefore, regulating informal debt-collection practices was left for a potential subsequent revision of the directive.

9.5.7.2 Questioning member states' opposition

Although these arguments are generally valid, it is doubtful that they were the main obstacles. If the issue was the absence of an impact assessment, it could have been easily surmounted by conducting one, assuming that the political will existed. The directive was not urgent, having been proposed in 2018 and already suffering delays. Therefore, it is hard to believe that conducting an impact assessment on proposed amendments would have had a negative effect.

It is also unlikely that MS opposed the amendments out of fear of interference in their legislative jurisdiction. In truth, some MS objected to similar measures in the 2002 CCD proposal because of their differing views on crediting ideology. However, the proposal concerned a directive that allowed enough flexibility for MS to achieve the EU legislators' goals.

Furthermore, if the MS truly loathed the idea of interference with their private laws, then the directive would not have included the introduction of two new contracts in national laws with mandatory content: the credit-servicing agreement and the outsourcing agreement (Chapter XVI). When I pointed out this aspect, DG FISMA representatives claimed that the MS requested the introduction of these new agreements, which contradicts their initial point.

Although I was not present at the Council's discussions and lack contradictory evidence, I find this unconvincing. The directive lacks specificity regarding the legal nature of the two contracts, likely leading to problems and fragmentation at the national and EU levels. If the MS had collectively requested the introduction of the new contracts in European private law, they would have advocated for more certainty and specificity. Therefore, it is likelier that the primary beneficiaries of the directive and the new contracts—credit servicers and credit purchasers—were able to influence their inclusion in the agenda.

9.5.7.3 The European Parliament's lack of political will and institutional power

The lack of political will (and institutional significance/power) is another explanation for the quasi-complete removal of the EP's amendments to the CSCPD. According to a staff member closely involved in drafting the proposals and negotiations, the EC's rejection of the amendments was meekly accepted by the EP, which failed to uphold its position and the interests of the European citizens it represents. The interviewee contended that the EP is a weak institution that rarely stands by its positions when confronted with opposition. It is worth noting that the EP vigorously opposed the 2002 CCD proposal to safeguard the financial industry's interests. However, consumer lobby groups do not exert a similar influence that could trigger an equally robust response.

The limited responses received and the reluctance of those contacted to provide more information make it challenging to give a definitive answer. I was often recommended to talk to someone else and pointed in another direction that proved to be another dead end. At times, even DG FISMA appeared uneasy when explaining why the directive turned out the way it did. Nonetheless, there are sufficient indications to suggest that the directive was crafted in the interest of the financial industry, implying a deliberate failure to implement adequate measures to tackle abusive practices in informal debt-collection.

9.6 Summary

This chapter delved into regulatory capture by the financial sector and its impact on EU policymaking, particularly in consumer credit and debt-collection regulation. It chronicled the EU's historical efforts to protect consumers from unfair informal debt-collection practices and detailed the consistent opposition to and dilution of these efforts by the financial lobby and certain MS. The chapter ultimately suggested that the absence of sufficient regulation of informal debt-collection practices at the EU level is deliberate and reflects the power imbalance between the financial industry and consumer advocacy groups.

The previous chapters suggested that a market of the size of the European debt market and actors enjoying such influence on EU and national lawmakers must be adequately regulated. This does not mean that there is currently no regulation or that no attempts have been made to bring debt-collection (the activity) and debt-collectors (the profession) within the confines of the law. However, at the EU level, such efforts have been largely unsuccessful due to a robust financial lobby against envisioned interventions. The next chapters tackle an alternative explanation, according to which the existing legal framework is sufficient to address abusive informal debt-collection adequately.

EU legislation on informal debt-collection was scarce until the Credit Servicers and Credit Purchasers Directive (CSCPD) was adopted in 2021. This is because the nature of the activity makes it difficult to encapsulate, especially in the context of consumer protection. Nevertheless, hints and references to it are found in some of the most important pieces of consumer legislation, which are addressed in the next chapters: the Unfair Commercial Practices Directive (UCPD), the Consumer Credit Directive (CCD), the Unfair Contract Terms Directive (UCTD), and the General Data Protection Regulation. The analysis reveals that the rules scattered across consumer-protection instruments cannot replace a sectoral approach.

X

ABUSIVE INFORMAL DEBT-COLLECTION AS AN UNFAIR COMMERCIAL PRACTICE

10.1 The Unfair Commercial Practices Directive

Directive 2005/29/EC on unfair business-to-consumer commercial practices in the internal market (the UCPD)[1] is the overarching piece of European Union (EU) legislation regulating unfair commercial practices in business-to-consumer transactions. As such, it applies to all commercial practices that occur before, during, and after a business-to-consumer transaction.

Consumer debt-collection activities are a service provided on the creditor's behalf, irrespective of whether it is a financial or a non-financial institution (such as a utility provider). Thus, the original contractual relationship between the creditor and the consumer-debtor lies at its foundation. Upon the consumer's default, a contractual relationship arises between the creditor (be it the aggrieved one or the subsequent purchaser) and the debt-collector.

Generally, there is no contractual relationship between the debt-collector and the consumer unless the debt-collector is also the creditor, which is rarely the case. Therefore, if the debt-collector behaved unfairly towards the consumer-debtor, a legitimate question under EU legislation is whether the consumer still enjoys protection against abusive practices in the absence of a contract. This question was answered in *Gelvora*[2] based on the legal framework of unfair commercial practices.

According to the UCPD, commercial practices occur not only during the marketing and supply stages but also after the transaction (after-sales stage), which can be brought into the directive's ambit.[3] Recital 13 of the UCPD also refers to 'unfair commercial practices which occur outside any contractual relationship between a trader and a consumer or following the conclusion of a contract and during its execution'. From this perspective, debt-collection activities are regarded as after-sales commercial practices because they are directly connected to the sale or supply of

[1] Directive No 2005/29/EC concerning unfair business-to-consumer commercial practices in the internal market [2005] OJ L149/22 (UCPD) 22–39.

[2] Case C-357/16 *UAB 'Gelvora' v Valstybinė vartotojų teisių apsaugos tarnyba* [2017] ECLI:EU:C:2017:573 (*Gelvora*) Judgment of 20 July 2017.

[3] UCPD (n 1) art 3(1).

EU Informal Debt-Collection Regulation. Cătălin-Gabriel Stănescu, Oxford University Press.
 DOI: 10.1093/oso/9780198966159.003.0010

products. There are no objective reasons to differentiate this assessment based on whether a trader outsources it or not.[4] As explained below, the Court of Justice of the EU (CJEU) also affirmed this position.

10.1.1 Case study: *Gelvora*

In 2017, the CJEU held that 'the legal relationship between a debt-collection agency and a debtor, who has defaulted under a consumer credit agreement and whose debt has been assigned to that agency, falls within the material scope of' the Unfair Commercial Practices Directive. More precisely, it reasoned that 'the practices in which that agency engages to recover the debt fall within the concept of "product" within the meaning of Article 2(c) of that directive' notwithstanding whether a court decision confirmed the debt and the decision was passed to a bailiff for enforcement.[5]

This dispute was among the few concerning informal debt-collection to reach the CJEU. Gelvora, a private Lithuanian debt-collection agency, was assigned portfolios of non-performing consumer debts by banks. Based on these assignments, Gelvora attempted informal (i.e. non-judicial) recovery from debtors. In some cases, these informal proceedings were paralleled by judicial ones carried out by state agents (bailiffs).[6]

In this context, several consumers complained to the Lithuanian State Consumer Rights Protection Authority, claiming that the company infringed the national transposition of the UCPD by engaging in unfair commercial practices.[7] The Authority found the allegations grounded and fined the debt-collection agency 3,475.44 euros.[8]

The main question raised by the case, and a key aspect of Gelvora's defence, was the legal nature of the relationship between a private debt-collection agency and a debtor who has failed to meet the terms of a consumer credit agreement and whose debt has been transferred to that agency. This would determine whether the consumer protections under the UCPD apply to the situation.[9]

In fining Gelvora, the Authority opined that informal debt-collection practices fall within the ambit of the UCPD (and the transposing national instrument). The collection agency disagreed. Gelvora appealed the Authority's decision before the Regional Administrative Court in Vilnius, but its action was dismissed as

[4] European Commission, Guidance on the interpretation and application of Directive 2005/29/EC of the European Parliament and of the Council concerning unfair business-to-consumer commercial practices in the internal market', C/2021/9320, OJ C 526, 29 December 2021 (2021 Guidance) 29.
[5] ibid para 32.
[6] ibid para 10.
[7] ibid para 11.
[8] ibid para 12.
[9] ibid para 18.

unfounded.[10] The court held that the relationship between the debtors and Gelvora was a consumer relationship. The company qualified as a 'trader' because it provided consumers with either a product or a service, namely debt management.[11] Gelvora appealed the regional court's decision to the Supreme Administrative Court of Lithuania, which referred the central question (and subsequent ones) to the CJEU.[12]

10.1.2 *Gelvora:* The Court of Justice of the European Union's interpretation of the Unfair Commercial Practices Directives on informal debt- collection

The CJEU grounded its reasoning in the broad formulation of the UCPD's concept of commercial practices,[13] which is defined as 'any act, omission, course of conduct or representation, commercial communication including advertising and marketing, by a trader, directly connected with the promotion, sale or supply of a product to consumers'.[14] It also referred to Recital 13's reading of UCPD Article 3, whereby the directive applies to unfair commercial practices by a business even outside a contractual relationship, before, after, or during the performance of the contract.[15] The keywords were 'directly connected with the sale of a product', which, in the court's view, covered 'any measure taken in relation to the conclusion of a contract, but also its performance, in particular, the measures taken to obtain payment for the product'.[16]

By applying its interpretation to the situation at hand, the CJEU found that the claims assigned to Gelvora originated in the supply of credit to consumers and, more precisely, instalment repayments to which interest at a previously agreed rate was added.[17] Consequently, debt-recovery activities could be regarded as a 'product' within the meaning of UCPD Article 2(c).[18]

Following the finding that informal debt-collection generally falls within the ambit of the UCPD, the CJEU considered whether the externalization of debt-collection activities to a third party would alter the result. Backed by the EC's 2016 Guidance on the Implementation/Application of the UCPD[19] and the position of several national courts, according to which debt-collection activities qualified as

[10] ibid paras 13 and 14.
[11] ibid para 15.
[12] ibid paras 16 and 17.
[13] UCPD (n 1) art 2(d).
[14] *Gelvora* (n 2) para 19.
[15] ibid para 20.
[16] ibid para 21.
[17] ibid para 22.
[18] ibid para 23.
[19] European Commission, Guidance on the implementation/application of Directive 2005/29/EC on unfair commercial practices [2016] SWD(2016)163 (2016 Guidance).

'after-sales commercial practices' and fell within the scope of the directive,[20] the CJEU's answer was negative:[21]

> although a debt-collection agency ... does not provide the consumer with a consumer credit service as such, the fact remains that the activity in which it engages, namely the recovery of debts which has been assigned to it, falls under the concept of 'commercial practice, which may be unfair, within the meaning of the Unfair Commercial Practices Directive, since the measures which it adopts are liable to influence the consumer's decision in respect of the payment of the product'.[22]

To reach this outcome, the court considered two main arguments: (1) the detrimental effects of potentially unfair/abusive debt-collection practices on the financial sector and (2) its negative impact on the effectiveness of consumer protection.

Regarding the first, the CJEU stated that the conditions in which a debt may be recovered from a consumer could decisively influence consumers' decisions to take out a loan.[23] At first glance, it is a protective measure for consumers. The court acknowledges the macroeconomic importance of consumers being active in the internal financial market. EU institutions deem consumer trust in the financial sector and institutions crucial for the health and functioning of the financial industry. Therefore, allowing unfair informal debt-collection practices to go unsanctioned could affect consumers' willingness to participate actively in the credit market. Tributary to market considerations, the CJEU seemed to believe that consumer protection is necessary but only because its absence might impair the functioning of the market. In other words, consumer protection is subordinate to market interests.

Regarding the second, the CJEU underscored that if debt-recovery activities were to be excluded from the application of the UCPD in cases where the original creditor assigned the debt to third parties, the effectiveness of the protection afforded to consumers by the directive would be called into question because professionals would be able to separate the debt-collection phase and circumvent the protective provisions of the directive.[24] Moreover, it added that initiating informal debt-collection activities in parallel to official enforcement proceedings through a bailiff could mislead the debtor regarding the nature of the procedure.[25] This behaviour would undermine the promise of a 'high level of consumer protection' and 'efficient enforcement' of EU consumer legislation.

[20] *Gelvora* (n 2) para 26.
[21] ibid para 24.
[22] ibid para 25.
[23] ibid para 27.
[24] ibid para 28.
[25] ibid para 30.

Both the CJEU's arguments are anchored in the directive, which sought to enhance consumer confidence and facilitate cross-border trade for businesses. However, the decision marked an extension of the UCPD's scope because, as the next subsection discusses, the directive was not designed to address informal debt-collection.

10.2 The Unfair Commercial Practices Directive's Coverage of Informal Debt-collection Practices

There is no early indication that the UCPD was meant to cover informal debt-collection practices. The analysis of the EC's policy and guidelines below shows that informal debt-collection was brought into the ambit of the UCPD by the judicial action of several member states (MS).

10.2.1 The absence of informal debt-collection practices in the European Commission's reports and communications

The EC's 2013 Communication on the application of the Unfair Commercial Practices Directive[26] did not mention debt-collection activities. Neither did the accompanying 2013 report on the application of the UCPD.[27] Position papers from European consumer organizations, such as BEUC,[28] were similarly silent. In the brief section on financial services, the organization supported the idea that 'specific rules to tackle unfair commercial practices in the financial services sector' could be 'developed at the national level or in targeted EU legislation'[29] but without mentioning debt-collection.

[26] European Commission, Communication on the application of the Unfair Commercial Practices Directive: Achieving a High Level of Consumer Protection. Building Trust in the Internal Market, COM(2013)138, 14 March 2013 <https://eur-lex.europa.eu/legal-content/EN/TXT/PDF/?uri=CELEX:52013DC0138> accessed 2 November 2023.

[27] European Commission, First Report on the application of Directive 2005/29/EC of the European Parliament and of the Council of 11 May 2005 concerning unfair business-to-consumer commercial practices in the internal market and amending Council Directive 84/450/EEC, Directives 97/7/EC, 98/27/EC and 2002/65/EC of the European Parliament and of the Council and Regulation (EC) No 2006/2004 of the European Parliament and of the Council, COM(2013)139 <https://eur-lex.europa.eu/legal-content/EN/TXT/PDF/?uri=CELEX:52013DC0139> accessed 2 November 2023.

[28] BEUC, *European Commission's Report on the Application of the Unfair Commercial Practices Directive* (BEUC Position Paper X/2013/049, 24 June 2013) <https://www.beuc.eu/sites/default/files/publications/2013-00457-01-e.pdf> accessed 2 November 2023.

[29] ibid 15.

The EC's 2013 Communication emphasized that the directive ensures high consumer protection across all sectors and serves as a safety net for issues not covered by other sector-specific EU rules.[30] However, debt-collection was evidently not a primary focus of the directive. In the realm of financial services, which were deemed critical sectors unaffected by the UCPD's maximum harmonization, the EC's primary concern was the lack of essential information during the advertising stage or the misleading description of financial products rather than the risk of abusive behaviour associated with the repayment of consumer debts.[31]

The reason behind the absence of any reference to debt-collection practices from the EC's report and communication must be questioned. Empirical evidence has already revealed that unfair debt-collection practices were a reality that some MS had to deal with. The 2011 study on the application of the UCPD to financial services and immovable property,[32] prepared by Civic Consulting, made several notes on it. Greece reported implementing a law focusing on the aggressive practices of companies when communicating with debtors.[33] When questioned about which product attracts the most common unfair practice complaints, the United Kingdom, an EU MS at the time, indicated 'a significant number of complaints' related to aggressive debt-collection, particularly concerning mortgages, secured loans, credit cards, and other loans.[34] The UK reporter underlined the position of one non-governmental organization, according to which these practices 'are of particular impact and importance' because they 'could have a detrimental impact on consumers' mental health'.[35] Similar concerns were raised by Slovakia, which noted that 'some creditors, and the debt-collection companies hired by them, have used inappropriate ways to collect financial claims'.[36] In all likelihood, the issue of abusive debt-collection practices was not confined solely to these MS. Still, it took another three years for the EC to acknowledge it in an official document.

30 European Commission, Communication on the application of the Unfair Commercial Practices Directive: Achieving a High Level of Consumer Protection. Building Trust in the Internal Market, COM(2013)138, 14 March 2013, 2.

31 ibid 6.

32 Civic Consulting, 'Study on the application of Directive 2005/29/EC on Unfair Commercial Practices in the EU, Part 1—Synthesis Report, Final Report' (*European Commission*, 2011) <https://op.europa.eu/en/publication-detail/-/publication/5550d564-65af-47c8-b7e4-a44020ad4a78#> accessed 02 November 2023.

33 ibid 57.

34 ibid 91 and 113.

35 ibid 91.

36 ibid 119. These inappropriate means of recovering debts included threatening to announce consumers' names in local media or print them on leaflets distributed in their home areas, coupled with frequent visits by debt-collectors to consumers' homes, annoying consumers with frequent phone calls, sending threatening mobile messages, and other practices.

10.2.2 The inclusion of informal debt-collection practices in the Unfair Commercial Practices Directive: The 2016 Guidance

The 2016 Guidance on the Implementation/Application of the UCPD[37] admitted that based on the suggestion of several national authorities, debt-collection activities 'should be regarded as after-sales commercial practices' irrespective of whether a trader has assigned a claim to a third party, given the direct connection of debt-collection to the sale or supply of products.[38]

It also noted that 'aggressive practices can occur in debt recovery, where third parties are mandated to collect debts',[39] although they would be equally damaging if the original creditor committed them. This position is backed by examples from Slovakia, Italy, and Poland,[40] in a non-exhaustive list. The 2016 Guidance also finds an implied ban on abusive debt-collection in No. 25 of Annex I to the UCPD, according to which 'conducting personal visits to the consumer's home and ignoring the consumer's request to leave or not to return except in the circumstances and to the extent justified, under national law, to enforce a contractual obligation' is unfair in all circumstances.[41] However, none of the above retained the attention of the European Parliament in its Overview of the EC's 2016 Guidance.[42]

10.2.3 Reaffirming the need to address abusive debt-collection

The necessity of addressing abusive debt-collection through the UCPD was reaffirmed in the 2017 Study for the Fitness Check of EU Consumer and Marketing Law[43] prepared by Civic Consulting. Based on suggestions from various national authorities, consumer organizations, and other stakeholders, the study listed many commercial practices proposed to be included on the UCPD's blacklist. Among them, Slovakia recorded 'practices related to the enforcement of consumer debts, particularly the use of humiliation in such contexts, e.g., by sending shaming notices in the envelops labelled as "how to get rid of debts" or addressed explicitly to "the debtor"'.[44]

[37] 2016 Guidance (n 19).

[38] ibid 6–7.

[39] ibid 78.

[40] ibid 7 and 51.

[41] ibid 7.

[42] Jana Valant, 'Application of the Unfair Commercial Practices Directive. Overview of the Commission's May 2016 Guidance Document' (*European Parliamentary Research Service*, January 2017) <https://www.europarl.europa.eu/RegData/etudes/IDAN/2017/595888/EPRS_IDA%282017%29595888_EN.pdf> accessed 2 November 2023.

[43] Civic Consulting, 'Study for the Fitness Check of EU consumer and marketing law. Final report Part 1—Main report' (*European Commission*, May 2017) <file:///C:/Users/SCG/Downloads/civic-study-fitness_check-consumer-law-part_1_44840.pdf> accessed 2 November 2023.

[44] ibid 47.

The suggestion to address abusive debt-collection was supported by more empirical evidence. The Consumer Market Study to Support the Fitness Check of EU Consumer and Marketing Law[45] cited European Consumer Complaints Registration System figures regarding the main reasons for complaints to this online tool. Invoicing/billing and debt-collection amounted to 7 per cent of the total complaints as of June 2016, more than double the 3 per cent of the total complaints in 2015.[46] Still, neither the suggestion nor the increase in consumer complaints was enough to convince the EU legislators, and the 2019 amendments did not make any specific reference to a ban on unfair debt-collection practices by the UCPD.

Nevertheless, by 2021, when the EC adopted the new guidance on its interpretation and application, the idea that the UCPD covers abusive debt-collection activities had solidified and become the norm at the MS level. In a pan-EU survey I conducted in 2020, thirteen respondents stated that the UCPD was used in their MS to tackle abusive debt-collection,[47] five of which[48] also had sectoral legislation. Four respondents answered negatively,[49] four said that they did not know,[50] and others[51] did not provide any information.[52] While the latter categories of responses could be explained by the respondents' level of personal knowledge, they could also indicate that national authorities did not deem the UCPD fit to deal adequately with abusive informal debt-collection practices.[53]

The CJEU's argument in *Gelvora* endorsed and encouraged the EC's position that debt-collection activities fall within the ambit of the UCPD. The arguments of the 2016 Guidance are replicated word for word in the 2021 Guidance, together with a circular reference to *Gelvora*,[54] now an EU judicial precedent.[55]

[45] GfK Belgium, 'Consumer Market Study to support the Fitness Check of EU consumer and marketing law. Final Report' (*GfK Belgium*, May 2017) <https://ec.europa.eu/newsroom/document.cfm?doc_id=44817> accessed 2 November 2023.

[46] ibid 66. In absolute numbers, the system registered 5,980 complaints as of June 2016 (from January 2016), compared to 13,176 complaints in 2015. The total number of complaints received was 90,484 as of June 2016 (from January 2016), compared to 499,228 in 2015.

[47] Belgium, Czechia, Denmark, Estonia, Finland, Germany, Italy, Latvia, the Netherlands, Poland, Slovakia, Slovenia, and Spain.

[48] Belgium, Denmark, Finland, Germany, and Latvia.

[49] Bulgaria, Ireland, Luxembourg, and Sweden.

[50] Austria, Croatia, Lithuania, and Portugal.

[51] Cyprus, France, Greece, Hungary, Malta, and Romania.

[52] Cătălin Gabriel Stănescu, 'Regulation of Abusive Debt Collection Practices in the EU Member States: An Empirical Account' (2021) 44(1) Journal of Consumer Policy 179, 188–89.

[53] ibid 190.

[54] 2021 Guidance (n 4) 29–30, 38.

[55] However, the 2021 Guidance goes further, with the help of new case law emerging from the MS. For instance, based on a Dutch case, a connection was found between professional diligence and abidance by national and international standards or codes of conduct concerning debt-collection, even though the company in question was not a member of the association. See: 2021 Guidance (n 4) 37 and n 153.

10.3 Lessons Learned and Impact on Consumer Protection

Besides clarifying the UCPD's scope, *Gelvora* illustrates many issues concerning the regulation of informal debt-collection practices in the EU at the Union and MS levels. The first is the apparent need to clarify the exact legal nature of informal debt-collection. *Gelvora* brings it under the broad umbrella of commercial practices, qualifying it as a 'product' under the directive. At the same time, the EC's Guidance on the Implementation/Application of the UCPD deemed it an after-sale service. As will become apparent later, debt-collection might qualify as an intermediation of consumer credit service in certain circumstances (see Chapter XI). In contrast, the CSCPD[56] defines it as a credit-servicing activity.[57] As already mentioned, divergent MS-level views further complicate the matter. Some MS consider it an 'ancillary' financial service, while others, notably Germany, catalogue it as a legal service that non-lawyers can perform.[58]

The second issue is ensuring protection against unfair informal debt-collection practices. In *Gelvora*, the national authority and, later, the CJEU had to rely on an extensive interpretation and application of the UCPD to ensure that consumers were protected. This situation stemmed from the fact that informal debt-collection was (and continues to be) largely unregulated via sector-specific legislation at the EU and MS levels.[59] Where sectorial legislation is absent, supervisory agencies and courts had to 'become creative' to curb abusive practices.[60] As mentioned in the EC's Guidance on the Implementation/Application of the UCPD, the directive had been used by some MS to tackle abusive debt-collection.[61] Still, empirical evaluations revealed that its impact remained minimal.[62] Two main reasons can be identified: (1) the regulatory blindness of the EU legislator and (2) over-reliance on national solutions, promoted by the minimal harmonization effect of the directive in connection with financial services. The UCPD came to play a role in addressing abusive debt-collection because several activist courts at the MS level used it as a substitute for absent sectorial legislation.

[56] Directive (EU) No 2021/2167 on credit servicers and credit purchasers [2021] OJ L438 (CSCPD).

[57] ibid art 3 (9)(a) and (b).

[58] Out-of-Court Legal Services (*Rechtsdienstleistungsgesetz*), published in Federal Law Gazette I 2007, p. 2840 (Germany) art 2. An English translation of an older version of the statute can be found at <https://www.gesetze-im-internet.de/englisch_rdg/index.html accessed 05.07.2024>. For details about the legal nature of debt-collection in Germany, see: David Markworth, 'Debt Collection Services in Germany. A Sector in Turmoil' in Cătălin Gabriel Stănescu (ed), *Regulation of Debt Collection in Europe: Understanding Informal Debt Collection* (Routledge 2023) 67–69.

[59] Stănescu (n 52).

[60] Jakub Kepinski, 'Regulation of Abusive Informal Debt Collection Practices: Poland' in Cătălin Gabriel Stănescu (ed), *Regulation of Debt Collection in Europe: Understanding Informal Debt Collection* (Routledge 2023) 110–12.

[61] 2016 Guidance (n 602) 7.

[62] Cătălin Gabriel Stănescu, 'Is the Unfair Commercial Practices Directive Fit to Effectively Tackle Abusive Debt Collection? A Critical Evaluation' (2020) 9(6) Journal of European Consumer and Market Law 235.

The third issue derives from the logic and priorities of European institutions. I contend that the internal market was and remains at the centre of the EU's debt-collection governance efforts. Ensuring a high level of consumer protection and efficient enforcement of consumer-protection rules are only secondary and generally subordinated to the primary goal of fostering and preserving the debt-commercialization market.[63] This is also evident in the CJEU's decision.

In its reasoning, the court's main concern was the potential negative impact of abusive informal debt-collection on the functioning of the internal (credit) market as aggrieved consumer-debtors might be discouraged from accessing loans. The starting point of the judgment in *Gelvora* is the EU legal context, namely, Recital 13 of the UCPD, which refers to the 'achievement of the Community's objectives through the removal of internal market barriers, replacement of divergent general clauses and legal principles at the MS level' and 'support[ing] consumer confidence'. The confidence in question concerns the adequate functioning of the internal market, which includes consumer protection and efficient enforcement.

As I detail in Chapter XIV, the CSCPD was adopted following the same logic of fostering the internal secondary market for NPLs through harmonization and standardization. At the same time, consumer protection is merely a by-product, an effect.[64] While one could object that the EU's intervention is constitutionally limited to proportionate and necessary measures for achieving its goals, the fact remains that consumer law is more likely a national law concern than an EU one.[65] However, even this statement is subject to qualifications regarding the regulation of informal debt-collection in MS. In these circumstances, one must wonder if the harmonization efforts in debt-collection will hurt rather than help consumer protection.

The fourth issue is intrinsic to the UCPD's scope. The UCPD is a normative act addressing unfair commercial practices aimed at consumers, meaning that all commercial transactions come within its ambit. *Gelvora* refers to credit agreements, but when it comes to unfair commercial practices related to debt-collection, these could also stem from utility agreements or any other type of consumer transactions. It is a maximum harmonization instrument which, however, has enabled MS to implement additional and more stringent protections in areas excluded from its coverage, such as financial services.[66]

[63] Hans-Wolfgang Micklitz, 'An Expanded and Systematized Community Consumer Law as Alternative or Complement?' (2002) 13 European Business Law Review 583, 588; Guido Comparato, *The Financialisation of the Citizen: Social and Financial Inclusion through European Private Law* (Hart Publishing 2018) 13, 185–86.

[64] Cătălin Gabriel Stănescu, 'The Impact of the Credit Servicing Directive on Regulating Abusive Informal Debt Collection in the European Union: A Step Forward or a Missed Opportunity?' (2023) 12(1) Journal of European Consumer and Market Law 4.

[65] Micklitz (n 63) 592–93.

[66] UCPD (n 1) art 3(9).

Interestingly, although the EC and the CJEU maintain that the UCPD's coverage extends to debt-collection activities, some MS have kept (or implemented) sectorial rules for informal debt-collection, such as Belgium, Denmark, Finland, Germany, Latvia, the Netherlands, Romania, and Sweden.[67] The reason is that the UCPD was not purposefully intended to comprehensively cover abusive debt-collection practices. Its effects in this area are primarily tangential and coincidental: it contains no rules concerning the authorization of debt-collectors, the validation of the debt, or the issue of added charges to the original debt (which are present in most sector-specific debt-collection laws and were also referred to in the proposed amendments to the CSCPD). Until the adoption of the Enforcement Directive,[68] it provided no individual remedy or private right to action to aggrieved consumer-debtors.[69]

10.4 Summary

This chapter delved into the application of the UCPD to informal debt-collection practices. The Gelvora case established that debt-collection activities are considered after-sales commercial practices, ensuring consumer protection even in the absence of a direct contractual relationship with debt-collectors. Emphasizing the UCPD's crucial yet limited role in safeguarding consumer rights and fostering market trust, the chapter underscored the necessity for explicit sector-specific regulation at both the EU and national levels to effectively address and prevent abusive debt-collection practices. The next chapter explores the relevance and impact of the CCD on debt-collection activities.

67 Stănescu (n 52).

68 Directive (EU) 2019/2161 amending Council Directive 93/13/EEC and Directives 98/6/EC, 2005/29/EC and 2011/83/EU of the European Parliament and of the Council as regards the better enforcement and modernization of Union consumer protection rules [2019] OJ L238/7 (Enforcement Directive).

69 Stănescu (n 62).

XI
CREDIT AND INTERMEDIATION OF RECOVERY: THE CONSUMER CREDIT DIRECTIVE'S INFLUENCE ON DEBT-COLLECTION PRACTICES

11.1 The 2008 Consumer Credit Directive

Directive 2008/48/EC on Credit Agreements for Consumers[1] (2008 CCD) was proposed by the European Commission (EC) in 2002 and adopted in 2008. It is still in force but will be replaced by Directive (EU) 2023/2225 on credit agreements for consumers (2023 CCD) on 20 November 2026.[2] The 2008 CCD had two main objectives: (1) harmonizing European Union (EU) rules on credit granted to consumers who borrow to finance purchases of goods and services and (2) opening up the EU consumer loan market while improving the transparency of contract terms and the level of consumer protection. The directive set rules for standard information to be included in advertising. Moreover, it specified that before consumers are bound by any credit agreement or offer, creditors (or credit intermediaries) must provide them with the information needed to compare different offers, allowing them to make an informed decision on whether to conclude a credit agreement.

Although there is no initial contractual relationship between debt-collectors and consumers, one such relationship can develop during collection efforts. Debt-collectors can enter into agreements with consumers concerning repayment plans of the original debt, an aspect acknowledged by most national sectoral laws and the Credit Servicers and Credit Purchasers Directive (CSCPD). In the case of claims arising from consumer credits accelerated by default, this option benefits both consumers and credit owners. Consumers can return to a repayment schedule that is easier to manage and comply with. Credit owners increase their chances of recovering an amount closer to the face value of the debt and secure the consumer's recognition of their claim, which is enforceable in court. The credit servicers also

[1] Directive 2008/48/EC on credit agreements for consumers [2008] OJ L133/66 (2008 CCD) 66–92.
[2] Directive (EU) 2023/2225 on credit agreements for consumers, PE/22/2023/REV/1 [2023] OJ L2023/2225 (2023 CCD).

EU Informal Debt-Collection Regulation. Cătălin-Gabriel Stănescu, Oxford University Press.
 DOI: 10.1093/oso/9780198966159.003.0011

benefit because any successful debt-collection or renegotiation allows them to claim a fee.

However, one may argue that by renegotiating and entering a payment schedule that involves deferred payments, the consumer is no longer in default under the initial credit agreement, which has been replaced with a new one. This ability of debt-collectors to renegotiate consumer debts, conclude instalment agreements on behalf of the creditors, and receive a fee for these services raises significant questions in EU consumer financial protection law, especially regarding the nature of repayment plans and debt-collectors' role and obligations vis-à-vis consumers in light of the CCD's provisions. Does the new agreement constitute credit, or is it merely a *sui generis* collection method? If the new deal constitutes credit, does the debt-collector act in a double credit servicer and credit intermediary capacity? And if so, what are the consequences? These questions arose in *Verein für Konsumenteninformation v INKO, Inkasso GmbH (INKO)*.[3]

11.1.1 Case study: *INKO*

The dispute started in Austria, where the Consumer Information Association brought an action against a debt-collector, INKO, concerning the latter's practice of concluding debt rescheduling agreements with consumers for the deferral of repayment without providing them with pre-contractual information.[4]

INKO was a debt-collection agency. Among the usual activities of its trade, it sent letters of demand to debtors on behalf of creditors, notifying them of the outstanding debt owed, accrued interest, and its fees. However, debtors were invited to either pay their debt within three days or fill out a pre-printed form indicating their acceptance of a rescheduling plan of their debt and return it to the agency. By entering into a formalized agreement, the debtors acknowledged the existence of the debt 'plus the filing costs and interest to be calculated for the resulting term'. Consumers undertook to pay their debt in monthly instalments of a determined amount following this plan. Based on the information available to the court, the payments first concerned INKO's fees and then the capital and interest.[5]

The Austrian Consumer Information Association objected to this practice and initiated legal action against INKO at the Commercial Court in Vienna. It

[3] Case C-127/15 *Verein für Konsumenteninformation v INKO, Inkasso GmbH* [2016] ECLI:EU:C:2016:934 (*INKO*) Judgment.
[4] ibid para 2.
[5] ibid (n 3) para 15.

sought an order restraining INKO from entering into agreements for deferred debt payments without providing the information required by the Austrian Law on Consumer Credit, which transposed the provisions of the CCD into national legislation.

Specifically, Paragraph 6(1) of the Austrian law stipulated that the lender must furnish the consumer with the necessary information to make an informed decision before any credit agreement or offer binds the consumer. This must include the type and total amount of credit, the conditions governing the drawdown, the duration of the credit agreement, the annual percentage rate of charge, and the total amount payable by the consumer.[6] Paragraph 6(2) clarified that these requirements 'also apply to credit intermediaries', except for those who are solely suppliers of goods or services in a 'subordinate role'.[7] Provisions of the Austrian Civil Code were also relevant, with Paragraph 1333 stating that 'in addition to statutory interest, the creditor may also seek the reimbursement of other damages caused to him by the fault of the debtor, in particular the necessary costs of extra-judicial enforcement or collection, provided these are reasonably proportionate to the claim pursued'.[8]

The first instance court granted the request, but the Regional Court of Vienna partially reversed the judgment in appeal.[9] Both parties then appealed the decision at the Supreme Court (the referring court),[10] which, by considering INKO's nature as a debt-collection agency, sought the guidance of the Court of Justice of the EU (CJEU) to ascertain whether a debt-collection agency that offers instalment agreements for the professional recovery of debts on behalf of its client and charges fees for this service to the debtors operates as a 'credit intermediary'[11] under the CCD.[12] This qualification would attract additional obligations, such as providing pre-contractual information to consumers concerning the new credit agreement.

In addition, it sought to determine whether the debt rescheduling agreements on deferred repayments concluded by INKO with consumers were to be considered 'free of charge' in light of the CCD[13] (since it is not claimed or proved that they exceed what is allowed under Austrian law) and, therefore, excluded from this directive's scope.[14] A positive answer would have shielded the debt-collector from the mandatory disclosures imposed by the CCD on credit intermediaries.

[6] ibid (n 3) paras 16 and 10.
[7] ibid (n 3) para 10.
[8] ibid (n 3) para 13.
[9] ibid (n 3) paras 17–18.
[10] ibid (n 3) para 19.
[11] ibid (n 3) paras 21 and 25(1).
[12] 2008 CCD (n 1) art 3(f).
[13] ibid art 2(2)(j).
[14] *INKO* (n 3) paras 22–25(2).

11.1.2 The Advocate-General's opinion on debt-collection agencies as credit intermediaries

In the preliminary remarks of her opinion,[15] Advocate-General (AG) Sharpston noted that the 2008 CCD does not contain 'any information to indicate whether debt-collectors ... *supply goods or services acting in an ancillary capacity*'[16] (emphasis added), as stated in Article 7 of the directive. Moreover, she observed that the classification of the legal arrangement between lenders, borrowers in default, and debt-collection agencies (and the applicable rules) differed across member states (MS).[17]

11.1.2.1 Debt-collectors as credit intermediaries

In the AG's view, a debt-collection agency providing such services would qualify as a credit intermediary under the CCD.[18] The AG juxtaposed the legal provisions with the case's facts to justify her interpretation. She found that if the debt-collection agency concluded credit agreements with consumers on behalf of the creditor, the wording was sufficiently broad to cover the debt-collector's activities[19] because all four conditions set in the CCD were met: the entity was (a) a natural or legal person, (b) not acting as a creditor, (c) operating in the course of its trade, business, or profession, and (d) charging a fee for its services.[20] The AG added that it makes more sense to require the debt-collector, not the creditor, to provide the pre-contractual information to the consumer because the debt-collector is the person (a) presenting or offering the new instalment agreement to the debtor, (b) undertaking the preparatory work concerning the agreement, and (c) concluding the agreement on behalf of the creditors, within the meaning of the directive.[21]

In addition, she argued that this interpretation would follow the twin aims of protecting consumers and creating a genuine internal market, as envisioned by the CCD.[22] If the debt-collection agency was deemed a credit intermediary under the directive, then it was required to provide the nineteen compulsory pre-contractual information points listed in the CCD in good time before the debtor was bound by the new credit agreement or offer, including as concerns the consequences of late payments or default in repaying the debt.[23] This would enable consumers to scrutinize and fully appreciate the outcomes of a subsequent default.[24] Conversely,

[15] ibid Opinion of Advocate-General Sharpston delivered on 21 July 2016 (1).
[16] ibid para 19.
[17] ibid para 20.
[18] ibid para 21.
[19] ibid para 26.
[20] ibid para 25.
[21] ibid para 29.
[22] ibid para 27.
[23] ibid para 29.
[24] ibid para 28.

not being provided with sufficient information and time to assess it deprived consumers of the statutory protections and exposed them to additional harm.

Regarding available time, the AG opined that giving defaulting consumers only three days to assess their position was inadequate. Therefore, the choice between full payment and entering into the instalment agreement was unlikely to be genuine.[25] What AG Sharpston noticed—but did not detail—was an abusive informal debt-collection practice, given the undue (additional) pressure it put on the consumer already experiencing a state of vulnerability.

INKO, the debt-collection agency, put forward two main arguments against an interpretation that would associate it with a credit intermediary under the CCD. First, it maintained that a credit intermediary merely brings lenders and borrowers together, which is different from what debt-collectors do: their activities are linked to the pre-existing credit agreement before the debt-collector presents an arrangement to the defaulting consumer. In other words, the repayment plan is not a new agreement; therefore, the obligations for credit intermediaries cannot be extended to debt-collectors. The Lithuanian government, which participated in the case, took a similar view.[26] Second, INKO argued that a broad understanding of the concept of credit intermediaries would apply to debt-collectors and professional activities excluded by the CCD, such as lawyers, who could also act as debt-recovery agents.[27]

The AG refuted all of INKO's arguments. It highlighted that there is no indication in the CCD that credit intermediation *must* occur before credit agreements are entered into. On the contrary, it was more consistent with the directive's wording not to restrict the notion of credit intermediary in this manner.[28] She also emphasized that the relevant agreement in the case was not the initial one between the lender and the borrower but the instalment agreement arranged by the debt-collector. If one accepted INKO's interpretation that debt-collectors are not credit intermediaries in such instances, then the borrowers would be deprived of the protection offered by the CCD as they would not receive the pre-contractual information before concluding the credit agreement for deferred payments.[29] Thus, she concluded that although 'debt-collection is not an activity associated with a more conventional type of credit intermediary', the term is general and covers several

[25] ibid para 28.
[26] ibid paras 32 and 35.
[27] ibid para 32. A third line of argumentation concerned the differences between the definition of credit intermediary under the CCD and the Consumer Mortgage Directive (CMD). Given that the latter specified that debt-collection agencies are not covered by its provisions, INKO claimed that a consistent interpretation of the two equivalent provisions requires debt-collectors to be excluded from the scope of the CCD as well. The AG rejected this perspective, noting that the CCD and CMD govern different legal relations (ibid para 34).
[28] ibid para 36.
[29] ibid para 36.

types of activities, including presenting instalment agreements to consumers on behalf of creditors to recover an outstanding debt for a fee.[30]

11.1.2.2 The meaning of 'free of charge' in debt-repayment plans

The AG also addressed at length the question of whether a credit agreement for the deferred payment, free of charge, of an existing debt under CCD's Article 2(2)(j) would be excluded from the scope of the directive. The AG again considered governmental submissions, with Germany and France expressing opposing views. On the one hand, Germany contended that an arrangement whereby a consumer pays a fee cannot be considered free of charge, even where the recovery costs under the instalment agreement are not greater than those of the initial one. The reason is simple: the costs in the initial agreement constitute charges for CCD Article 2(2)(j) purposes. On the other hand, France argued that instalment agreements give rise to extra costs for consumers where (a) a consumer pays more under such agreement than they would have paid if repayment had been organized by other means and (b) the debt-collector's costs are borne directly or indirectly by the consumer. The EC also submitted that it would be necessary to determine whether the consumer faces more significant charges under the instalment agreement than they would have without it.[31]

Answering the question required determining the meaning of 'free of charge' in Article 2(2)(j) of the directive and whether INKO arrangements fell within that provision. The AG's starting point was the absence of a definition of 'free of charge' in the directive, followed by the observation that the phrase could not be interpreted coherently in isolation but in connection with the following one, 'and without any other charges',[32] which is also associated with the definition of 'total cost of credit to the consumer' under CCD's Article 3(g). That definition is worded broadly to include 'all the costs, including interest, commissions, taxes and *any other kind of fees* which the consumer must pay in connection with the credit agreement, and which are known to the creditor' (emphasis added). As the AG noted, this is 'sufficiently broad to incorporate *recovery costs* incurred where a borrower is in default, under the initial agreement, whether those costs are charged by the lender himself or by a debt-collector acting on his behalf' (emphasis added).[33]

The ensuing discussion is generally relevant to debt-collection because lenders often delegate debt recovery to third parties in return for a fee or at a discount.[34] The reason is that it is easier and more efficient than trying to service the debts themselves. Given that debt-collection is associated with costs in case of default, credit agreements contain provisions making defaulting consumers responsible

[30] ibid paras 33 and 37.
[31] ibid para 39.
[32] ibid para 41.
[33] ibid para 41.
[34] ibid para 43.

for covering them. Thus, the AG argued, the process cannot be considered 'free' to the borrowers. The facts of the case supported this view: INKO did not deny that it charged fees for its services, and the sample agreement submitted to the national courts revealed that the borrower bore the recovery costs.[35]

What follows in AG's reasoning is simple and logical. The debt-collector services the debt for a fee. Therefore, the instalment agreement offered to consumers cannot be said to be free of charge. Given that there are financial implications for consumers, they should be able to make an informed choice, which can be done only under the auspices of the directive.[36] Concurrently, the method of payment is irrelevant; thus, whether the consumer pays the cost to the creditor who then pays the debt-collector or to the debt-collector directly is of no consequence for CCD Article 2(2)(f) if the ultimate responsibility for payment lies with the consumer. Similarly irrelevant is whether the quantum of recovery fees should be higher than those of the initial agreement, for the directive does not make such a distinction. This condition, the AG contended, would be incompatible with the consumer-protection standard of the CCD: that of a properly and fully informed consumer better placed to take responsibility for their borrowing agreements.[37]

AG Sharpston's opinion meticulously addressed the classification and obligations of debt-collection agencies under the CCD, which would have significantly impacted informal debt-collectors. She posited that debt-collectors qualify as credit intermediaries if they conclude credit agreements on behalf of creditors, necessitating the provision of pre-contractual information to consumers. Her arguments reinforced a broad understanding of credit intermediation, aligning with the directive's dual aims of consumer protection and market integrity. This comprehensive interpretation would have prevented potential exploitation by debt-collectors and ensured robust consumer safeguards in the context of informal debt-collection practices. Unfortunately, the CJEU did not adopt the same view.

11.1.3 The Court of Justice of the European Union shields debt-collectors from additional obligations vis-à-vis consumers

The CJEU's judgement concurred with the AG on the second account and nuanced the first. It noted that regarding consumer credit, the CCD sought to establish complete and mandatory harmonization in several key areas to ensure a high and equivalent level of protection for all EU consumers.[38] It also endorsed the AG's opinion that the concept of the credit agreement 'is particularly broad and covers

[35] ibid paras 43–44.
[36] ibid para 45.
[37] ibid para 51.
[38] ibid (n 3) para 27.

an agreement ... which provides for the rescheduling of repayments of an existing debt',[39] which helps to meet the objective of consumer protection.[40] This objective cannot be called into question by the cumulative amounts of interest and costs provided for by a deferred payment agreement, even if those amounts do not exceed those that would be payable otherwise.[41] Because, in the case at hand, the new agreement obligated the consumer to pay the costs of a credit-recovery agency, which were not provided for by the initial agreement, it could not be regarded as being linked to a deferred payment that had been agreed to 'free of charge'.[42]

On the first question, the CJEU concluded that a collection agency that acts on behalf of the lender to collect unpaid credit, interest, and costs must be considered a 'credit intermediary' under the CCD[43] unless the national court determines that this role was undertaken in an 'ancillary capacity', as per Article 7 of the CCD. The determination can be made based on Recital 24 of the 2008 CCD, which states that 'Suppliers of goods and services may be deemed, for example, to be acting as credit intermediaries in an ancillary capacity if their activity as credit intermediaries is not the main purpose of their trade, business or profession'. However, the wording is not particularly helpful, and courts may take different stances on the matter, enhancing the risk of fragmentation.

Prima facie, based on the CJEU's wording, most debt-collectors may not qualify as credit intermediaries because concluding deferred payment agreements is not the primary purpose of their trade, business, or profession. However, I believe that this interpretation is incorrect. Instead, I think national courts should assess whether entering into such agreements with consumers is an occasional occurrence or a regular part of the debt-collector's practice (even if it is infrequent).[44]

Either way, the only effect of the above is to insulate debt-collectors from additional obligations vis-à-vis consumers. Otherwise, the CJEU (along with the directive's wording) is clear that the consumer faced with a repayment schedule should receive all relevant pre-contractual information.[45] It is merely a question of whether the source of that information is the debt-collector or the creditor. Recital 24 and Article 7 of the 2008 CCD specify that, in cases where the suppliers of services act as credit intermediaries in an ancillary capacity, the creditor remains

[39] ibid (n 3) para 30.
[40] ibid (n 3) para 35.
[41] ibid (n 3) para 40.
[42] ibid (n 3) para 39.
[43] ibid (n 3) para 44.
[44] A similar issue occurred in the US regarding the definition of debt-collectors in the Fair Debt Collection Practices Act, which includes any attorney or other type of debt-collector 'who regularly collects or attempts to collect, directly or indirectly, [consumer] debts owed or due or asserted to be owed or due another'. Regularity appeared to be a key concept, which the courts had to define. The criterion was engagement in debt-collection in more than isolated instances or collecting debt more than a handful of times in a year, although the burden of proof fell on the consumer. For a list of relevant US cases see: National Consumer Law Center, *Fair Debt Collection*, vol 1 (9th edn, 2018) 159, n 336–40.
[45] *INKO* (n 3) paras 47–52.

responsible for ensuring that the consumer receives the complete pre-contractual information. Whether or not this occurs in debt-collection and what the resulting consequences are is an entirely separate issue.

11.2 The Aftermath

The adoption of the 2021 CSCPD and the 2023 CCD revision raise the questions of whether the CJEU's decision in *INKO* still constitutes 'good law' and whether there is still a link between the CCD and debt-collection.

11.2.1 Credit servicers and credit intermediaries

The CSCPD acknowledges that renegotiations with the borrower are part of the credit servicers' activity range. However, the definition indicates that credit servicers and credit intermediaries are mutually exclusive. According to the CSCPD, credit-servicing activities mean, among other things,

> renegotiating with the borrower, under national law, any terms and conditions related to a creditor's rights under a credit agreement, or of the credit agreement itself, in line with the instructions given by the credit purchaser, where the credit servicer is not a credit intermediary as defined in Art 3. Point (f) of Directive 2008/48/EC or Art 4, point 5, of Directive 2014/17/EU.[46] (emphasis added)

Since the CSCPD does not specify what happens when the credit servicer *is* a credit intermediary, conditionality infers that the intermediary role would supersede that of servicer in such cases.

In close connection, the recitals of the CSCPD state that the directive

> is without prejudice to the rules of Union and national law governing *credit origination*, including in cases when credit servicers can be considered to engage in credit intermediation as well as any national rules imposing additional requirements in respect of a credit purchaser or a credit servicer as concerns the renegotiation of the credit agreement's terms and conditions.[47] (emphasis added)

[46] Directive (EU) No 2021/2167 on credit servicers and credit purchasers [2021] OJ L438 (CSCPD) art 3(9)(b).

[47] ibid recital 16.

This suggests a willingness to accept potential overlap or confusion between the two roles at the Union or national level and a hesitation to clearly distinguish between them.

Conversely, the above may indicate that credit *origination* (including intermediation) differs from credit *regeneration*, with the former occurring *ante*-default and the latter being a *post*-default consequence. This understanding, which restates some of the defences advanced by INKO in the case discussed above, would be more in line with Article 3(9)(b) of the CSCPD but grossly contradict the findings[48] and the ruling of the CJEU.[49] Therefore, I posit that the first interpretation—that of potential overlap/confusion between credit servicers and credit intermediaries—should be adopted.

11.2.2 Forbearance measures and debt-collection

The repeal of the 2008 CCD and adoption of the 2023 CCD did not alter the CJEU's findings in *INKO*. The provisions of Recital 24 of the 2008 CCD are now restated in Recital 43 of the 2023 CCD, and those of Article 7 of the 2008 CCD are now included in Article 10(10) of the 2023 CCD. However, the 2023 CCD adds more weight to forbearance measures, extending the term of the credit agreement, changing the type of credit agreement, deferring payment of all or part of the instalment repayment for a period, reducing the borrowing rate, offering a payment holiday, partial repayments, currency conversions and partial forgiveness, and debt consolidation—although these remain at the discretion of the creditor.[50]

The relevance of forbearance measures to debt-collection stems from several elements. First, such measures would be a preliminary step to debt-collection (informal enforcement), to be exercised reasonably, where appropriate.[51] The considerable discretion left to creditors undermines most of the positive effect such a step could have on defaulting consumers. Still, it also creates a basis for creditors to settle many workable (but defaulted) accounts directly with the consumers. Second, one may wonder whether debt-collectors, acting as agents for the creditor, could play a role in forbearance measures such as those described in INKO or whether these are now deemed separate, preliminary steps to debt-collection. Whether informal debt-collection is part of an enforcement proceeding could determine the outcome. Third, Article 35(3) and (4) of the 2023 CCD states that where MS allow creditors to define and impose additional charges on the consumer arising from a default, which generally includes debt-collection charges, those MS may require

48 *INKO* (n 3) para 44.
49 ibid point 2 of the ruling.
50 2023 CCD (n 2) recital 80.
51 ibid art 35 (1).

that such charges are not greater than necessary to compensate the creditor for the costs it has incurred and are allowed to place caps on these charges.

This last provision could tremendously impact debt-collection activities because debt-collection charges remain one of the most contentious issues in debt-collection; however, the effect will likely vary from MS to MS. Several jurisdictions with sectoral legislation, such as Finland[52] or the Netherlands,[53] have already imposed caps on debt-collection charges. The Finnish example even prompted countries without such legislation, such as Estonia, to adopt similar restrictions.[54] At the same time, others, such as Romania,[55] banned such charges altogether. It should be noted that the CCD addresses the charges pre-imposed by creditors on defaulting consumers, but debt-collectors could still impose additional ones.

11.2.3 Debtor databases under the 2023 Consumer Credit Directive

Another critical factor concerns registering defaulting consumer-debtors in public or private databases. Since it can have severe implications for the consumer—usually resulting in the denial of any other credit applications—registering consumer-debtors in such a database is a powerful pressuring tool for creditors or debt-collectors in extracting repayment (see Chapter XIII).

To this point, the 2008 CCD only provided that in the interest of cross-border credit, access to national databases should be granted non-discriminatorily to all creditors in the EU to assess consumers' creditworthiness. Access could only be limited by other EU legislation or if the information was contrary to public policy or security objectives. Unencumbered database access was granted solely in the interest of creditors (i.e. to assess consumers' creditworthiness and prevent any competitive advantage among creditors).[56] Under the 2008 CCD, the only right available to the consumer was to be informed in case a creditor rejected their credit application based on the consultation of said databases.[57] In practice, consumers could find out that they were registered in a debtors' database only *ex post facto* once their application had been reviewed, with the risk of being rejected based on incorrect information.

52 Law 513/1999 (Finland) Section 10a.

53 Decision of 27 March 2012 on reimbursing extrajudicial debt-collection expenses (Netherlands) art 2.

54 Karin Sein, 'Abusive Debt Recovery Practices in Estonia' in Cătălin Gabriel Stănescu (ed), *Regulation of Debt Collection in Europe: Understanding Informal Debt Collection* (Routledge 2023) 106.

55 Government Emergency Ordinance 50/2010, published in the Official Gazette 389/2010 (Romania) art 71^2.

56 2008 CCD (n 1) recital 28.

57 ibid art 9.

The 2023 CCD fills in some of the gaps surrounding debtor databases in the EU by introducing two new rights for consumer-debtors: (1) the right to be informed within thirty days of the registration of any arrears in credit repayment and of their rights under the General Data Protection Regulation[58] and (2) the right to challenge the content of these databases, including the information that third parties can obtain from them.[59] These rights will enable consumers to know if they are recorded in a debtor database and to challenge any inaccurate information *ex ante* potential credit applications, provided that the MS implements adequate and swift complaint procedures. Even so, it is safe to conclude that the impact of the CCD on debt-collection regulation and its usefulness to aggrieved consumers remains limited.

11.3 Summary

The chapter provided an in-depth analysis of the 2008 CCD and its impact on debt-collection, with a specific focus on the *INKO* case. It sought to determine whether debt-collection agencies should be categorized as credit intermediaries under the CCD when negotiating repayment plans. While the AG's opinion supported this classification, arguing that debt-collectors should furnish pre-contractual information to consumers, the CJEU granted national courts the authority to decide whether debt-collectors operate in an ancillary capacity, thereby exempting them from additional obligations. The chapter also examined the 2023 CCD revisions, which underscore the importance of transparency and consumer protection in debt-collection practices, highlighting the persistent challenges in safeguarding consumer rights. Following this thorough exploration of the CCD and its implications for debt-collection, the next chapter delves into the role of the Unfair Contract Terms Directive in assessing the fairness of contractual terms regarding debt recovery.

[58] 2023 CCD (n 2) art 19(7). For implications concerning the General Data Protection Regulation, see Subsection 13.3.

[59] 2023 CCD (n 2) art 19(8).

XII
CONTRACTUAL PITFALLS: THE UNFAIR CONTRACT TERMS DIRECTIVE AND DEBT-COLLECTION

12.1 The Unfair Contract Terms Directive

Chapters X and XI showed that debts originate from a contractual relationship between the creditor and the consumer and new ones could arise from repayment plans concluded with the debt-collector. However, these agreements are commonly based on standard formats imposed on the consumer, prompting the question of whether they could be contested based on European Union (EU) legislation regarding the fairness of consumer contract terms. This issue was the focal point in the *Provident Polska* cases,[1] in which the Court of Justice of the EU (CJEU) examined whether contractual terms concerning debt-collection activities that might be considered invasive and infringe on the debtor's privacy can be invalidated as unfair.

Council Directive 93/13/EEC, or the Unfair Contract Terms Directive (UCTD),[2] protects consumers against unfair standard contract terms imposed by traders. It applies to all types of business-to-consumer contracts, including credit agreements. The UCTD has a double objective: adequately protecting consumers—as the typically weaker party—against unfair contract terms that are used by sellers or suppliers and have not been individually negotiated, and contributing to the establishment of the internal market through the minimum harmonization of the national rules aiming at this protection. As such, it is a central instrument for achieving fairness in the internal market.

[1] Case C-717/21 *Provident Polska SA v VF* [2022] (2022/C 359/71) (*Provident Polska 1*) Summary of the request for a preliminary ruling pursuant to Article 98(1) of the Rules of Procedure of the Court of Justice <https://curia.europa.eu/juris/showPdf.jsf?text=debt%2Bcollection&docid=253321&pageIndex=0&doclang=EN&mode=req&dir=&occ=first&part=1&cid=5318309> accessed 28 July 2023; Case C-321/22 *ZL, KU, KM v Provident Polska* [2023] ECLI:EU:C:2023:911 (*Provident Polska 2*) Summary of the request for a preliminary ruling pursuant to Article 98(1) of the Rules of Procedure of the Court of Justice, available at https://curia.europa.eu/juris/showPdf.jsf;jsessionid=274E9A991886256F0B2A92320764EC05?text=&docid=261941&pageIndex=0&doclang=en&mode=req&dir=&occ=first&part=1&cid=15010985> accessed 5 July 2024.

[2] Council Directive 93/13/EEC of 5 April 1993 on unfair terms in consumer contracts [1993] OJ L95/29 (UCTD) 29–34.

EU Informal Debt-Collection Regulation. Cătălin-Gabriel Stănescu, Oxford University Press.
 DOI: 10.1093/oso/9780198966159.003.0012

The UCTD aims to rectify situations of unequal bargaining power between parties in a contract, which may be caused by differences in information, expertise, or negotiating strength related to the contract terms. Specifically, by declaring unfair contract terms non-binding under Article 6(1), the UCTD seeks to restore a fair balance between the parties by eliminating the unfair terms that disadvantage consumers. Additionally, the UCTD aims to discourage sellers or suppliers from using unfair terms in the future.[3]

12.1.1 Case study: *Provident Polska*—Can contracts legalize abusive debt-collection practices?

In 2021, a Polish court filed a request for a preliminary ruling with the CJEU on a claim for the payment of a sum of money due to two outstanding loans under a contract including terms subject to an examination of their fairness. Concretely, in the *Provident Polska 1* case, the Polish court asked whether Article 7 of the Charter of Fundamental Rights of the EU, which expresses a fundamental right protecting the place of residence, has any bearing on the interpretation of the concept of a significant imbalance, under which a consumer credit contract may be performed by instalment payments collected by the seller or supplier exclusively at the consumer's place of residence.[4]

The case was never heard,[5] but a similar question was raised again in a subsequent request for a preliminary ruling with the CJEU, *Provident Polska 2*, which was decided in 2023.[6] Here, the referring court drew a link between its own inquiry and the aforementioned question, asking about the possibility of deeming unfair the standard contractual terms stipulating that loan repayment can solely occur in cash, facilitated by a Provident employee, during weekly visits at the borrower's residence.[7] The facts of the two Polish cases are very similar and concern a significant player (Provident Polska) in the non-bank lending market in Poland, which has been offering a 'home loan service' for many years and has made it a recognizable brand of its financial offer.

[3] European Commission, Guidance on the interpretation and application of Council Directive 93/13/EEC on unfair terms in consumer contracts', 2019/C 323/04, OJ C323, 27 September 2019 (2019 Guidance on UCTD) 9.

[4] *Provident Polska 1* (n 1) Summary of request, para 16, 19–20.

[5] *Provident Polska 1* (n 1) Order of the President of the Court of 29 March 2022 (2022/C 359/71) <https://eur-lex.europa.eu/legal-content/EN/TXT/PDF/?uri=CELEX:62021CB0685> accessed 5 July 2024.

[6] *Provident Polska 2* (n 1) Judgment of the Court of 23 November 2023.

[7] *Provident Polska 2* (n 1) Summary of request, para 42.

12.1.2 *Provident Polska 1*: Facts

In *Provident Polska 1*, the consumer, VF, concluded two loan contracts with Provident Polska in 2018. In both instances the consumer signed a loan application, printed on a standard form used by the lender, under which he made unconditional declarations expressing his consent to receive correspondence and visits from Provident staff at his residence for purposes related to all loan contracts. The contract forms also set the basic terms concerning the loan amount, commissions, fees, interest rate, and other costs.[8]

Under the loan contract forms, the consumer undertook to repay the loan in instalments solely in cash to an adviser during the latter's weekly visits to the consumer's residence. As per the contract, the lender was 'obliged' vis-à-vis the borrower to visit the latter's residence weekly to 'enable' him to pay the instalments at that place. The form also included a provision regarding the consumer's consent to visits from an employee of the creditor's at their place of residence as a condition to exercise their 'right to repay' the loan in cash.[9] The form also mentioned the possibility of repaying due amounts to the creditor's account, but 'solely and exclusively' when the consumer could not pay the loan instalments during the house calls for reasons beyond his control.[10] None of the contractual terms were negotiated.[11]

When the consumer defaulted on the loans, the crediting company acted against him in the regional court, claiming the outstanding balance plus default interest and procedural costs. The consumer retorted that the action should be dismissed in its entirety and that the proceedings should be stayed for the duration of ongoing criminal proceedings, where he alleged that he was the victim of fraud. In subsequent hearings, the consumer contended that the parties had not agreed on the commissions charged since the creditor imposed them. In addition, he argued that he was not able to negotiate the method for repaying the loan given the imposition of the terms regarding repayment at his place of residence.[12]

12.1.3 *Provident Polska 1*: The position of the referring national court

Both Polish courts filed requests for a preliminary ruling. In *Provident Polska 1*, the court's starting point was the right to respect for a person's private and family life, home, and communication, as laid down in the Charter of Fundamental Rights.[13]

[8] *Provident Polska 1* (n 1) para 1.
[9] ibid para 2.
[10] ibid para 3.
[11] ibid para 4.
[12] ibid paras 5 and 7.
[13] *Provident Polska 1* (n 1) para 8.

It then noted that the term at issue—the creditor's 'obligation' to make periodic visits to the consumer's place of residence to collect due repayments of the loan—appeared to be designed as an obligation to carry out a certain level of activity, which was 'legitimized' by the consumer's prior consent through the standard loan application form and the loan agreement form, over the content of which the consumer had no influence. In other words, the time and place of contract performance were transferred to the private sphere of the debtor, which enjoyed special legal protection under the Charter of Fundamental Rights. Therefore, in the view of the referring court, it became necessary to assess the relationship between the provisions governing consumer protection against unfair contract terms and the provisions defining the substance of the fundamental right arising from the Charter.[14]

As mentioned, the system developed by the UCTD is based on the premise that the consumer is in a weak position vis-à-vis the seller/supplier in terms of both bargaining power and knowledge level. Accordingly, the directive provides that unfair terms are not binding on consumers.[15] In the view of the referring court, while the CJEU had repeatedly addressed the interpretation of concepts such as good practice or significant imbalance, it had not established the necessary criteria for defining the substance of these concepts when they intersect with the fundamental right referred to in the Charter.[16]

The referring court was troubled by what it perceived as behaviour contrary to good practice that creates a significant imbalance within the meaning of the UCTD. Because the previous case law of the CJEU specified that a considerable imbalance could not be limited to a quantitative economic evaluation and could result from a sufficiently severe impairment of the consumer's legal situation,[17] the referring court set out to consider the implications of the house visits for debt-collection purposes at the consumer-debtor's place of residence.

In analysing the consequences of the disputed contractual terms, the referring court retained that

> while the granting of access to the consumer's place of residence by itself does not necessarily lead immediately to abuse directly seeking to infringe a person's rights as an individual ... the collection of the debt by the seller or supplier at the debtor's place of residence doubtless also gives rise to a certain pressure on the consumer.[18]

[14] ibid para 9.
[15] UCTD (n 2) art 6(1).
[16] *Provident Polska 1* (n 1) para 11.
[17] ibid para 12.
[18] ibid para 13.

In the view of the referring court, 'the mere transgression of the "intransgressible boundaries of privacy" defined by the area of the residence infringed the consumer's territorial autonomy by making it de facto accessible to the creditor'.[19]

Moreover, said transgression of privacy boundaries occurred based on pre-consent given by a consumer, recorded in a standard contract and preceded by a standard credit application, which appeared to indicate only the choice of payment by house calls. Although prior consent could be withdrawn at any time, the contract did not indicate how repayment was to be made after consent was withdrawn, which undoubtedly made matters difficult for the consumer. Finally, the creditor's 'obligation', under the agreement, to make visits legitimized, in the eyes of the consumer, the direct contact with the creditor at the consumer's residence.[20]

Furthermore, it can be argued that the benefits stemming from the fact that home collections make it easier and more convenient for consumers (especially in environments where digital exclusion affects a considerable proportion of consumers[21]) to repay their debts directly to the creditor without leaving their home are disproportionate to the level of infringement of their right to privacy. That is because when entering the contract, the consumer cannot be expected to foresee all the consequences (mainly the actual pressure) resulting from compliance with the creditor's house calls at their residence.[22]

Notwithstanding these considerations, the referring court found uncertainty as to whether shifting the time at which a consumer contract is performed from the common sphere of the lender's economic activity to the consumer's private space is, by nature, contrary to good practice and creates a significant imbalance.[23] It also highlighted a certain 'relativization' of the concept of imbalance based on criteria developed by case law.[24]

Hence, the Polish court sought guidance on the question of whether any relativization of the conditions laid down in Articles 3(1) and 4(1) of the UCTD is necessary to assess the unfairness of a contractual term where a non-negotiated term of a consumer contract encroaches directly on the private sphere covered by the fundamental right inscribed in Article 7 of the Charter. Put differently: would Article 7 of the Charter constitute a sufficient standard for assessing the unfairness of a consumer contract term under Article 3(1) of the UCTD in a situation where the contract is performed by transgressing the private sphere?[25]

[19] ibid para 13.
[20] ibid para 14.
[21] Sabrina Rochemont, 'The Payments Revolution. Toward Financial Exclusion or Inclusion' in Cătălin Gabriel Stănescu and Adimi A. Gikay (eds), *Discrimination, Vulnerable Consumers and Financial Inclusion. Fair Access to Financial Services* (Routledge 2021) 132.
[22] *Provident Polska 1* (n 1) paras 14–15.
[23] *Provident Polska 1* (n 1) para 16.
[24] ibid para 18.
[25] ibid para 20.

12.1.4 *Provident Polska 2*: Facts

In *Provident Polska 2*, ZL, KU, and KM concluded consumer credit agreements with Provident Polska or its legal predecessor in 2019 and 2020.[26] According to the agreements, all of them had to pay significant amounts in non-interest costs to the creditor, usually between 70 per cent and 90 per cent of the loan. The consumers brought individual actions before Polish courts, seeking declaratory judgments that the contractual terms providing for non-interest costs were unfair and, therefore, unenforceable against them. They notably alleged that the fees and commissions were disproportionate to the amount of the loan and constituted the lender's principal source of revenue.[27]

In all three instances, the loan agreements provided that the amounts were due in weekly payments that were payable only in cash, in hand, to an agent of the lender during visits at the borrower's home.[28]

Provident Polska rejected the consumers' assertions and brought a counter-claim against each of them, seeking an order that they pay the remaining sums corresponding to the challenged fees and commissions provided for in the loan agreement. In response, the consumers contended that the counter-claims should also be dismissed given the unfairness of the terms on which they were based.[29]

12.1.5 *Provident Polska 2*: The position of the referring national court

The second referring court firmly believed that the contractual term concerning weekly payments performed at the borrower's home was unfair, for several reasons. First, in the court's view, the purpose of stipulating that the loan may only be repaid in cash to the defendant's employee and preventing the consumer from repaying the loan by bank transfer in an era of cashless transactions was to 'exert emotional pressure on the consumer to settle his or her liabilities in a timely fashion'.[30] Second, the court opined that the relevant provisions concerning the parties' obligations 'are not expressed in plain, intelligible language' for 'the general framework of those visits, their duration and permissible actions by the company's employee in the consumer's home and so on are not stipulated'.[31] Third, in the view of the referring court, businesses that arrogate such far-reaching rights in interfering with the consumer's private life should provide them with sufficient warnings regarding

[26] *Provident Polska 2* (n 1) Judgment of the Court, paras 17–23.
[27] ibid paras 27–28.
[28] ibid paras 21 and 24.
[29] ibid para 30.
[30] *Provident Polska 2* (n 1) Summary of referred questions, para 43.
[31] ibid.

the potentially dangerous consequences of visits by a stranger to their home, primarily when the creditor employs that stranger.[32]

Convinced that forcing upon consumers the sole option of cash collection during house calls is an unfair contractual term, the referring court in *Provident Polska 2* sought to determine whether the contract could survive the term's removal or replace it with other means of repayment.[33] Given that *Provident Polska 1* was removed from the registry of the CJEU in 2022, the only pertinent references stem from *Provident Polska 2*, which was adjudicated by the CJEU in 2023.

12.1.6 *Provident Polska 2*: The Advocate-General's position on the connection between unfair contract terms and informal debt-collection

In their opinion (which does not address all questions raised by the Polish court), Advocate-General Pikamäe argued that, insofar as the principle of effectiveness is concerned, it must be interpreted to preclude any national provisions that would subject the consumer to a need to prove a legal interest for their action to find unfair terms unenforceable.[34]

At first glance, there is little conspicuous connection between unfair contract terms in consumer contracts and debt-collection because consumers rarely enter into contracts with debt-collectors. Nevertheless, this connection exists in several situations, as became apparent in the CJEU's UCTD-related case law[35] or recent requests for preliminary rulings,[36] such as the ones reported above.

First, the original contract may contain potentially unfair terms imposed on the consumer, such as excessive and unreasonable fees and commissions (as in the *Provident Polska* cases) or disproportionate financial consequences of default, including those of debt recovery (e.g. *Aziz*, *Radlinger and Radlingerová*, and *Impuls Leasing Romania*). The problem is relevant, especially when considering that empirical studies revealed that unconscionable charges and debt-collection costs, as

[32] ibid.

[33] ibid paras 44–46.

[34] *Provident Polska 2* (n 1) Opinion of Advocate-General Pikamäe, EU:C:2023:514.

[35] Case C-45/11 *Mohamed Aziz v Caixa d'Estalvis de Catalunya, Tarragona i Manresa (Catalunyacaixa)* [2013] EU:C:2013:164 (*Aziz*); Case C-32/14 *ERSTE Bank Hungary Zrt v Attila Sugar* [2015] EU:C:2015:637 (*ERSTE Bank*); Case C-421/14 *Banco Primus SA v Jesús Gutiérrez García* [2017] EU:C:2017:60 (*Banco Primus*); Case C-377/17 *Radlinger and Radlingerová v FINWAY a.s.* [2016] EU:C:2016:283 (*Radlinger and Radlingerová*); Case C-448/17 *EOS KSI Slovensko s.r.o. v Jan Danko and Margita Dankova* [2018] EU:C:2018:745; Case C-725/19 *IO v Impuls Leasing Romania IFN SAE* [2022] ECLI:EU:C:2022:396 *(Impuls Leasing Romania)*.

[36] *Provident Polska 2* (n 1); Case C-170/21 *Profi Credit Bulgaria EOOD v TIT* [2022] ECLI:EU:C:2022:518; Case C-192/20, *Prima banka Slovensko v HD* [2021] ECLI:EU:C:2021:48.

well as mistaken or misleading amounts, were the top complaints pertaining to debt-collection.[37]

Second, the subsequent contract (e.g. a repayment plan agreed upon during debt-collection) may contain unfair terms, such as excessive fees, including recovery costs (without legal grounds), or the modification of financial consequences in case of default, among others. This can result from the weaker position of consumers (when dealing with professionals) and their vulnerable state (being in default and unable to meet their original contractual obligations and facing the risk of negative credit ratings, etc).

Third, consumers may be unable to exercise their rights under the UCTD because creditors or debt-collectors resort to special procedures that, under national law, prevent consumers or courts from complaining about or assessing on their own motion the fairness of contractual terms (e.g. *Aziz*, *EOS KSI Slovensko*, *Impuls Leasing Romania*, or *Provident Polska*).

12.1.7 *Provident Polska 2*: The reasoning and findings of the Court of Justice of the European Union

The CJEU took a multi-step, nuanced approach in answering whether the provisions of the UCTD, particularly Article 6(1), preclude declaring a loan agreement null and void if an essential term setting the payment arrangements is found to be unfair. The court's analysis emphasized that Article 6(1) aims to remove unfair terms while allowing the contract to continue provided that it can do so without said terms, thus restoring the real balance between the parties.[38] MS are responsible for defining the detailed rules, ensuring that consumer protection remains paramount when determining the contract's continuation.[39]

The court further elaborated that the principle of proportionality must guide the annulment of contracts, ensuring that measures do not exceed what is necessary to protect consumers.[40] The national court should consider whether the contract can continue without the unfair terms, potentially substituting them with supplementary provisions of national law to avoid disproportionately negative consequences for consumers.[41] In this case, it was noted that the invalidity of the entire contract would not disadvantage the consumers,[42] which meant that the

[37] Olivier Jérusalmy, Paul Fox, and Nicolas Hercelin, 'Is the Human Dignity of Individual Debtors at Risk?' (*Finance Watch*, 2020) <https://www.finance-watch.org/wp-content/uploads/2020/01/Report_Human-dignity_final_with-annex.pdf>; Cătălin Gabriel Stănescu, 'Regulation of Abusive Debt Collection Practices in the EU Member States: An Empirical Account' (2021) 44(1) Journal of Consumer Policy 195.

[38] *Provident Polska 2* (n 1) Judgment, para 81.

[39] ibid para 83.

[40] ibid paras 84–85.

[41] ibid para 87.

[42] ibid para 88.

contract could be annulled, freeing the consumer of the financial burden it implied. The court clarified that if an unfair term can be removed without altering the contract's essence, the contract should remain valid, ensuring consumer protection while maintaining contractual integrity.[43]

Ultimately, the court concluded that Article 6(1) does not preclude declaring a loan agreement null and void if the unfair term cannot be separated and the agreement cannot persist without it.[44] However, if the term is separable and its removal does not affect the core repayment obligations, the contract should not be invalidated entirely.[45] In the CJEU's view, this interpretation ensures the elimination of unfair terms while preserving the contractual relationship where feasible, aligning with the directive's objectives of fairness and legal certainty.[46]

Notably, the CJEU clearly emphasized that, in its opinion, the presumably unfair payment provision in Provident Polska contracts was 'ancillary to' and, therefore, severable from the elements of the contract that define the substance of that term, such as the determination of the amounts to be paid and the dates on which those payments must be made.[47] Tributary to the usual market considerations, the CJEU clarified that while certain collection practices, such as those employed by Provident Polska, may be unfair, payment obligations cannot be avoided. If possible, the substance of the contract must not be affected:[48] 'the consumer continues to be obliged to perform his or her repayment obligation in accordance with the other conditions laid down in that term by choosing any method of payment from among those which are permissible under national law.'[49] The lesson is simple: abusive debt-collection may be punished, but it will not discharge the payment obligation, no matter how harsh it is. The creditors' interests are safe.

12.2 Unfair Terms in Consumer Loan Agreements and Informal Debt-collection in Light of the Court of Justice of the European Union's Case Law

The situation described in the *Provident Polska* cases qualifies as (informal) debt-collection, even if the debt has yet to default and the creditor services it on its own. Their relevance stems from (1) how the loan agreement, in which the debt originates, was conceived and (2) potential circumventions of statutory protections by the contract. As shown, just like most credit agreements, the contract contained

43 ibid paras 89–93.
44 ibid para 96.
45 ibid para 94.
46 ibid para 95.
47 ibid para 93.
48 ibid para 96.
49 ibid para 93.

detailed provisions about the repayment method, related commissions and costs, and the consequences of default (late fees, penalty charges, etc), but also a pre-default approval of house calls for repayment, with a potential negative impact on the consumer-debtors' privacy.

These terms become even more critical if the debt is externalized to a professional debt-collector because they will continue to influence what the debt-collector can ask or do and what the consumer must do. However, since most of these terms are pre-imposed on the consumer, one may wonder if they could be considered unfair and what consequences they may have. A more detailed look at the UCTD and the CJEU's case law should help find an answer.

The directive states that unfair terms are not binding on consumers[50] due to the consumers' weaker position relative to the seller or supplier in terms of both bargaining power and knowledge levels, which makes them prone to agree to contractual terms drawn up in advance by the seller or supplier without being able to influence their content.[51] This imbalance is deemed so detrimental that the CJEU has stated on several occasions that national courts must investigate on their own motion (a) whether a term falls within the UCTD's ambit and (b) whether this term is unfair.[52] Most importantly, a national court that has found that a contractual term is unfair is not obliged to wait for the consumer to submit a statement requesting that the unfair term be declared invalid as long as the principle of *audi alteram partem*[53] is observed.[54]

Yet, in *ERSTE Bank,* the CJEU held that the

> effective legal protection guaranteed by [the UCTD] is based on the premise that one of the parties to the contract will bring an action before the national courts,[55] although it will be for the national courts to determine whether ... procedural rules of actions in its own national system ... guarantee effective legal protection to the consumer.[56]

This premise forces consumers to act only *ex post* after suffering the consequences of a potentially unfair term, which is disproportionate on multiple levels and reduces the 'effectiveness' of the protection, especially when faced with either fast-track self-help mechanisms (like in *ERSTE v Sugar*) and informal/non-judicial debt-collection (like in *Provident*) or judicial ones (like in *Aziz, EOS KSI Slovensko,*

[50] UCTD (n 2) art 6(1).
[51] *ERSTE Bank* (n 35) paras 40–41.
[52] ibid para 39.
[53] *Audi alteram partem* (or *audiatur et altera pars*) is a Latin phrase meaning 'listen to the other side' (or 'let the other side be heard as well'). According to this principle, no person should be judged without a fair hearing in which each party is given the opportunity to respond to the evidence against them.
[54] *ERSTE Bank* (n 35) para 42.
[55] ibid para 63.
[56] ibid para 64.

and *Impuls Leasing Romania*). The danger that the consumer is left only with *ex post* protection or even dissuaded from acting due to a lack of financial resources necessary to pay for judicial fees or required judicial guarantees was acknowledged by the CJEU in *Aziz* concerning enforcement against mortgaged immovable property[57] and *Impuls Leasing Romania* on the enforcement of unsecured claims consisting of unpaid invoices, court fees, penalties, differences in exchange rates, and insurance and debt-collection costs exceeding several times the amount of the principal.[58]

Of relevance to debt-collection cases is also the CJEU's answer to the fifth and sixth referred questions in *Radlinger and Radlingerová* regarding whether the UCTD can be used to assess whether the amount of compensation required of a consumer in default is disproportionally high, within the meaning of point 1(e) of the Annex to the directive. The CJEU held that to assess this, it is necessary to evaluate the cumulative effect of all the penalty clauses in the contract in question, regardless of whether the creditor insists that they all be satisfied in full.[59] Moreover, if necessary, the national courts must exclude all terms found to be unfair under UCTD Article 6(1) to ensure that they do not bind the consumer.[60] In other words, should the penalties associated with the contract (including debt-collection) be disproportionately high and, thus, unfair, they should be removed from the agreement.

In light of the above, two challenges remain. First, the consumer must somehow bring an action against said contract or terms, and the court must find that the amount of compensation for default is disproportionately high. As *Radlinger and Radlingerová* clarifies, in establishing whether a term is unfair for this reason, the courts must consider the nature of the goods and services for which the contract was concluded and refer to all the circumstances that affected the conclusion of the contract.[61]

Second, the CJEU deems it necessary to assess the cumulative effect of *all* such terms in an agreement between a consumer and a seller or supplier. Such an assessment is justified because all those terms are applicable regardless of whether the creditor insists they all be entirely performed.[62] This also means that even if only the cumulative effect of the sanctions makes them disproportionate, all relevant contract terms must be considered unfair.

57 *Aziz* (n 35) paras 60–64.
58 *Impuls Leasing Romania* (n 35) paras 55, 57, and 59.
59 *Radlinger and Radlingerová* (n 35) paras 92–101.
60 ibid para 101.
61 ibid para 94.
62 ibid para 95.

12.3 Analysis of Fairness and Proportionality of Default Compensation under the 2019 Unfair Contract Terms Directive Guidance

The above still does not elucidate what will be deemed 'disproportionately high' and how national courts, in their factual case-by-case analysis, are to determine that a compensation in case of default is unfair. The EC's 2019 UCTD Guidance may provide some help. What must be remembered is that for the sanctions or consequences attached to the consumer's contractual default not to cause a significant imbalance to the detriment of the consumer, they 'have to be justified in light of the importance of the consumer's obligation and the seriousness of the failure to comply with it (*Aziz*[63] or *Banco Primus*[64])'—or, better put, proportionate.

Among the factors summarized by the 2019 UCTD Guidance, those about default interests and costs are of greater relevance to debt-collection. The CJEU has addressed the test of fairness concerning default interest in *Aziz*, stating that in evaluating a contractual clause, national courts must examine the pertinent national law and the default interest rates, compared to the statutory interest rates, to ensure their suitability for achieving the objectives set by the MS, as outlined by EU law.[65]

Thus, the CJEU advises national courts to resort to several benchmarks for the contractual terms subjected to their evaluation:

1) The general/default rules that would govern the contract in the absence of a specific provision. They may be those of the Civil Code (where available)—*lex generalis*—or the law governing statutory interests or debt-collection charges (where available)—*lex specialis*. 'Or' suggests that should no such general and specific rules governing the issue of default interest be available, the courts could—alternatively—compare the terms under advisement with market terms. However, one could easily argue that this would not indicate fairness or proportionality if disproportionate charges were the actual market practice.[66]
2) Juxtaposing the contractual default rate with the statutory one to determine whether (a) it is appropriate to secure the attainment of its objectives and (b) it does not go beyond what is necessary to achieve them. The comparison serves to determine whether the contractual term is punitive in effect or not.

63 *Aziz* (n 35) para 73.
64 *Banco Primus* (n 35) para 66.
65 *Aziz* (n 35) para 74.
66 See *Aziz* (n 35) para 31(2)(b), where the referring Spanish court indicated that the setting of default interest rates—in this case, exceeding 18%—that were consistent with the criteria for determining default interest in other consumer contracts (consumer credit) and would be regarded as unfair in other types of consumer contracts were accepted in contracts relating to immovable property due to the absence of any clear legal limit.

The test might not always be sufficient, especially concerning outsourced debt-collection. The contractual terms may be quite vague (e.g. providing that the consumer must cover all costs associated with debt-collection), which brings the issue of transparency to the forefront. The shortcomings of the CJEU's test would also be exacerbated by the absence or type of sectoral debt-collection legislation in each MS because similar situations could lead to different outcomes.

As regards transparency, the 2019 Guidance explains that it would not automatically lead to the unfairness of a given contract term. However, several judgments refer to lack of transparency as an essential element in assessing the unfairness, at least of particular types of contract terms. These include, for example, those allowing the seller or supplier to change the rates to be paid by consumers in long-term contracts, that is, terms that determine the consumer's core obligations in loan agreements or choice-of-law clauses.

Summing up, the guidance states that, depending on the content of the contract term, its potential unfairness can be closely related to its lack of transparency, or the lack of transparency of a contract term may even indicate its unfairness. For instance, this may be the case where consumers cannot understand the consequences of a term or are misled:

> Indeed, where consumers are put in a disadvantageous position based on contract terms which are unclear, hidden or misleading, or where explanations necessary to understand their implications are not provided, it is unlikely that the seller or supplier was dealing fairly or equitably with the consumer and took their legitimate interests into account.[67]

It is fair to speculate that a broad clause that leaves open the issue of costs stemming from debt-collection in a manner that would make them unconscionable to the consumer could be challenged under the UCTD.

However, this might not necessarily be the case if the existing general or sectoral legislation impacts or clarifies this provision. Based on the test adopted by the CJEU regarding default interest, and depending on whether the MS has legislation applicable to either default interest or debt-collection, several situations could be distinguished:

1) The MS has sectoral legislation governing debt-collection, explicitly enabling the debt-collector to charge fees for its efforts—for instance, in Finland, where the law provided for maximal fees correlated to the amount of the debt.[68] In this case, the unfairness of debt-collection costs would have to be evaluated within the confines of that law.

[67] 2019 Guidance on UCTD (n 3) 35.
[68] Law 513/1999 (Finland) Section 10a.

2) The MS has (specific) legislation governing the charge of debt-collection fees, even if these are contained in an act that is separate from the one governing debt-collection—for instance, in Denmark, where the legislator adopted a separate order on out-of-court recovery costs for late payments concerning maximal fees relative to the claimed amount for third-party debt-collection and internal debt-collection.[69]
3) The MS has general legislation governing interest rates in case of default but no indication of the possibility of adding debt-collection fees (without banning it either)—for instance, in Belgium, where the law allows only the collection of charges specified in the contract,[70] which could include debt-collection fees.
4) The MS has general legislation governing interest rates in case of default but bans added informal debt-collection fees—for instance, Romania has detailed provisions regarding penalizing statutory interest rates and judicial enforcement costs but bans any other penalties or informal debt-collection charges added by debt-collection entities.[71] Similarly, in Greece, creditors who delegate credit information activities to third parties cannot collect the associated costs from debtors.[72]

12.4 Summary

The chapter delved into the UCTD's role in safeguarding consumers from unfair contract terms that enable intrusive debt-collection, with a focus on two cases involving Provident Polska. These cases examined whether requiring loan repayments through home visits infringed on consumers' privacy and imposed undue pressure on them. The findings emphasized that such terms could be considered unfair if they create a significant imbalance disfavouring the consumer. This underscores the significance of fairness, transparency, and the protection of fundamental rights in consumer contracts. Looking ahead, the next chapter presents a deeper exploration of the protection of debtor privacy and personal data vis-à-vis informal debt-collection under the General Data Protection Regulation.

[69] BEK 601 of 12/07/2002 (last amended by BEK 719 of 03/06/2024) (Denmark).

[70] Law 62/2002 (Belgium) art 5.

[71] Government Emergency Ordinance 50/2010, published in the Official Gazette 389/2010 (Romania) arts 38 and 71^{2}.

[72] Law 3578/2009 (Greece) art 4(7).

XIII
PRIVACY CONCERNS: THE GENERAL DATA PROTECTION REGULATION'S IMPACT ON INFORMAL DEBT-COLLECTION

13.1 Debt-collection and Data Protection

The previous chapter highlighted how contractually mandated home visits for loan repayments pose significant dangers to a debtor's privacy. However, those are not the only privacy-related concerns stemming from informal debt-collection practices. Creditors and debt-collectors have other powerful weapons, such as reporting a defaulting debtor to a credit bureau.

These organizations collect, use, and disclose information that may be utilized in assessing a consumer's creditworthiness regarding future credit applications and sell it to interested parties for a fee. Credit bureaus acquire information from numerous types of data providers, from creditors and debt-collectors to vendors and public databases (court records, insolvency registries, etc.) or social media. In addition, credit bureaus assign credit scores to the surveyed consumers based on the latter's credit history, which histories have become essential predictors of whether a consumer will later qualify for credit and on what terms. In turn, debt-collectors use credit scores provided by credit bureaus to feed their information technology-enabled (IT) statistical modelling of the evolution of delinquent debt to predict the outcome of debt-collection.[1]

Problems may arise when people are reported to credit bureaus for insignificant amounts, challenged or already paid debts, or when debts are attributed to the wrong person. Such abusive or wrongful reports can tremendously impact a person's ability to access credit. Moreover, once registered by a credit bureau, the data tends to linger for years, thus affecting a consumer's credit score for an extended period, which is not always justified by the consumer's actions or the risks they present.

[1] Lukasz A Drozd and Ricardo Serrano-Padial, 'Modelling the Revolving Revolution: The Debt Collection Channel' (2017) 107(3) The American Economic Review 897, 898.

EU Informal Debt-Collection Regulation. Cătălin-Gabriel Stănescu, Oxford University Press.
 DOI: 10.1093/oso/9780198966159.003.0013

The risks posed to consumers and the negative impact of lingering data are exacerbated by the legal requirements for creditors to conduct creditworthiness assessments of potential customers by consulting the relevant private and public databases, even in member states (MS) where they are not established. The Consumer Credit Directive,[2] the Consumer Mortgage Directive,[3] and the Regulation on Insolvency Proceedings[4] are prime legal instruments enabling creditors to access information on European Union (EU) consumer-debtors anywhere inside the Union. The official explanation is that efficient credit reporting systems can provide creditors with access to information that complements data received from borrowers, thus allowing well-informed credit decisions and better credit availability to creditworthy borrowers.[5] However, the purposes and effects of data sharing go beyond creditworthiness assessments. The Credit Servicers and Credit Purchasers Directive (CSCPD) also expanded this right to credit purchasers and credit servicers to enable them to assess the value of a creditor's rights.[6]

Both creditors and debt-collectors were already using such information concerning consumers for credit granting or between themselves for debt portfolio purchases. Research has shown that the emergence of IT-enabled statistical modelling to predict the outcome of recovery efforts has led to extensive use of large databases[7] coupled with the production of information.[8] What has changed is the implementation of the creditors' and debt-collectors' right to unencumbered access to databases in all MS. In other words, the CSCPD provided debt buyers and debt-collectors with a data gold mine.

Nonetheless, it is, to a certain extent, a 'Greek gift' with unforeseen consequences. Given the apparent connections between privacy protection, personal data, and debt-collection arising from debt-collectors' processing of personal data, this section examines the role of credit bureaus in debt-collection and the potential implications of the GDPR on informal debt-collection. These aspects are addressed in the *Schufa* case, which is discussed below.

2 Directive 2008/48/EC on credit agreements for consumers [2008] OJ L133/66 (2008 CCD) recitals 26 and 28 and art 8(1).

3 Directive 2014/17/EU on credit agreements for consumers relating to residential immovable property [2014] OJ L60/34 (CMD) recitals 55 and 59 and art 21(1) and (2).

4 Regulation (EU) 2015/848 on insolvency proceedings [2015] OJ 2015 L141, recital 76 and art 79(4) and (5).

5 European Commission, Consumer Financial Services Action Plan: Better Products, More Choice, COM(2017)139, 11.

6 Directive (EU) No 2021/2167 on credit servicers and credit purchasers [2021] OJ L438 (CSCPD) recital 36 and art 15(1).

7 Drozd and Serrano-Padial (n 1) 898; Johannes Kriebel and Kevin Yam, 'Forecasting Recoveries in Debt Collection: Debt Collectors and Information Production' (2020) 26 European Financial Management 537, 537–59.

8 Kriebel and Yam (n 7) 557.

13.2 The General Data Protection Regulation

The General Data Protection Regulation 2016/679[9] (GDPR) is a comprehensive data-protection law of the EU that governs personal data collection, processing, storage, and transfer. Although it is an EU legal instrument, it imposes obligations on public institutions and private companies anywhere if they target or collect data related to people in the EU. Its goals are to strengthen individuals' control and rights over their personal information and simplify business regulation regarding the collection and processing of personal data.

Under the GDPR, personal data refers to any information that could directly or indirectly identify a living person.[10] Examples of personal data include a person's name, phone number, and address. Other types of personal data encompass a person's interests and information about past purchases, health, online behaviour, and debts. Data processing involves various activities, such as collecting, organizing, storing, sharing, disclosing, and deleting data.[11] Every organization that handles personal data must ensure that the personal data it processes meets the requirements outlined in the GDPR and observes its basic principles.[12]

13.2.1 Case study: *Schufa*

Some of the issues associated with the prolonged presence of former debtors in credit bureau databases and their compatibility with the requirements and guiding principles of the GDPR arose in the joint cases of UF[13] and AB[14] against Schufa Holding AG (*Schufa*). This private credit information agency records and stores information from public registries in its databases, including information concerning the discharge of remaining debts. This information is deleted three years after registration per internal procedures and a code of conduct drawn up by the association of agencies providing credit information and approved by the competent supervisory authority.[15]

UF and AB were granted early discharge from remaining debts by judicial decisions delivered in 2020 and 2021, respectively.[16] As per applicable German insolvency law, the publication of data from insolvency proceedings must be erased

[9] Regulation (EU) 2016/679 on the protection of natural persons with regard to the processing of personal data and on the free movement of such data [2016] OJ L119/1 (GDPR) 1–88.

[10] GDPR (n 9) art 4(1).

[11] ibid art 4(2).

[12] ibid arts 5 and 6.

[13] Joined cases C-26/22 and C-64/22 *UF, AB v Land Hesse, joined party: SCHUFA Holding* [2023] ECLI:EU:C:2023:958 (*Schufa*) Case C-26/22.

[14] ibid, Case C-64/22.

[15] *Schufa* (n 13) para 26.

[16] ibid para 25.

no later than six months after the proceedings are terminated.[17] However, because the same data was still available in Schufa's databases, the two petitioners asked the credit rating agency to delete the decisions regarding the discharge of their remaining debts from its records. Schufa refused, claiming that the six-month limitation did not apply to it and that its activity was GDPR-compliant.[18] The subsequent complaints to the competent supervisory authority were promptly dismissed.[19] Consequently, UF and AB brought actions before the administrative court,[20] which referred several questions to the Court of Justice of the EU (CJEU).[21] The Advocate-General (AG) delivered his opinion in March 2023,[22] and the CJEU rendered a decision in December of the same year.[23]

The case raised five questions. The first two concerned the role of the supervisory authorities vis-à-vis the obligation to examine complaints and the scope of judicial review of their decisions. While interesting, they are beyond the scope of this book and will not be discussed here. The remaining three addressed (1) the compliance of the practice of credit bureaus with the principles governing the processing of personal data enshrined in the GDPR (namely, lawfulness, purpose limitation, and data minimization), (2) the data subjects' recourse to the right of erasure, and (3) the recourse to a code of conduct within the meaning of the GDPR, which sets time limits for review and erasure that exceed the retention periods for public registries. The three are addressed in separate subsections below.

13.2.2 *Schufa*: The Advocate-General's analysis of the impact of credit bureaus' personal data processing on debtors

In his opinion, AG Pikamäe started with several preliminary remarks, acknowledging the role of credit information agencies in allowing providers of financial services to evaluate their clients' creditworthiness and the inherent risks associated with contractual commitments, as requested by EU legislation.[24] He also noted the parallel existence of public (official) registers operated by public authorities and private databases managed by private agencies. This leads to competition between systems and legal conflicts if the legal arrangements governing these registries differ significantly.[25] Regulatory disparities can pose significant

[17] ibid para 24.
[18] ibid para 27.
[19] ibid paras 28–29.
[20] ibid para 30.
[21] ibid paras 34–45.
[22] *Schufa* (n 13) Opinion of Advocate-General Pikamäe of 16 March 2023 (1), ECLI:EU:C:2023:222 (*Schufa* Opinion).
[23] *Schufa* (n 13) Judgment of The Court (First Chamber) of 7 December 2023, ECLI:EU:C:2023:958 (*Schufa* Judgment).
[24] *Schufa* Opinion (n 13) para 31.
[25] ibid para 32.

challenges, especially when they impact data protection. Whether the entity overseeing the database is public or private, it is essential to uphold the interests of data subjects in managing and recording their data. Because information concerning an individual's financial status is sensitive with regard to personal data protection and privacy, it necessitates particular vigilance.[26]

The ensuing analysis is too lengthy to cover comprehensively, but several considerations are worth mentioning to understand the impact of personal data processing by credit bureaus and other private entities on debtors. For instance, in his discussion of compliance with the principle of lawfulness, the AG adopted a three-step approach: looking into the existence of a data controller's 'legitimate interest',[27] the need to process the data for the purposes of the legitimate interest,[28] and balancing the different interests (those of the data controller and the data subject) at stake.[29] The latter appears to be the crux of this analysis, and it is also assessed based on four criteria: the controller's legitimate interest,[30] the impact of processing on data subjects,[31] provisional balance,[32] and additional safeguards.[33] The second criterion receives the most attention, and the period after which data must be erased is the relevant factor. In the AG's words, 'the longer the period for which data are stored in the databases of private credit information agencies, the greater the consequences for the data subject'.[34] From this perspective, in the case at hand, data storage beyond the six months established by the German legislator seemed to have an a priori significant negative impact on the data subject.

The parallel presence of personal data in public and private databases was also deemed to seriously interfere with the data subject's fundamental rights because it increased the potential number of users having access to the data. The fact that data was stored and made available in parallel private databases was held to have a further impact on the individual's private life, in addition to the negative consequences of those data being available in the public records.[35] In the view of the AG, the potentially sensitive nature of the data also had to be considered given that CJEU case law had already emphasized that personal data concerning debt recovery is sensitive to the data subject's private life. Therefore, making such data available to unlimited users had to be regarded as a significant interference with the data subject's fundamental rights.[36] Finally, one had to consider the time factor. Here, the AG questioned how the storage of sensitive personal data could be

[26] ibid para 32.
[27] ibid paras 59–64.
[28] ibid paras 65–68.
[29] ibid paras 69–78.
[30] ibid para 70.
[31] ibid paras 71–74.
[32] ibid para 75.
[33] ibid para 76.
[34] ibid para 71.
[35] ibid para 72.
[36] ibid para 73.

justified for three years when the national legislature deemed a much shorter period of six months sufficient to protect the interests of economic operators.[37]

In conclusion, the AG found that 'the considerable negative consequences that the storage of data will have on the data subject after the period of six months ... seem to override the commercial interest of the private agency and its clients in storing the data after that period', especially in cases where the granted discharge from remaining debts is intended to allow the beneficiary to re-enter economic life.[38] In its judgment, the CJEU acquiesced to the AG's arguments.[39] This position seems to suggest that the data of consumer-debtors who either managed to repay (albeit with a delay) or got a discharge of their debts should not be kept for too long in a private database, to allow them to return to the market as active subjects. It is not only their fundamental rights but also market interests that prevail.

The issue of the potential consequences of prolonged data processing for data subjects was again raised in the AG's analysis of the credit bureau's compliance with purpose limitation and data minimization principles. The AG noted that 'information concerning insolvency proceedings will always be used as a negative factor in a future assessment of the creditworthiness and ability to pay of the natural person concerned, which has a significant impact on that person's rights'.[40] In particular, 'a false picture of their economic situation can produce detrimental effects for data subjects by complicating significantly the exercise of their freedoms or even by stigmatising them in society', which may result in data subjects being 'denied goods and services' or suffering 'unjustified discrimination'.[41]

Because of these consequences, the AG returned to the time factor to find that the processing of personal data by private agencies beyond what is prescribed by law for public registers is 'excessive and penalises the data subject de facto, even though nothing of the kind is envisaged by the law', especially when the discharge of debt is meant to allow the beneficiary to re-enter economic life. In the AG's view, this objective would be frustrated if credit bureaus were authorized to store personal data after the data has been erased from public registries, which may even amount to a circumvention of national legislation.[42] Finally, the AG considered it 'disproportionate to reuse a past situation which has already been given a legal clarification' in future evaluations rather than using updated factors for risk assessment to get a more precise and objective evaluation of the data subject's economic situation.[43]

[37] ibid para 74.
[38] ibid para 75.
[39] *Schufa* Judgment (n 13) paras 93–98.
[40] *Schufa* Opinion (n 13) para 83.
[41] ibid para 83.
[42] ibid para 85.
[43] ibid para 86.

It should be mentioned here that the AG's considerations are valid not only regarding information on insolvency but also any debt-recovery proceedings. Even in situations where the consumer has defaulted on their debt, assuming that the debt has been repaid or rescheduled, maintaining information about the default for a prolonged period not only informs potential creditors but also punishes the debtor for past actions by reducing their capacity to access credit or obtain fair terms. As the AG highlighted several times, this stigmatizes and denies debtors re-entry to the market. Practically, it pushes consumers to seek credit from loan sharks or other short-term, high-interest solutions, which ultimately condemns them to further over-indebtedness and debt peonage.[44]

13.2.3 An existential threat? The impact of the General Data Protection Regulation and *Schufa* on the debt-collection industry

This effect is intentional from the perspective of aggrieved creditors and debt-collectors because the looming threat of credit reporting and its potential consequences may incentivize the debtor to repay. Nevertheless, if, even after the debt is repaid, rescheduled, or discharged, debtors' data remains in credit bureaus and debt-collector databases, they face the risk of debt peonage as their economic choices diminish or worsen dramatically.

Thus, the decision in *Schufa* may have more far-reaching consequences than enabling data subjects to seek the deletion of their data from privately held databases of credit reporting agencies (or debt-collectors) once such data has been removed from public records. Still, matters were open to interpretation where personal data was not found in public databases or the law did not provide a specific term for deletion from such public registries. National debt-collection associations, such as BDIU, already assumed that personal data can be lawfully collected and processed if a contract is still performing and the debt is enforced.[45] The remaining question is how long could this data be stored and processed after the account has been closed. If the CJEU's decision in *Schufa* is any indication, the answer is 'not long'.

It is no wonder that the GDPR caused tremors in the debt-collection industry from its inception and continues to be perceived as an existential threat.[46]

44 On this, see also the Polish court's arguments in: Case C-321/22 *ZL, KU, KM v Provident Polska* [2023] ECLI:EU:C:2023:911 (*Provident Polska 2*) Summary, paras 34–36. These led to the conclusion that 'even if the first loan is relatively small, but is taken out on very unfavourable terms, this pushes the consumer into a spiral of (exponentially rising) debt'.

45 BDIU, 'White paper on the requirements of the GDPR to business activities of debt-collection agencies' (*FENCA*) <https://fenca.org/images/pdf/NL_Summer_17/BDIU_White_Paper_GDPR.pdf?acm=2891_46> accessed on 19 January 2024.

46 As noted by FENCA, the 'GDPR gave rise to serious legal and operational uncertainties in the debt-collection industry. In many discussions with its member associations and affiliated debt-collection firms, FENCA noticed that GDPR's abstract requirements are a major challenge for the industry.' See also: FENCA, 'Comments on the European Commission draft Regulation on Data

Data is the lifeblood of debt-collectors: they could not chase non-paying consumers without it. The Federation of European National Collection Associations (FENCA) has lobbied EU institutions extensively regarding any proposed amendments improving personal data protection that might have impacted their business, always expressing 'serious concerns'.[47] According to their 2013 position paper, any modification of rules regarding consent or the right to be forgotten in favour of the data subject should have been deleted.[48] The ability to retrieve data from credit information agencies (credit bureaus) to profile potential creditors or current debtors was also supposed to remain unencumbered.[49]

In 2015, the dangers posed by the GDPR were deemed even higher. FENCA sought clarifications and amendments to enable the industry to continue collecting and processing debtors' data outside the envisioned legal framework. Most of their explanations stemmed from practical considerations: the potential illegitimacy of processing debtors' data or the ease with which they could locate the debtor and extract payment. Their comments about the proposed provisions regarding the reasons behind the collection of data, maintaining accurate and up-to-date data, lawful processing and legitimate interests, the burden of proof vis-à-vis consent, or the right to be forgotten reveal, once again, deep concerns not only about compliance costs but also about the existence and functioning of their business model.[50]

More apprehension was expressed in 2017 in response to the ePrivacy Regulation, stemming from the fact that, in most cases, creditors transferred the data necessary for debt management and recovery to a debt purchaser or debt-collector agency in electronic form. Implementing the regulation would have confronted debt-collectors with additional rules regarding data handling that went further than those advanced by the GDPR. FENCA's recommendations suggested a complete alignment of the ePrivacy Regulation (a *lex specialis*) with the GDPR (*lex generalis*), stating that the *lex specialis* should not increase the preconditions of the *lex generalis* because this would cause detriment to customers of debt-collectors, which contradicts the very logic of a derogatory regime. Measures regarding reminders about the possibility of withdrawing consent or limiting unsolicited communications were rejected in full by the industry because unsolicited mail, emails, or phone calls are at the very centre of its activity.[51]

Protection COM(2012) 11 final' (*FENCA*, 2015) <https://fenca.eu/images/pdf/2015/fenca_data_protection_com.pdf> accessed 19 January 2024.

[47] FENCA, 'Position paper on the Data Protection—Recast' (*FENCA*, 11 April 2013) <https://fenca.eu/images/pdf/2013/position-paper-on-data-protection.pdf> accessed 19 January 2024.

[48] ibid.

[49] ibid.

[50] ibid.

[51] FENCA, 'Comments of Fenca (Federation of European Collection Associations) on the ePrivacy Regulation concerning the respect of private life and the protection of personal data in electronic communications' (*FENCA*) <https://fenca.eu/images/pdf/FENCA-Position-on-ePrivacy.pdf> accessed 19 January 2024.

The best illustration of the disturbance caused by the adoption of a more stringent legal framework for personal data protection is FENCA's implementation of a code of conduct concerning personal data protection just a few months after the GDPR entered into force. In contrast, the adoption of a general code of conduct for its members took six years (and an additional nine for a revision).[52] National codes of conduct regarding the GDPR also appeared. The German Association of Debt-Collection Companies (BDIU) published two best practice guides—one in 2018 and an updated version in 2019.[53]

Most concerns proved unfounded. A white paper from BDIU held, with specific qualifications, that under the GDPR, debt-collectors can still collect and process personal data for debt recovery. Moreover, processing without consent continued to be legal as long as it was necessary to enforce third-party rights or for contract performance, and profiling remained possible for debt-collection agencies.[54] These positions were also reflected and developed in the Best Practice Guide 2.0.[55] Nevertheless, the repercussions of *Schufa* are expected to significantly affect the industry. Consequently, industry stakeholders have reinitiated lobbying efforts to mitigate its potential impact on their business model. In April 2024, BDIU submitted a position paper concerning the amendments to the Federal Data Protection Act, aiming to secure language that would shield the industry as much as possible from the effects of the CJEU's decision.[56]

13.3 The Way Forward: The Misuse of Debtors' Personal Data in Light of the General Data Protection Regulation and the Credit Servicers and Credit Purchasers Directive

However, evidence from practice shows that the branches of German debt-collection agency mammoths, such as EOS, were slow to react and implement said best practices guides. In October 2023, the Croatian Personal Data Protection Agency imposed an administrative fine of 5.47 million euros on EOS Matrix d.o.o.

[52] FENCA, '2008 Code of Conduct' (FENCA) <https://juliorosonvsbbva.files.wordpress.com/2010/05/fenca-code-of-conduct.pdf> accessed 19 January 2024.

[53] BDIU, 'Die Europäische Datenschutz-Grundverordnung Best Practice Guide 2.0, Leitfaden für den Bereich' (*BDIU*, 20 November 2019) <https://www.inkasso.de/fileadmin/user_upload/mitgliederinformationen/BestPracticeGuideZweiPunktNull_BDIU_DSGVOimForderungsmanagement.pdf> accessed 19 January 2024.

[54] ibid.

[55] ibid.

[56] BDIU, 'Stellungnahme Entwurf der Bundesregierung eines Ersten Gesetzes zur Änderung des Bundesdatenschutzgesetzes' (*BDIU*, 9 April 2024) <https://www.inkasso.de/fileadmin/user_upload/stellungnahmen/2024_04_09_BDIU_Stellungnahme_zum_RegE_BDSG_AendG.pdf> accessed 10 July 2024.

as data controller for several violations of the GDPR,[57] including: the lack of appropriate technical measures to protect the personal data of data subjects contained in the storage systems;[58] the processing, without a legal basis, of data belonging to data subjects who were not in a debtor–creditor relationship;[59] the processing of personal data of a particular category (i.e. health data) of the data subjects without determining a legal basis;[60] failure to inform the data subject in a transparent and prescribed manner of the processing of their health data in the privacy policies;[61] failure to identify a legal basis for recording telephone conversations with the data subjects from May 2018 to January 2019;[62] and failure to inform data subjects understandably and clearly about the recording of telephone conversations.[63]

The details of the case are revealing and worrisome. The investigation was triggered by the receipt of an anonymous complaint and an attached USB stick containing the personal data of more than 181,000 natural persons (debtors) purchased by EOS Matrix d.o.o. based on a cession agreement. Of these, 294 were minors when the database was compiled. During the supervisory procedure, the Croatian agency established that the debt-collection agency also processed the personal data of persons who were neither debtors nor legal representatives of inheritors in debtor–creditor relationships (including their first and last name, residential address, and telephone number).

Particularly concerning was that the agents of the debt-collection agency actively recorded comments about the debtor's state of health and monitored such information down to the details of individual diagnoses, which included terminal illnesses, thus exposing their privacy to the maximum extent possible. The debt-collector's defence that the data subjects volunteered such data was rejected. The supervisory authority stated that for the debt-collector to be able to record someone's health information actively, the data subject themselves should have manifestly made public such data (through means of public communication or social networks)—a logic that did not apply to phone conversations between two people, which could be considered confidential. Worse, had it not been for an anonymous informant, the extent and nature of the violations committed by the debt-collection agency would not have been known.

The company's privacy policies between 2018 and 2020 were found to be misleading or outright false. Although all telephone conversations had been recorded

[57] Croatian Personal Data Protection Agency, 'Debt Collection Agency EOS Matrix d.o.o Imposed with an Administrative Fine in the Amount of 5.47 Million EUR' (*AZOP*, 5 October 2023) <https://azop.hr/debt-collection-agency-eos-matrix-d-o-o-imposed-with-administrative-fine-in-the-amount-of-5-47-million-euros/> accessed 20 January 2024.

[58] GDPR (n 9) arts 32 (1)(b) and (2).

[59] ibid art 6(1).

[60] ibid arts 6(1) and 9(2).

[61] The practice was contrary to GDPR (n 9) arts 12(1) and 13(1) and (2).

[62] GDPR (n 9) arts 6(1) and 5(2).

[63] ibid art 12(1).

since 2014, data subjects were only told that this 'may be' a possibility, creating ambiguity as to whether they were indeed recorded and giving data subjects the impression that this only occurred in certain circumstances. On this, the supervisory authority found that while privacy policies stated that EOS Matrix d.o.o. does not and will not process health data, it actively processed such data provided in telephone conversations.

As mentioned, the CSCPD expands the right to access databases across the Union to credit servicers and credit purchasers but restates that both the GDPR and the Regulation on the protection of personal data processed by public bodies[64] apply to the processing of personal data for debt-collection and purchasing.[65] Thus, debt buyers and collectors must have adequate governance arrangements and internal control mechanisms to comply with personal data-protection rules.[66]

There is more than a general reference to the GDPR because the CSCPD also contains specific obligations related to personal data protection. When handling personal data in accordance with the directive, it is important to specify the exact purpose, refer to the relevant legal basis, adhere to the security requirements outlined in the GDPR, and uphold the principles of necessity, proportionality, purpose limitation, and transparent and proportionate data-retention periods.[67] In addition, data protection by design and data protection by default should be embedded in all data-processing systems developed and used within the framework of the directive. Finally, the industry is encouraged to create its own code of conduct.[68]

Even more specific obligations concern the contractual relationship between the debt buyer and the debt-collector. For example, the mandatory content of the 'credit-servicing agreement' includes 'an undertaking by the parties to comply with Union and national law applicable ... including regarding ... data protection'.[69] At the same time, the failure of a debt-collector's governance arrangements and internal control mechanisms to ensure respect for borrowers' rights and compliance with data-protection rules may become grounds for administrative penalties and remedial action,[70] which, under the GDPR, can reach 20 million euros or 4 per cent of the total worldwide turnover of the preceding financial year (whichever is higher).[71]

64 Regulation (EU) 2018/1725 on the protection of natural persons regarding the processing of personal data by the Union institutions, bodies, offices and agencies and on the free movement of such data [2018] OJ L295/39 (Regulation on the protection of personal data processed by public bodies).
65 CSCPD (n 6) recitals 36 and 51 and art 25.
66 ibid recital 28 and art 5(1)(e).
67 ibid recital 51 and art 25.
68 ibid recital 51 and art 40.
69 CSCPD (n 6) art 11(2)(d).
70 ibid art 23(1)(b).
71 GDPR (n 9) art 83 (4)–(6).

Despite the above, the CSCPD could significantly impact *Schufa* by enabling debt purchasers and collectors to retain substantial amounts of personal data from consumer-debtors beyond what could constitute a necessary period.[72] This would be accomplished by mandating them to store various records, including relevant correspondence with the borrower, for a minimum of five years and a maximum of ten years.[73] The provision to make such records available to competent authorities upon request suggests that the logic is to ensure archival evidence for the sake of supervision and, subsequently, consumer protection. In practice, the provision also ensures a convenient legal basis for the prolonged collection and processing of the debtor's personal data without the risk of interference from data-protection agencies.

Still, the story of the GDPR's threat to the debt-collection business does not end here. In November 2022, a Polish court asked the CJEU whether the provisions of Article 5(1)(a) read in conjunction with Article 6(1)(a),(c), (e), and (2) of the GDPR preclude a provision of national law that allows the sale, for debt-collection purposes, of a database containing personal data if the data subject did not consent to such a sale.[74] At the time of writing, the case is still pending.[75] Without going into a deeper discussion, it suffices to say that should the question be answered positively, it would undermine the entire basis of non-performing loan transactions and other debt portfolios at both the member state and EU levels. Given the market considerations behind the repeated restatement of the right of credit servicers and purchasers to access databases throughout the Union and the financial interests surrounding the European Commission's efforts to create a harmonized and functional secondary non-performing loan market, it seems unlikely that the CJEU will render a decision that might affect them.

[72] For objections from the European Data Protection Supervisor, see: European Data Protection Supervisor, 'Formal Comments of the EDPS on the Proposal for a Directive of the European Parliament and of the Council on Credit Servicers, Credit Purchasers and the Recovery of Collateral' (*European Data Protection Supervisor*, 24 January 2019) <https://www.edps.europa.eu/sites/default/files/publication/19-01-24_comments_proposal_directive_european_parliament_en.pdf>; European Data Protection Supervisor, 'Formal Comments on the Draft Proposal for a Commission Implementing Regulation laying down Implementing Technical Standards for the Application of Article 15(1) of Directive(U) 2021/2167 with regard to the Templates to be used by Credit Institutions for the provision to Buyers of Information on their Credit Exposures in the Banking Book' (*European Data Protection Supervisor*, 25 July 2023) <https://www.edps.europa.eu/system/files/2023-07/2023-0712_formal_comments_en.pdf> accessed 22 July 2024.

[73] CSCPD (n 6) art 11(4)(a).

[74] Case C-693/22, Request for a preliminary ruling from the Sąd Rejonowy dla m.st. Warszawy w Warszawie (Poland) lodged on 10 November 2022 [2023] (2023/C 35/43).

[75] For a good summary, see: Bird & Bird, 'CJEU will rule on whether bailiffs can sell databases with personal data in enforcement proceedings' (*Bird & Bird*, 31 January 2024) <https://www.twobirds.com/en/insights/2024/poland/cjeu-will-rule-on-whether-bailiffs-can-sell-databases-with-personal-data-in-enforcement-proceedings> accessed 5 July 2024.

13.4 Summary

This chapter delved into the pivotal role of the GDPR in safeguarding personal data in debt-collection, primarily focusing on the *Schufa* case. It underscored the profound impact of extended data retention by credit bureaus on debtor privacy, emphasizing the imperative to strictly adhere to GDPR principles of lawfulness, purpose limitation, and data minimization. The chapter highlighted that retaining outdated debtor information can lead to unwarranted discrimination and impede individuals' reintegration into economic life. Furthermore, it detailed how the GDPR presents challenges to the debt-collection industry's business model by imposing limits on data-retention periods and enforcing rigorous compliance measures.

The preceding analysis of EU legislation and case law pertinent to debt-collection evaluated the effectiveness of these instruments in regulating debt-collection practices and protecting consumers from abusive debt-collection practices. It revealed that while specific measures affecting informal debt-collection can be found in the EU's general consumer protection instruments, these are fragmented, technical, and inadequate to comprehensively address the issue.

The next chapters further explore the deficiencies and potential impact of the CSCPD on national regulatory frameworks. They explore the intricate effects of the Credit Servicers, Credit Purchasers Directive (CSCPD). They critically examine the CSCPD's impact on debt-collection regulation in the European Union (EU) and its member states (MS), focusing on four primary concerns: the minimal emphasis on consumer protection, the standardized licensing regime for debt-collectors, the complex legal and supervisory framework surrounding credit servicers and purchasers, and the directive's enforcement mechanisms.

The analysis concludes that although the directive may streamline specific aspects of the debt-collection market and address non-performing loan (NPL) challenges, it fails to adequately protect consumers, leading to increased regulatory complexity and potential for abuse. In the first step, this chapter reveals that the directive does not primarily serve as a consumer protection instrument, leading to the absence of robust consumer safeguards. Instead, it aims to simplify market access for debt-collectors across the EU while increasing legal complexity for consumers and potentially exacerbating legal fragmentation in debt-collection regulation. This deliberately unbalanced approach undermines consumer protection while benefiting the debt-collection industry.

XIV
A DIRECTIVE FOR THE INDUSTRY: THE CREDIT SERVICERS AND CREDIT PURCHASERS DIRECTIVE

14.1 The Reasons for Adopting the Credit Servicers and Credit Purchasers Directive

As mentioned in Chapter IX, informal debt-collection did not reappear on the EU's regulatory agenda[1] until the Council of the European Union's Action Plan to tackle NPLs in Europe. Although the two issues of consumer credit and NPLs may seem unrelated, they are connected, albeit for different regulatory reasons. Following the financial crisis (which coincidentally unfolded at the time that the EU adopted the blunted 2008 Consumer Credit Directive), the loss of jobs and the decline in real incomes affected consumers' ability to repay their debts.[2] The ensuing high ratio of NPLs threatened the stability of the financial industry and economic recovery (see Chapter XII).[3] The result has been a need for faster and more efficient extra-judicial enforcement.

Consequently, the Council of the European Union tasked the European Commission (EC) with developing a European approach to foster the growth of secondary NPL markets while safeguarding consumers' rights. Additionally, the Council sought to simplify and potentially harmonize the licensing requirements

[1] Some provisions that could apply to debt-collection did surface in the application of other EU instruments, such as the Unfair Commercial Practices Directive, the Unfair Contract Terms Directive, the 2008 Consumer Credit Directive, or the General Data Protection Regulation, but none of these were specifically designed with debt-collection in mind. For details, see Chapters X–XIII.

[2] Joe Deville, *Lived Economies of Default* (Routledge, 2015); Federico Ferretti, *Comparative Aspects of Consumer Over-Indebtedness. A View from the UK, Germany, Greece, and Italy* (Eleven International Publishing 2016); Sarah Brown, *The Regulation of Consumer Credit. A Transatlantic Analysis* (Edward Elgar 2019).

[3] Corrado Macchiarelli, Renato Giacon, Andromachi Georgosouli, and Mara Monti, 'Why nonperforming loans are still putting the European banking union at risk' (*LSE EUROPP*, 27 March 2019) <https://blogs.lse.ac.uk/europpblog/2019/03/27/why-non-performing-loans-are-still-putting-the-european-banking-union-at-risk/> accessed 20 Dec 2020; Gian Boeddu, Jenniger Chien, Ivor Istuk, and Ligia Lopes, 'Protecting financial consumers during the COVID-19 crisis' (*World Bank Blogs*, 8 May 2020) <https://blogs.worldbank.org/en/psd/protecting-financial-consumers-during-covid-19-crisis>.

EU Informal Debt-Collection Regulation. Cătălin-Gabriel Stănescu, Oxford University Press.
 DOI: 10.1093/oso/9780198966159.003.0014

for third-party loan servicers and consider legislative action in this regard.[4] Subsequently, the EC introduced measures to address the risks of elevated NPL levels in Europe, including a proposal for a directive on credit servicers, credit purchasers, and collateral recovery.

The next sections discuss the CSCPD's primary focus—the protection of the financial system—and highlight the secondary status of consumer protection measures. In doing so, they demonstrate that regulatory measures for debt-collection activities do not match the regulation of the credit servicer profession.

14.2 Protecting the Financial System, Not the Consumer

The CSCPD is not directly concerned with borrower and consumer protection. Any positive impact of the directive is merely ancillary to its main objectives. The Union's priority is to create a comprehensive strategy to tackle the issue of NPLs, especially preventing future build-ups.[5]

The reasons are multifold. Some are general, such as completing the banking union, preventing potential spill-over effects among MS and the Union at large, enhancing the resilience of the economic and monetary union to adverse shocks through cross-border risk-sharing, and fostering job creation and economic growth within the EU. Others are more specific, including strengthening the banking union, ensuring competition in the banking sector, preserving financial stability, and promoting lending.[6] The CSCPD falls within two complementary areas of policy action: 'developing secondary markets for distressed assets' and 'reform of restructuring, insolvency, and debt recovery frameworks'.[7]

14.3 Boosting Debt Outsourcing and the Creation of a 'Debtor Society'

Adopting the CSCPD was necessary given the new prudential rules implemented through Regulation (EU) 2019/630,[8] which require credit institutions to set aside sufficient resources when new loans become non-performing. In the EC's view,

[4] Council of the European Union, 'Council conclusions on Action plan to tackle non-performing loans in Europe' (11 July 2017) Press Release <https://www.consilium.europa.eu/en/press/press-releases/2017/07/11/conclusions-non-performing-loans/> accessed 2 February 2024.

[5] Directive (EU) No 2021/2167 on credit servicers and credit purchasers [2021] OJ L438 (CSCPD) recital 1.

[6] CSCPD (n 5) recitals 1 and 2.

[7] ibid recital 3.

[8] Regulation (EU) 2019/630 of the European Parliament and of the Council of 17 April 2019 amending Regulation (EU) No 575/2013 as regards minimum loss coverage for non-performing exposures [2019] OJ L111, 4.

these prudential rules should encourage early intervention to address NPLs and prevent 'excessive accumulation' by enabling their sale in 'efficient, competitive and transparent secondary markets to other operators'.[9] From a macro-prudential standpoint, these views appear justified, which is why the CSCPD was designed to improve credit sale conditions to third parties.[10]

However, this is only part of the story. The other part is that the CSCPD significantly bolsters debt-recovery activities carried out by specialized debt-collectors and debt purchasers with 'the *necessary* risk appetite and expertise to manage' them.[11] There is something ominous about the language used as it sometimes goes beyond the original intentions of the directive and even contradicts them. On the one hand, it implies that debt-collection is not a business suitable for everyone, but only for those with the stomach and financial resources for it. On the other hand, it effectively allows credit institutions to disregard responsible lending by promptly outsourcing debt-collection to professional entities ready to do what is deemed 'necessary' and then resume business as usual. This creates a foundation for a 'debtor society', where debt is created, discarded, and created again in recurrent cycles.

Consequently, the adoption of the CSCPD in its current form has faced criticism. As observed by the European Economic and Social Committee (EESC), the existing prudential rules and the overall design of the directive 'force' banks to sell NPLs quickly instead of allowing financially distressed debtors to return to a more stable financial situation.[12] This contradicts the emphasis placed on forbearance measures laid out by the 2014 Consumer Mortgage Directive[13] and the 2023 revised CCD.[14] The EESC believes that NPL levels reflect the severe impact of indebtedness on families and small and medium enterprises, adding a strong social dimension to the matter.[15]

[9] CSCPD (n 5) recital 6.

[10] ibid recital 7, first thesis.

[11] CSCPD (n 5) recital 7, second thesis.

[12] European Economic and Social Committee, 'Opinion on Proposal for a Regulation of the European Parliament and of the Council on amending Regulation (EU) No 575/2013 as regards minimum loss coverage for non-performing exposures [COM(2018) 134 final—2018/0060 (COD)] Proposal for a Directive of the European Parliament and of the Council on credit servicers, credit purchasers and the recovery of collateral [COM(2018) 135 final—2018/0063 (COD)] OJ C 367 43, Sections 1.8 and 4.1.1–4.1.5.

[13] Directive 2014/17/EU on credit agreements for consumers relating to residential immovable property [2014] OJ L60/34 (CMD) 34–85.

[14] Directive (EU) 2023/2225 on credit agreements for consumers, PE/22/2023/REV/1 [2023] OJ L2023/2225 (2023 CCD).

[15] European Economic and Social Committee, 'Opinion on Proposal for a Regulation of the European Parliament and of the Council on amending Regulation (EU) No 575/2013 as regards minimum loss coverage for non-performing exposures [COM(2018) 134 final—2018/0060 (COD)] Proposal for a Directive of the European Parliament and of the Council on credit servicers, credit purchasers and the recovery of collateral [COM(2018) 135 final—2018/0063 (COD)] OJ C 367 43, Section 3.5.

Treating all NPLs in bulk (a one-size-fits-all approach) may exacerbate the social and economic consequences,[16] and the EESC suggests that regulators should prioritize consumer and worker protection and refrain from incentivizing the sale of NPLs.[17] As rightfully noted, 'the transfer of a loan means that the debtor must deal with a non-financial company with different personnel, working methods and purpose', which would justify an appropriate set of measures and recommendations to protect debtors.[18] Unfortunately, the final text of the directive did not include sufficient measures to protect debtors, putting the responsibility on the MS.

Furthermore, the EC's 2023 Study on Consumer Over-Indebtedness pointed out that an overly stimulative regulatory framework facilitating the trading of NPLs could deter creditors from lending responsibly because the risk of non-repayment could easily be transferred to a third party without significantly affecting the bank's profitability.[19]

This echoed a statement of Gunnar Beck, a member of the European Parliament (MEP), who argued that 'creating an internal secondary market for NPLs and establishing national asset management companies only creates more favourable conditions for banks to contain the consequences of their bad investment decisions, without actually reducing the probability of bad investment decisions'.[20] He cautioned that the '[f]urther harmonisation of the Banking Union and further integration of European financial markets does not solve this problem at all' but 'will only make the euro area more vulnerable to speculation by foreign credit purchasers'.[21] His words were disregarded.

14.4 *Qui prodest*? The Main Beneficiaries

Yet, the primary beneficiaries of the CSCPD are not crediting institutions but credit servicers and credit purchasers. According to the EC, these entities, rather than banks, are unable to 'reap the benefits of the internal market due to barriers erected by divergent national regimes in the absence of a dedicated and coherent regulatory and supervisory regime'.[22] It is they who suffer higher 'compliance costs'

[16] ibid Section 4.1.5.

[17] ibid.

[18] ibid.

[19] European Commission, 'Study on European Consumers' Over-indebtedness, and Its Implications. Final Report' (*European Commission*, June 2023) 251.

[20] European Parliament, 'Report on the proposal for a Directive of the European Parliament and of the Council on credit servicers, credit purchasers and the recovery of collateral (COM(2018)0135–C8-0115/2018-2018/0063A(COD), Committee on Economic and Monetary Affairs, A9-0003/2021' (*European Parliament*, 14 January 2021) 46.

[21] ibid.

[22] CSCPD (n 5) recitals 10 and 13.

when trying to purchase credit across borders in the Union[23] and can only operate in a few MS, limiting their competitive opportunities.[24]

14.4.1 Harmonizing entry requirements

Concerning the removal of obstacles to NPL transfers, the EC sought to establish a standardized EU-wide authorization system for credit servicers.[25] This makes for a ground-breaking piece of sectoral legislation at the EU level, dedicated to a particular category of service providers.[26] The directive acknowledges the lack of uniform standards for regulating debt-collection,[27] indicating the EC's intent to oversee the activity. However, the CSCPD's provisions offer limited support for this objective.

The EU legislator also highlights conflicting rules governing credit purchasers, leading to increased compliance costs,[28] limited competition,[29] and market inefficiencies, such as low NPL trading volumes and prices for NPL portfolios.[30] The most significant disparity arises from the varying requirements for obtaining authorization as a credit institution.

Ultimately, MS with sectoral legislation for credit-servicing activities that are equivalent to or stricter than the CSCPD must automatically recognize existing entities as authorized credit servicers. This allows established debt-collectors to continue their activity unencumbered by the transposition of the directive's rules.[31] These measures result in clearer, simpler, standardized entry rules and reinforce the position of existing market players, which have a competitive advantage over new market entrants.

Viewing the EU debt transfer regime as a property system highlights the significance of competent authorities, envisioned by the CSCPD as a facilitating bureaucracy with limited consideration for debtor protection. Variations are expected given that empirical data shows that national laws have elected or created different structures based on specific interests.

Unfortunately for consumers, this bureaucracy will function alongside the existing bureaucracy and have a different focus. For instance, most states have trade registries, consumer protection agencies, and financial supervisory authorities.

[23] ibid recital 10.
[24] ibid recitals 10, 14, and 15.
[25] CSCPD (n 5) recital 9.
[26] Cătălin Gabriel Stănescu, 'The Impact of the Credit Servicing Directive on Regulating Abusive Informal Debt Collection in the European Union: A Step Forward or a Missed Opportunity?' (2023) 12(1) Journal of European Consumer and Market Law 4.
[27] CSCPD (n 5) recital 10.
[28] ibid recital 10.
[29] ibid recitals 10 and 15.
[30] ibid recitals 11 and 15.
[31] ibid recital 25 and art 32(2).

Whereas the corporate form must be registered in trade registries, the authorization procedure will be handled by a parallel authority maintaining its own records, and supervision will be entrusted to other authorities with their own records. Contrary to the CSCPD's aims, there is duplication, but it is intended to ease market functionality rather than supervision. This did not stop debt-collection industry representatives from criticizing the system and lobbying for a change of the appointed authorities that were deemed 'dangerous', as in Germany.[32]

Despite industry criticism, the role of the CSCPD-related bureaucracy is to serve the interests of the CSCPD's addressees. Instead of complex and diverse national application processes, credit servicers and purchasers will benefit from a simple and standard application procedure in an MS of their choosing without the risk of additional and diverse requirements for operating in another MS. The examination and authorization of one office will be recognized by other authorities, saving labour, time, and costs. Simultaneously, credit servicers and purchasers will enjoy a multilateral approach to administration and the stringency of national rules, allowing them to identify and choose the least debtor-friendly jurisdiction. They will have the opportunity to shop not just for debt portfolios but also for forums.[33]

14.4.2 Strengthening market functionality

The other primary concern is market functionality, with the apparent beneficiaries being the credit institutions. The limited participation of credit purchasers has led to low demand, weak competition, and low bid prices for portfolios, discouraging credit institutions from selling NPLs.[34] This assertion emphasizes the 'clear Union dimension' of the issue[35] and justifies the EU's intervention under the guise of 'market development' and 'completion of the banking union and capital-markets union'.[36]

However, there is little evidence to substantiate this claim other than references to the 'small volume' of national NPL markets. On the contrary, empirical evidence indicates a significant increase in debt buying and collection following the financial crisis and even during the COVID-19 pandemic, with a notable cross-border dimension. As MEP Gunnar Beck pointed out, 'the regional concentration of NPLs does not justify far-reaching harmonisation, especially vis-à-vis countries with already sufficiently developed secondary markets'.[37]

32 See the example of BDIU in Chapter VIII, Subsection 8.3.
33 Stănescu (n 26).
34 CSCPD (n 5) recital 11.
35 ibid recital 16 and 61.
36 ibid recital 11.
37 European Parliament (n 20) 46.

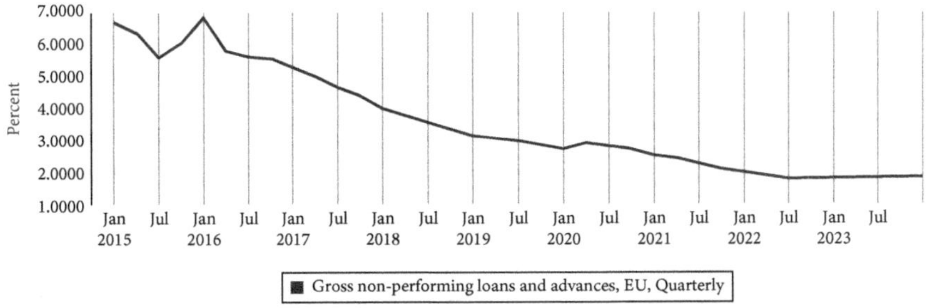

Figure 14.1 Gross NPL ratios of total gross loans and advances in EU27, 2015–2023.
Source: ESCB.

The European Banking Authority (EBA) reported a steady decline in NPL levels in the EU between 2015 and 2023. In 2015, banks reporting to the EBA had accumulated almost 1.2 trillion euros in NPLs (6% of total gross loans and advances). However, by 2019, the total NPL volume had fallen to 636 billion euros (3%).[38] The NPL ratio further declined to 1.82 per cent by 2023 but saw a slight increase to 1.91 per cent by the beginning of 2024, totalling approximately 403 billion euros[39] (see Figure 14.1). The positive results until 2023 were attributed to various factors, including 'sales, write-offs, cash collections and ... foreclosures', as well as 'increased investor appetite for NPLs'.[40] The market scale, amounting to 600 billion euros, reflects its substantial size and functionality.

Regarding consumer loans, the EBA also noted improved NPL ratios for households during the same period.[41] In 2015, NPLs to households[42] totalled 396 billion euros (5.5%), which reduced to 250 billion euros (3.1%) by 2019, putting the consumer NPL market at more than 145 billion euros over four years[43] (a quarter of the total NPL market). This data contradicts the statements in the CSCPD's Recitals, suggesting that the true justification for the directive's adoption may lie elsewhere.

The directive anticipates the establishment of Union-wide secondary markets that are 'efficient, competitive and transparent' to enable credit institutions to 'perform their role of financing the economy'.[44] In essence, these markets for

[38] European Banking Authority, 'Report on NPLs. Progress Made and Challenges Ahead' (European Banking Authority, 2019) 11 <https://www.eba.europa.eu/sites/default/documents/files/document_library/Risk%20Analysis%20and%20Data/Risk%20Assessment%20Reports/2019//Final%20EBA%20Report%20on%20NPLs-for%20publication_final.pdf> accessed 30 March 2023.

[39] European Central Bank, 'ECB publishes consolidated banking data for end-December 2023' (*European Central Bank*, 13 June 2024) Press Release <https://www.ecb.europa.eu/press/pr/date/2024/html/ecb.pr240613~2a1d054108.en.html> accessed 15 July 2024.

[40] ibid 16.

[41] ibid 8 and 28.

[42] However, according to the same report, NPLs for consumer credits stood at 5.6% in 2019, despite improvements over the previous years: ibid 24.

[43] ibid 23.

[44] CSCPD (n 5) recital 11.

trading (consumer) debts are fostered to allow credit institutions to create more consumer debt.

14.5 Ancillary Borrower and Consumer Protection

Borrower and consumer protection is a secondary objective, following the primary goals of facilitating debt-collection and fostering secondary debt markets.[45] This protection is restricted to what the directive deems necessary for achieving these objectives. The term 'consumer' is introduced later in the recitals,[46] primarily in connection with other EU or national normative acts, indicating that the CSCPD aims to maintain existing rights regarding debt-collection rather than establish new ones.[47]

In general, creditors and their representatives must comply with EU law in their dealings with consumers to ensure the protection of consumer rights,[48] even in cases of contract novation[49] or assignment of account.[50] These rights are derived from EU legislation and national transpositions (i.e. creditors' duty to take forbearance measures and consider the consumer's rights and interests[51]) and contractual obligations[52] and should be seen as reaffirmations of existing rights.

As a result, most consumer protection is a by-product of other CSCPD goals.[53] Debt-collectors' vetting and prior authorization can benefit all stakeholders, including (consumer-)debtors, despite the potential for circumvention. Similarly, the general requirement to act in good faith and treat debtors fairly can positively impact consumers[54] even though these measures are not explicitly designed solely for their benefit. The CSCPD does not include such measures and delegates this task to the MS.

14.5.1 Obligations for debt-collectors and debt buyers

Recital 20 of the CSCPD outlines a set of obligations to be observed by all debt buyers and collectors in their dealings with borrowers, including consumers.

[45] Stănescu (n 26). Following my article, the EC's Study on European Consumers' Over-Indebtedness and Its Implications also acknowledged the indirect effect of the CSCPD on consumers, mainly after it is transposed into national legislation: European Commission (n 19) 247.

[46] The first mention of consumers is in CSCPD (n 5) recital 19.

[47] CSCPD (n 5) recitals 21 and 54.

[48] ibid recital 19.

[49] ibid recital 55 and 57.

[50] ibid recital 57.

[51] ibid recital 56.

[52] ibid recitals 21, 40, 46, 49, and 57.

[53] Stănescu (n 26).

[54] CSCPD (n 5) recitals 20, 28, and 32.

These obligations include acting in good faith, treating borrowers fairly,[55] respecting their privacy, and providing accurate information. Additionally, there are prohibitions against harassing borrowers and providing misleading information. Some of these obligations are tied to consumer protection rules arising from other EU legislation, such as the 2008 Consumer Credit Directive (CCD) and the 2014 Consumer Mortgage Directive, which, among others, impose minimum disclosures and transparency obligations, or the Unfair Commercial Practices Directive, which bans misleading, harassing, and coercive behaviour towards consumers.[56]

Further provisions benefiting consumers can be identified in the subsequent restatement of the rights under Articles 7 (right to privacy) and 47 of the Charter of Fundamental Rights of the EU (right to a fair and public trial) coupled with the possibility of resorting to legal aid, which embodies general legal principles such as access to justice and procedural fairness. The same principles can be identified in the recommendation that debt-collectors implement appropriate governance, internal control mechanisms, and procedures for recording and handling complaints.[57]

The vetting process for the management or administrative organs of credit servicers and the requirements for conducting business competently and responsibly[58] aim to uphold professionalism and accountability. In the view of the EU legislator, all are necessary to 'avoid a reduction in borrower protection' and 'promote trust',[59] but one would be mistaken to believe that they serve the limited and dedicated purpose of protecting borrowers.

Instead, these measures seek to protect the interests of stakeholders in the NPL market, including credit institutions and credit purchasers. For example, managerial vetting and professionalism assure debt buyers (credit purchasers) and creditors that they are dealing with a trustworthy entity and minimize their exposure to reputational damage, especially because, according to the CSCPD, liability lies primarily with the beneficiary.[60] Registration and disclosure requirements[61] promote transparency and facilitate accountability efforts for all involved parties.[62] Furthermore, the maintenance of separate accounts was implemented to mitigate fraud or insolvency risks from the debt-collectors' side.[63]

[55] A reference to fair treatment of consumers is also found in CSCPD (n 5) recital 56.

[56] CSCPD (n 5) recital 21. Mandatory disclosures towards consumers are also referred to in CSCPD (n 5) recital 53.

[57] CSCPD (n 5) recital 28.

[58] CSCPD (n 5) recitals 27 and 28.

[59] ibid recital 27.

[60] ibid recitals 27, 28, and 32.

[61] ibid recitals 33 and 37.

[62] ibid recital 30. Of particular interest is the disclosure to the borrower of the outsourcing of debt-collection activities, as per CSCPD (n 5) recital 32.

[63] CSCPD (n 5) recital 29.

14.5.2 Transparency and accountability

Transparency stemming from creditors' disclosures or the authorization procedures of national supervisory agencies eases the activity of debt buyers, that is, debt-collectors. By giving debt buyers access to the information necessary to assess portfolios of non-performing agreements and the likelihood of recovery, the CSCPD enables them to conduct thorough due diligence and make reasonable price offers to creditors.[64] Simultaneously, by providing clear, proportionate, uniform, and harmonized authorization criteria to debt-collectors, the CSCPD simplifies their administrative and compliance burdens, thereby fostering the creation and functioning of the debt-collection market.

Transparency plays a crucial role in supervision and enforcement. It is closely tied to the principle of accountability, although the objectives may not always be apparent and the approaches may be convoluted. National public registries or lists are to be established to ensure that the number and identity of authorized credit servicers are known.[65] However, this could have been achieved more effectively by creating a centralized EU register, granting all parties quicker and more transparent access to information at a lower cost.[66] Additionally, extensive communications on the cross-border activities of debt-collectors are to be exchanged among competent authorities in the MS within reasonable timeframes.[67] Nevertheless, there is a risk that these obligations may lead to substantial expenses for authorities, potentially diminishing their monitoring and enforcement resources.

Credit purchasers must notify the relevant authorities in their home MS when they enlist the services of debt-collectors, credit institutions, or non-credit institutions supervised by another MS's competent authority. This notification allows the authorities to effectively oversee the credit servicer's or institution's activity concerning the borrower. If the purchaser hires a credit servicer or institution different from the one initially reported, they must inform the competent authorities again.[68] Although these disclosures are intended to enhance supervision, the system is too complex and resource-consuming to be genuinely effective for consumers.

In addition, credit institutions and credit purchasers have reporting obligations regarding the total outstanding balance of the transferred credit portfolios, the number and size of the included credits, and whether the transfer comprises credit agreements concluded with consumers on a biannual or quarterly basis. This

[64] CSCPD (n 5) recitals 36–38.
[65] ibid recital 30.
[66] Stănescu (n 26).
[67] CSCPD (n 5) recital 33.
[68] CSCPD (n 5) recital 45.

transparency is aimed at harmonizing and monitoring the transfer of credit agreements within the Union,[69] clearing the current opacity surrounding the size of the debt-collection market. Still, the specific purpose of this data remains unclear.

14.5.3 Further concerns about consumer protection

Finally, some worry that even the meek CSCPD provisions supposed to protect consumers might inadvertently harm them. The EC's 2023 Study on Consumer Over-Indebtedness highlighted that although the CSCPD includes measures to protect consumers from the negative impacts of NPL transfers on the secondary market, such as being informed of the change in creditor (Article 28 of CSCPD), consumers do not have the right to veto or oppose the transaction.[70]

The study also raised the point that forbearance measures and the possibility for MS to impose caps on default charges could be interpreted as preventing a decrease in the level of protection of over-indebted consumers' interests. On the one hand, the report stressed that whether lenders exercise reasonable forbearance (and what this will mean in practice) is not harmonized at the EU level and will depend on national transposition. On the other hand, the study noted that the CSCPD left the definition of the quantum of the 'cap' to the discretion of national legislators. As a result, the regulatory framework relating to the imposition of excessive charges on consumers may vary among MS, and the protective effect may even be undermined where MS introduce a very high cap.[71] Though unable to fully evaluate the extent of the CSCPD's impact on over-indebted consumers, the study warned of a risk of 'unintended effects'.

14.6 Summary

The chapter provided an in-depth examination of the CSCPD, revealing its primary objective of stabilizing the financial system and fostering secondary markets for NPLs, often at the expense of robust consumer protection measures. It showed that while the directive simplifies market access for established debt-collectors and purchasers, it also introduces a complex legal landscape that could exacerbate regulatory fragmentation and weaken consumer safeguards.

The next chapter further explores the legal and supervisory framework established by the CSCPD. It delves into the dual mechanisms of contractual and

[69] ibid recital 37.
[70] European Commission (n 19) 248; Stănescu (n 26).
[71] European Commission (n 19) 249.

administrative supervision, scrutinizing how these frameworks operate and their implications for credit servicers and debtors. By navigating this legal maze, the book uncovers the inherent weaknesses and operational complexities that undermine the directive's effectiveness in protecting consumer rights and ensuring fair debt-collection practices.

XV
PROHIBITED BEHAVIOUR UNDER THE CREDIT SERVICERS AND CREDIT PURCHASERS DIRECTIVE

15.1 Prohibited Behaviour of the Credit Servicer

This section addresses the prohibited behaviours of credit servicers, primarily focusing on violations of licensing and behavioural obligations post-licence issuance.

15.1.1 Failure to maintain archival evidence

The CSCPD sanctions the failure to comply with the requirements, in the national provisions transposing Article 11, regarding the contractual relationship between a credit servicer and a credit purchaser.[1] The potential sanctions are outlined in Article 11(4) and (5) and pertain to the credit servicer's obligations (a) to keep and maintain various records (i.e. relevant correspondence with the credit purchaser and the borrower, relevant instructions received from the credit purchasers or the credit-servicing agreement) for a period of five to ten years from the date on which the credit-servicing agreement is terminated and (b) to make these records available to competent authorities upon request.

Importantly, although these obligations are also present in Article 12(3) and (4), non-compliance with them is not specified as a sanctionable situation under the CSCPD. This may result in extensive databases of debtors' personal information being created under the guise of fulfilling legal obligations that are intended to benefit consumers.

15.1.2 Breach of the mandatory content of an outsourcing agreement (Article 12)

The issue at hand revolves around the reference to an infringement caused by the outsourcing agreement. To clarify, the non-compliance of the outsourcing

1 Directive (EU) No 2021/2167 on credit servicers and credit purchasers [2021] OJ L438 (CSCPD).

EU Informal Debt-Collection Regulation. Cătălin-Gabriel Stănescu, Oxford University Press.
 DOI: 10.1093/oso/9780198966159.003.0015

agreement is penalized here, as opposed to that of the credit servicer. Therefore, the crucial section is Article 12(1), which delineates the conditions to be met by the agreement. Penalties can be inferred if (a) there is no written statement concerning the credit service provider's obligation to adhere to the relevant legal requirements transposing the directive or applicable national laws concerning creditor's rights, (b) all credit-servicing activities are outsourced, (c) there is a change in the contractual relationship between the credit servicer and the credit purchaser, (d) the credit servicer does not comply with the authorization requirements outlined in Article 5(1), (e) it hinders the oversight of a credit servicer by competent authorities, (f) there is no direct access to all pertinent information concerning the outsourced credit-servicing activities, or (g) there is a lack of expertise or resources to continue the outsourced credit-servicing activities after the outsourcing ceases.

Notable points include the absence of protection for debtors and the imposition of administrative sanctions on a contractual relationship. Given that the competent authority would have to oversee and enforce the credit purchaser's rights under the credit-servicing agreement throughout the outsourcing agreement, it is likely that the supervising authorities will not be those responsible for consumer protection but rather those tasked with rather financial regulation, which are typically creditor-friendly.

15.1.3 Breach of licence duties

Credit servicers can violate their licence obligations in several ways. The first includes not respecting the borrowers' rights under the credit agreement or the General Data Protection Regulation's (GDPR) personal data-protection rules. The CSCPD mandates that credit servicers must have robust governance arrangements and effective internal control mechanisms, encompassing risk management and accounting procedures.[2] Crucially, these structures and mechanisms must be established before receiving authorization. Authorization being granted means that they were thoroughly reviewed and found compliant. Therefore, if credit servicers fail to uphold these requirements while conducting their operations, their authorization should be revoked.[3] Imposing any other penalty would potentially allow credit servicers to exploit the system after obtaining their authorization.

A second potential breach could arise from implementing an inadequate policy for the proper treatment of borrowers.[4] The provision references a pre-condition for authorization, which includes rules for the protection and fair and diligent treatment of borrowers, taking into account their financial situation. It also suggests

[2] ibid art 5(1)(e).
[3] ibid art 8(1)(e).
[4] ibid art 5(1)(f).

referring such borrowers to available debt advice or social services. However, the CSCPD does not provide clear guidelines on what constitutes a policy for borrower protection or fair and diligent treatment. This lack of clarity leaves the task to individual MS, potentially leading to legal fragmentation.

The only guidance provided is that creditors and credit servicers should consider the borrowers' financial situation; further details are not provided. Arguably, the European Union (EU) legislator had in mind the forbearance measures listed in the Consumer Credit Directive or the Consumer Mortgage Directive, given the references made throughout the CSCPD. However, empirical evidence suggests that financial institutions rarely employ these measures.[5] For this reason, it is doubtful they will be of much use during debt-collection, a more advanced phase of default.

Similarly, because having such a policy is a precondition for authorization, its adequacy was presumably checked before authorization was granted. The current sanction applies to situations where the original policy was removed or improperly amended, rendering it inadequate for its intended purpose. In this case, the penalty should be the withdrawal of the authorization. Therefore, the directive focuses on formality rather than substance, as it considers the inadequacy of the policy rather than how it was implemented.

A third scenario could occur if internal procedures[6] are implemented without incorporating provisions for documenting and resolving borrower complaints in accordance with national regulations implementing the directive. In this situation, the credit servicer may be held accountable for failing to comply with pre-authorization requirements at a later time, maybe due to changes in internal procedures or failure to follow their provisions (such as misplacing, not recording, or deleting borrower complaints). At first glance, such non-compliance should also lead to the revocation of the licence.[7]

A fourth violation of the CSCPD can occur when a credit servicer allows individuals who do not meet the legal requirements[8] to become or remain members of its management or administrative team. This violation stems from the failure to conduct proper background checks on these key team members before authorization. Individuals in these roles are expected to have a 'sufficiently good repute', evidenced by 'a clean police record' in areas such as property, financial services and activities, money laundering, usury, fraud, tax crimes, violations of professional secrecy or physical integrity and any other offences under laws relating to companies, bankruptcy, insolvency, or consumer protection.[9] They should also

[5] Finance Watch, 'Tackling Causes of Over-Indebtedness in the EU Consumer Credit Market' (*Finance Watch*, March 2022) 24.
[6] Outlined in CSCPD (n 1) art 5(1)(g).
[7] CSCPD (n 1) art 8(1)(e).
[8] ibid art 5(1)(b).
[9] ibid recital 27 and art 5(1)(b)(i).

have demonstrated 'transparency, openness and cooperativeness in their past business dealings with supervisory or regulatory authorities'.[10] If it is discovered that non-compliant members are part of the leadership of the credit servicers, revoking authorization would be entirely justified.[11] This requirement would benefit consumer-debtors, but it should have been extended to the entirety of the credit servicer's staff, not just its managerial bodies, given that consumers rarely deal with them directly.

A fifth violation can arise if credit servicers fail to adhere to the national provisions transposing the CSCPD and mandating the establishment and maintenance of transparent and effective procedures for addressing borrower complaints without charging any fees.[12] Credit servicers must also document the complaints and the actions taken to resolve them. This provision[13] is a more detailed version of the one mentioned above,[14] emphasizing the fair treatment of borrowers and the proper recording of their complaints. Non-compliance with these requirements could result in the loss of the authorization. This implies that mishandling the borrower's complaint could carry a more severe penalty than 'mishandling' the borrower (i.e., subjecting them to unlawful behaviour), making the imposition of such sanctions unlikely.

The sixth breach pertains to receiving and holding funds from borrowers when such actions are forbidden in an MS.[15] The CSCPD does not outline or imply any specific sanctions for violating this prohibition. However, read in conjunction with the next provision,[16] it becomes apparent that receiving funds from borrowers when this is not permitted might lead to the commingling of the credit servicers' funds with the credit purchaser's funds, exposing the latter to potential fraud or insolvency risk of the former. In essence, this serves as a protective measure for the creditor. The likely sanction should be the withdrawal of authorization.[17]

Finally, failure to comply with the requirements outlined in the national provisions transposing Article 6(2) of the CSCPD presents a connected but reversed situation. When MS allow credit servicers to hold funds, the directive imposes pre-authorization requirements. This entails credit servicers having a separate account in a credit institution, where all funds received from borrowers are credited and held until their transfer to the relevant credit purchaser. Additionally, credit servicers must provide receipts or letters of discharge to borrowers, on paper or

[10] ibid art 5(1)(b)(iii).
[11] ibid art 8(1)(e).
[12] CSCPD (n 1) art 24.
[13] ibid.
[14] ibid art 5(1)(f) and (g).
[15] ibid art 6(1)(b).
[16] ibid art 6(2).
[17] Based on the corroborated reading of CSCPD (n 1) art 6(2) and (3) and art 8(1)(e).

any other durable medium, whenever they receive funds from the borrower to acknowledge the amounts received.

As part of the pre-authorization procedure, non-compliance with the obligation to maintain separate accounts could, in theory, result in the withholding of the authorization.[18] However, it is unclear whether this sanction will cover purely formal violations, such as the closure of the separate account, or situations involving the amalgamation of funds by not using the separate account. The matter will have to be addressed at the national level.

The penalty for failing to furnish borrowers with discharge documents for their payments requires further clarification. This particular scenario is not explicitly included in the reasons for revoking an authorization.[19] The only circumstance in which such non-compliance with the directive's requirements would be considered a severe violation of the applicable rules is if it breaches the national provisions transposing the directive or other consumer protection laws in the host MS or the MS where the credit was granted.

Once more, the disparity between the protections afforded to the creditor (the credit purchaser) and those extended to the borrower (the consumer-debtor) is evident. Maintaining a separate account primarily serves the creditor's interests, whereas providing evidence of debt discharge mainly safeguards the debtor's interests. Nonetheless, even if fraudulent conduct leads to the immediate termination of the credit servicer's operations, there may still be debate over whether defrauding paying borrowers constitutes a severe violation of local regulations.

15.1.4 Breaches of behavioural duties towards borrowers

The CSCPD outlines two primary behavioural duties that can attract credit servicers' liability in case of non-compliance. The first involves compliance with the national provisions transposing Article 10. This article holds critical provisions benefiting consumer-debtors and borrowers, guaranteeing them the rights to be treated in good faith, fairly, and professionally; to receive honest, straightforward, and truthful information; to have their personal data and privacy respected and protected; and to be communicated with in a manner that does not constitute harassment, coercion, or undue influence.

However, authorization can only be revoked in cases of 'serious infringement' of applicable rules, including the national provisions transposing the CSCPD or other consumer protection rules of the host MS and the MS where the credit was granted. The definition of 'serious infringement' is left to the MS, potentially resulting in legal fragmentation and a lack of harmonized protection standards.

18 CSCPD (n 1) art 8(1)(e).
19 ibid.

Notably, whereas a breach of mere formalities, such as the lack of an internal policy to treat borrowers fairly, can lead to the immediate withdrawal of the licence, violations of legal protections will only incur the same penalty if deemed sufficiently 'serious'.

The second duty concerns refraining from serious infringements of the applicable rules, including the national provisions transposing the CSCPD, or other consumer protection rules, such as relevant rules of the host MS and the MS where the credit was granted.[20] Although this provision lacks the specificity of the previous ones, it stands out as one of the few provisions focused on safeguarding borrowers, particularly consumer-debtors. The provision is found in Article 8, which addresses the withdrawal of authorization, implying that debt-collectors could face termination of activities for breaching borrowers' rights.

Nevertheless, this provision remains primarily of theoretical significance as the application of this penalty is limited to 'serious infringements', which are not explicitly defined in the directive but could (and should) be outlined in national legislation. Further, each case will necessitate an individual assessment of the circumstances, subject to judicial review and interpretation at the national level. This is likely to result in varying outcomes and, consequently, discrepancies in the level of protection provided.

15.2 Prohibited Behaviour of Credit Purchasers

This section details the prohibited behaviour of credit purchasers or their designated representatives,[21] if applicable.

15.2.1 Failure to communicate the mandatory information

This refers to breaches related to the information required by national regulations implementing Articles 18 and 20. According to Article 18, if credit purchasers use an entity not covered by the CSCPD[22] or a credit servicer for credit-servicing activities related to the transferred creditor's rights under a non-performing credit agreement, they must inform the competent authorities of their home MS of the entity's or credit servicer's identity and address. This information should be provided no later than the commencement of credit-servicing activities. A similar obligation applies when the entity or credit servicer is replaced.

[20] CSCPD (n 1) art 8(1)(f).
[21] ibid art 19.
[22] CSCPD (n 1) art 2(5)(i)–(iii).

Under Article 20, credit purchasers transferring a creditor's rights under non-performing credit agreements must inform the competent authorities of their home MS on a biannual basis[23] of the new credit purchaser's legal entity identifier (LEI) and, if applicable, its representative. In cases where such an identifier does not exist, they must provide the identity of the new credit purchaser or the members of the new credit purchaser's management or administrative organ and the persons holding qualifying stakes in the latest credit purchaser, as well as the address of the new credit purchaser. Additionally, credit purchasers are required to inform the competent authorities of their home MS of the aggregate outstanding balance of the creditor's rights under the transferred non-performing credit agreement, the number and size of the creditor's rights under the transferred non-performing credit agreement, whether the transfer includes a creditor's rights arising from credit agreements with consumers, and the types of assets securing the non-performing credit agreement. These obligations are related to the monitoring interests of MS and do not imply any potential sanctions for non-compliance.

15.2.2 Failure to appoint an entity or a credit servicer to perform credit-servicing activities

This obligation stems from the national provisions transposing Article 17, according to which credit purchasers who are domiciled or with a registered/head office in the EU must appoint an entity referred to in Article 2(5) point (a)(i)–(iii)[24] or a credit servicer to perform credit-servicing activities under non-performing credit agreements concluded with consumers.[25] For credit purchasers located outside the Union or without a registered office in the Union, their representative must appoint an entity or a credit servicer to perform credit-servicing activities under non-performing credit agreements concluded with natural persons (including consumers and independent workers) as well as micro and small and medium-sized enterprises[26] (SMEs).[27]

This provision pertains to accountability and encompasses several aspects. First, if credit purchasers deal with consumers, they are not allowed to collect their own debts. They have to engage a professional debt-collector (a credit servicer) or one of the regulated entities mentioned in Article 2. Second, foreign credit purchasers face higher standards: their ability to collect debts is further restricted,

[23] MS also have the right to request said information on a quarterly basis, whenever the competent authorities deem necessary, including to better monitor a high number of transfers that might occur during a crisis period. CSCPD (n 1) art 20(2).

[24] CSCPD (n 1) art 2(5) point (a)(i)–(iii).

[25] ibid art 17(1)(a).

[26] As defined by the Annex to Commission Recommendation 2003/361/EC, art 2.

[27] CSCPD (n 1) art 17(1)(b).

excluding independent workers and micro and SMEs. Third, the identity of the appointee(s) must be disclosed to competent authorities of their home MS[28] for monitoring and supervision purposes.

Will this positively impact consumers? Is it a consumer protection mechanism? It certainly seems that way. However, it is important to note that the liability is (re-) allocated between the credit purchaser and the credit servicer. These limitations protect credit purchasers from liability while exposing credit servicers.

15.2.3 Failure of non-European Union credit purchasers to designate a representative

This breach concerns the failure to adhere to the national provisions implementing the requirement[29] for a credit purchaser not domiciled in the EU or without a registered office in the EU to designate in writing a representative who is domiciled in the EU or with a registered/head office in the EU. The representative will be held fully responsible for ensuring compliance with the obligations imposed on the credit purchaser. Nonetheless, the specific sanction for non-compliance remains to be determined at the MS level.

15.2.4 Failure to act in good faith and other obligations towards borrowers

This situation pertains to failure to comply with national provisions that mandate credit purchasers to conduct their dealings with borrowers in good faith and professionally,[30] providing accurate and truthful information, respecting and protecting their privacy, and refraining from harassing, coercing, or unduly influencing them. The obligations outlined for credit servicers apply here as well, except for potential sanctions for non-compliance.

15.3 Prohibited Behaviour of Other Parties

The CSCPD also encompasses sanctions for non-compliance by other involved parties.

[28] ibid art 18(1) and (2).
[29] CSCPD (n 1) art 19.
[30] ibid art 10.

15.3.1 Severe violations of the law by the credit service provider

The credit service provider to whom the credit-servicing activities were outsourced will be held accountable for any serious infringement of applicable legal provisions, including national laws transposing the directive.[31] For equality of treatment and consistency, credit service providers are only liable for severe breaches of the law.

This provision requires further qualifications because, as per the directive, credit servicers must ensure that outsourcing their credit-servicing activities does not lead to undue operational risk or non-compliance with EU or national law requirements by the credit service providers.[32] Additionally, they are fully responsible for complying with all obligations under national law that implement the directive.[33]

The type of liability involved here is ambiguous. The credit servicer's ultimate liability implies that it has assumed the role of the principal in the outsourcing agreement, with the credit service provider acting as its agent. This interpretation is supported by the requirement for the written outsourcing agreement to stipulate that the credit service provider must adhere to the relevant legal provisions. A diligent credit servicer could avoid primary/direct liability and transfer it to the credit service provider. It is plausible that a split-liability arrangement could be established, such that a credit service provider engaging in prohibited behaviour could be sanctioned and enjoined to refrain from it while the credit servicer would bear the more significant consequences, such as moral damages and reparation. The determination of liability status would be made at the national level, with MS deciding whether it constitutes joint and severable liability or subsequent liability (guarantee).

15.3.2 Failure to provide the mandatory information required of credit institutions

Credit institutions must disclose specific information to credit purchasers.[34] Failure to do so may attract liability. This obligation includes providing information about a creditor's rights under a non-performing credit agreement, the non-performing credit agreement itself, and any applicable collateral. The information is essential for credit purchasers to assess the value of the rights and the likelihood of recovery before entering into a transfer contract.[35] The disclosure must comply

[31] CSCPD (n 1) art 23 (1)(a).
[32] ibid recital 31.
[33] ibid art 12(1).
[34] Under the national provisions transposing CSCPD (n 1) art 15.
[35] ibid art 15(1).

with the requirements of two regulations, (EU) 2016/679 (the GDPR) and (EU) 2018/1725, which protect individuals regarding the processing of personal data by EU institutions, bodies, offices, and agencies.[36]

Furthermore, credit institutions transferring creditors' rights under non-performing credit agreements or the non-performing credit agreements themselves must disclose certain information to the competent authorities of the host MS. This information includes the credit purchaser's or their representative's LEI, the identity of the credit purchaser or the members of its managing/administrative body and the persons who hold qualifying holdings, and their addresses. Additionally, the disclosure must include the aggregate outstanding balance of the creditor's rights under the non-performing credit agreements, the number and size of the creditor's rights, and whether the transfer includes creditor rights arising from non-performing credit agreements concluded with consumers. Finally, the disclosure must specify the types of assets used to secure the non-performing credit agreements (where applicable). This provision is intended to ensure transparency in credit transfers.

Competent authorities must observe and protect credit purchasers' interests in transfers of non-performing loan (NPL) portfolios. This aligns with the EU legislator's aim to promote the development of secondary NPL markets. The mention of the GDPR and other data-protection instruments serves to reassure individuals whose data is being transferred. However, the parties involved in NPL transactions have broad access to personal data and discretion in determining its legitimate use for the intended purpose.

15.3.3 Failure to disclose mandatory information by supervised credit and non-credit institutions

Entities mentioned under Article 2(5) point (a)(i) or (iii) are subject to sanctions per the CSCPD for non-compliance with national provisions transposing Article 10. These entities include credit institutions established in the EU and non-credit institutions supervised by competent authorities of an MS when performing activities in that state.[37] Typically, these entities are not covered by the CSCPD when they service a creditor's rights. The obligation pertains to the mandatory initial disclosure following the transfer of creditor's rights under a non-performing

[36] Regulation (EU) 2018/1725 on the protection of natural persons regarding the processing of personal data by the Union institutions, bodies, offices and agencies and on the free movement of such data [2018] OJ L295/39 (Regulation on the protection of personal data processed by public bodies).

[37] Directive 2008/48/EC on credit agreements for consumers [2008] OJ L133/66 (2008 CCD) art 20 or Directive 2014/17/EU on credit agreements for consumers relating to residential immovable property [2014] OJ L60/34 (CMD) art 35.

agreement to credit purchasers, *always* before the performance of the first debt-collection activity by the Article 2(5) entity.[38]

Importantly, the initial exclusion of specific entities from the scope of the CSCPD is limited to administrative requirements, such as authorization. However, the directive's language is ambiguous. Article 10(1) of the CSCPD only imposes the obligation to treat borrowers fairly on credit purchasers and credit servicers, without explicitly mentioning the entities in Article 2(5)(i) and (iii). This omission could mean that the protective measures concerning borrowers will not apply in their case.

This is a significant issue because Article 17 allows credit purchasers to choose between the entities listed in Article 2(5) and credit servicers when seeking to enforce their rights under non-performing agreements concluded with consumers/natural persons. This choice could effectively allow them to bypass the CSCPD's meek protections for borrowers.

15.4 Summary

The chapter revealed that the CSCPD primarily focuses on formalities and administrative requirements rather than substantial borrower protection. Prohibited behaviours are mainly centred on maintaining records, internal governance, and adherence to pre-authorization requirements. The directive's emphasis on transparency and accountability appears to protect creditors more than debtors, exposing a significant disparity in protection levels. The chapter also underscored the potential for legal fragmentation and varying levels of protection due to the directive's reliance on national implementations and the absence of a clear definition of 'serious infringements'.

With this comprehensive understanding of the prohibited behaviours outlined in the CSCPD, the next chapter provides an in-depth analysis of enforcement and supervision mechanisms. It investigates the functions of contractual and administrative tools as well as the roles of competent authorities in guaranteeing compliance.

[38] CSCPD (n 1) art 10(2).

XVI
SUPERVISION AND COMPLIANCE IN THE CREDIT SERVICERS AND CREDIT PURCHASERS DIRECTIVE

16.1 Navigating a Legal Maze

The Credit Servicers and Credit Purchasers Directive's (CSCPD) supervisory mechanism perfectly illustrates the imbalance between credit servicers' and debtors' rights.[1] It comprises a *contractual* component, where the credit purchaser is responsible for monitoring compliance, and an *administrative* component based on the country-of-origin principle, overseen by the competent authorities of the home member state (MS) and, sometimes, co-shared with those of the host MS.

Both of these mechanisms possess inherent weaknesses that compromise their effectiveness. Moreover, their operational complexity contrasts with the simplicity of the credit servicers' authorization process and their ability to operate across borders. On the one hand, the contractual mechanism reverses the liability from the debt-collector to the debt-collection beneficiary, putting ultimate responsibility for any potential abuse on the debt-collector. On the other hand, the administrative mechanism based on the country-of-origin principle[2] entrusts the supervision of the debt-collector's behaviour to the competent authorities of the home MS, reversing the jurisdiction over tortious action, which is typically granted to the state where the harmful event took place.[3] As the next sections show, the design of the supervisory mechanism not only does not enhance debtor protection but deliberately diminishes and delays the debtors' ability to seek and obtain relief.

16.1.1 Contractual supervision and compliance

The CSCPD is based on a nexus of contracts between the stakeholders. Moreover, it introduced a new standard contract in the national legislation of the MS.[4] This

[1] Directive (EU) No 2021/2167 on credit servicers and credit purchasers [2021] OJ L438 (CSCPD).
[2] Trevor C Hartley, 'Basic Principles of Jurisdiction in Private International Law: The European Union, The United States and England' (2022) 71(1) International & Comparative Law Quarterly 211.
[3] ibid.
[4] Whether this new legislated contract is a *sui generis* contract (as the directive suggests) or merely a type of agency agreement is to be determined elsewhere.

EU Informal Debt-Collection Regulation. Cătălin-Gabriel Stănescu, Oxford University Press.
 DOI: 10.1093/oso/9780198966159.003.0016

is supported by the provisions of credit-servicing agreements regulated by the CSCPD's Article 11. However, the parties' compliance is left to each European Union (EU) jurisdiction. Party autonomy is severely reduced given that they must observe strict obligations prescribed by the directive and its transposition into national law.

16.1.1.1 The contractual nexus of the Credit Servicers and Credit Purchasers Directive

The original contract is the credit agreement concluded between the original creditor (i.e. the credit institution that provided the credit[5]) and the borrower, broadly defined as a legal or natural person who entered into a credit agreement with a credit institution, including its legal successor or assignee.[6] This agreement involves the former granting credit to the latter 'in the form of a deferred payment, a loan or other similar financial accommodation'.[7] The borrower may be a consumer,[8] leading to the application of specific provisions for consumer protection under EU and national law.

The subsequent contract is the credit-purchase agreement concluded between the original creditor and the credit purchaser (i.e. any natural or legal person other than a credit institution) by which the purchaser acquires the creditor's rights under a non-performing credit agreement[9] in the course of its trade, business, or profession, as per relevant EU and national law.[10]

Should the credit purchaser attempt to collect the debt arising from the non-performing agreement by using the services of a professional credit servicer (i.e. a legal person that, in the course of its business, manages and enforces the rights and obligations related to a creditor's rights under a non-performing credit agreement on behalf of a credit purchaser and carries out at least one or more credit-servicing activities,[11] as defined by the directive[12]), they will conclude a written credit-servicing agreement, by which the two parties will agree on the services to be provided by the credit servicer on behalf of the credit purchaser.

[5] CSCPD art 3(2).
[6] CSCPD (n 1) art 3(3).
[7] CSCPD (n 1) art 3(4).
[8] A consumer is defined as a natural person who, in credit agreements covered by the directive, is acting for purposes that are outside his trade, business, or profession. CSCPD (n 1) art 3(12).
[9] ibid art 3(13).
[10] ibid art 3(6).
[11] ibid art 3(8).
[12] Credit-servicing activities are grouped into four main categories: (a) collecting or recovering from the borrower any payments due to the creditor; (b) renegotiating with the borrower any terms and conditions related to the creditor's rights, in line with the instructions given by the credit purchaser, where the credit servicer is not a credit intermediary as defined by EU law; (c) administering any complaints relating to the creditor's rights under the credit agreement; and (d) informing the borrower of any changes in interest rates or charges or any payments due related to a creditor's rights under the credit agreement. CSCPD (n 1) art 3(9).

While the credit purchaser hires the credit servicer to perform credit-servicing activities, the servicer can enter into a written outsourcing agreement with a third-party credit service provider to conduct some, but not all, of the credit-servicing activities.[13] This outsourcing agreement is governed by Article 12 of the CSCPD, but the directive does not prescribe specific content for it; it only subjects the contract to certain conditions.

16.1.1.2 Legal implications and obligations in credit-servicing agreements

The key provisions in the credit-servicing agreement's content pertain to the requirement for the parties to adhere to EU and national laws concerning a creditor's rights under a credit agreement as well as the credit agreement itself. They include compliance with consumer and data-protection regulations.[14] Furthermore, the agreement should contain a clause mandating the fair and diligent treatment of borrowers.[15]

Although it may seem redundant to include these obligations in the agreement given that the parties are already obliged to comply with the law, explicitly restating these obligations holds legal significance. It transforms potentially abusive debt-collection practices into a contractual liability, which will run parallel to (but not fully overlap with) any potential administrative (contraventional) and civil liabilities arising from the CSCPD or (consumer-)debtor protection legislation (i.e. the Unfair Commercial Practices Directive or national fair debt-collection practices laws).

The provision effectively increases the supervision of the credit servicer, placing it under the oversight of the competent authorities in both the home and host MS as well as under that of the credit purchaser. The CSCPD maintains that even when the credit servicer is entrusted with managing and enforcing the credit agreement, the credit purchaser retains ultimate responsibility under the contract and the law.[16]

The credit-servicing agreement is crucial because it serves as written evidence and limits the credit purchaser's liability to the agreed-upon credit-servicing activities.[17] Any activities carried out by the credit servicer beyond the contractual terms will hold the servicer liable, but not necessarily the credit purchaser, as long as the latter can demonstrate that the former acted outside the agreement.

16.1.1.3 Outsourcing of credit-servicing activities and its impact on liability

Additionally, the credit purchaser's liability may be limited when the credit servicer outsources credit-servicing activities. According to the CSCPD, if the credit

13 ibid art 3(7).
14 ibid art 11(2)(d).
15 ibid art 11(2)(e).
16 CSCPD (n 1) recital 32.
17 ibid art 11(2)(a).

servicer utilizes a credit service provider for any credit-servicing activities, the credit servicer retains full responsibility for complying with all obligations under national provisions transposing the directive.[18] Because the legal requirement does not explicitly address contractual obligations, outsourcing certain activities to a third party does not automatically absolve the credit purchaser of their ultimate responsibility.

Despite this, the extent of the credit purchaser's liability is mitigated by the directive's stipulation that the credit servicer must ensure the credit service provider's compliance with relevant legal provisions. Additionally, the outsourcing agreement should not alter the contractual relationship between the credit servicer and the credit purchaser and the obligations of the credit servicer to the credit purchaser or borrowers.[19] Credit servicers are responsible for ensuring that outsourcing credit-servicing activities does not result in excessive operational risk or non-compliance by the credit service provider.[20]

Seeing as contractual liability does not travel down the contractual chain, monitoring does. As a result, the credit purchaser's primary concern is overseeing contractual performance and the credit servicer's compliance with contractual (and legal) obligations. Conversely, the credit servicer is concerned with scrutinizing the credit service provider's contractual performance.

16.1.1.4 Record-keeping requirements and implications for compliance

The CSCPD requires MS to ensure that credit servicers keep specific records for evidentiary purposes. These records encompass relevant correspondence between the credit purchaser and the borrower, instructions received from the credit purchaser regarding each non-performing credit agreement managed and enforced by the credit servicer on behalf of the credit purchaser, and the credit-servicing agreement. These records should be retained for a minimum of five to ten years following the termination of the credit-servicing agreement.[21] Credit service providers are also subject to this obligation, with the period calculated from the termination of the outsourcing agreement.[22] The implications of these provisions for consumers' rights under the GDPR were already discussed (see Chapter 13, Subsection 13.3), so they will not be restated here.

The directive stipulates that credit servicers and credit service providers must make these records available to the competent authorities.[23] Therefore, the archival obligations imposed on them are also intended to facilitate administrative

[18] ibid art 12(1).
[19] CSCPD (n 1) art 12(1)(a) and (c) and recital 31.
[20] ibid recital 31.
[21] CSCPD (n 1) art 11 (4).
[22] ibid art 12(3).
[23] ibid art 11(5) and art 12(4).

compliance. It logically follows that contractual and administrative liability complement each other, and one could be utilized as evidence for the other or vice versa.

16.1.1.5 Operational issues regarding borrower protection

The situation then becomes somewhat unclear. The aforementioned provisions are designed to assist the contractual parties in determining and assigning contractual (and potentially legal) responsibilities. Additionally, the directive addresses 'borrower' and 'consumer' protection, although borrowers (including consumers) are privy to the credit-servicing and credit-outsourcing agreements.

If the purpose is to protect borrowers and consumers via a contract, this is a straightforward extension of contractual limits like the one adopted by the Court of Justice of the EU (CJEU) in *Gelvora* (see Chapter 10, Subsection 10.1.2). In this case, the CJEU expressed concerns that outsourcing debt-collection activities to third parties could undermine the Unfair Commercial Practices Directive, consequently diminishing the level of consumer protection outlined in the directive.[24] This raises the question of why the EU legislator, instead of establishing an appropriate protective regime for borrowers and consumers, chose to push the boundaries of contractual limits, which challenge the fundamental principles of private law.

Other practical questions arise, such as what role and benefits can be derived from contractual provisions by involved parties. Subsequent inquiries concern the practical steps leading to contractual liability and their consequences. If borrowers are subjected to unfair debt-collection practices, to whom should they address their complaints—the credit servicer or the credit purchaser? The directive mandates credit servicers to establish effective internal procedures for handling borrower complaints,[25] but the same obligation does not bind credit purchasers. In such a scenario, should a credit purchaser forward the borrower's complaint to the credit servicer for investigation, or should it conduct its own investigation? If the credit servicer rejects the borrower's complaint, should the borrower 'appeal' to the credit purchaser, or can the credit purchaser 'rely' on the credit servicer's decision? Should the credit purchaser proactively monitor the activities of the credit servicer, or should it intervene only when prompted by borrower complaints? Assuming that the credit purchaser finds evidence of non-compliance by the credit servicer, which circumstances must be present and how many violations must be documented before the agreement can be terminated? Some of these questions could be addressed through meticulous contract drafting. Still, without clear

[24] Case C-357/16 *UAB 'Gelvora' v Valstybinė vartotojų teisių apsaugos tarnyba* [2017] ECLI:EU:C:2017:573 (*Gelvora*) paras 28, 30.

[25] CSCPD (n 1) recital 49.

guidelines, outcomes may vary depending on the parties' diligence and the competence of their legal advisors.

Further operational issues emerge from the differing interests and positions of the parties vis-à-vis borrowers. Credit purchasers are professional entities specialized in managing financial assets. They profit by gambling on the risk of non-payment,[26] purchasing NPL portfolios at a discount with the expectation of recovering more than their initial investment. Protecting the borrower is not a top priority for them. By holding them ultimately responsible as the primary beneficiaries of the credit-servicing agreement, the EU legislator aimed to make them equally invested in ensuring fair and professional credit-servicing activities. However, it is unlikely that consumers would be able to make a contractual claim against a credit purchaser for a credit servicer's non-compliance. It seems more likely that the intention aimed to enable credit purchasers to better manage risks arising from administrative supervision and avoid the repercussions of administrative enforcement by passing them down to their contractors and sub-contractors.

Another argument against the borrower-friendliness of contractual liability is the complexity that arises in cross-border settings. In such cases, it will be challenging for an aggrieved borrower or consumer to pursue a network of credit purchasers, credit servicers, and credit service providers, especially if they are registered in different home states. This creates a complex web of actors and jurisdictions that borrowers will find challenging to navigate. Consequently, any claims of contractual liability would have to be resolved in court through lengthy and expensive procedures, in which the credit purchasers and credit servicers may show little interest unless some form of administrative sanction has already been imposed on one of them.

16.1.2 Administrative supervision

The CSCPD's extensive administrative supervision and enforcement provisions should encourage and benefit borrowers. However, these provisions are dispersed throughout the directive: the general ones are consolidated under Title IV (Supervision), while those specifically applicable to cross-border credit servicers are found in Title II (Credit Servicers). Unfortunately, as the next sections indicate, these provisions establish a complex system unlikely to provide aggrieved borrowers with the necessary efficiency and adequate remedies.

The CSCPD recommends that MS empower their competent authorities with 'appropriate' administrative penalties and remedial measures applicable to a comprehensive, albeit not exhaustive, list of situations.[27] There is no definition of

[26] CSCPD (n 1) recital 7.
[27] CSCPD (n 1) art 23(1).

appropriateness; however, the directive recommends that the penalties and measures be effective, proportionate, and dissuasive and include authorization withdrawals, cease and desist orders, and monetary fines.[28]

16.1.2.1 The effectiveness requirement

The CSCPD urges MS to effectively implement administrative penalties and remedial measures.[29] It is unclear how MS will achieve this as existing empirical evidence suggests that administrative enforcement effectiveness is an issue. Furthermore, limited regulatory resources in some MS may weaken administrative enforcement due to insufficient expertise and financial resources. Industry representatives doubt that all MS will have the necessary budget, expertise, and operational capacity to meet all the directive's requirements.[30]

Empirical evidence indicates that even MS with experience and financial capabilities struggle to confront major or systemic fair debt-collection violations and must rely on third-party finances and expertise. For instance, the Danish Financial Supervisory Authority ordered Danske Bank to conduct and fund an impartial inquiry into its over-collection from thousands of customers over several years.[31] Although this is an innovative solution, it suggests that administrative enforcement may not be as reliable as EU legislators believe. More broadly, a report from the Public Audit Chamber of Romania revealed that although the National Authority for Consumer Protection imposes fines, institutional obstacles and a lack of cooperation mean that barely a fifth of the fines are collected from wrongdoers.[32]

16.1.2.2 The proportionality requirement

The proportionality assessment may be based on the 'relevant circumstances' expressly mentioned in the directive. These include the severity and duration of the infringement; the level of responsibility of the credit servicer, credit purchaser, or the latter's representative; the financial strength of the credit servicer or purchaser; the amount of profits gained or losses avoided due to the infringement; the losses caused to third parties by the breach (as far as those can be determined); the degree of cooperation with the competent authorities shown by the credit servicer and

[28] ibid art 23(2).

[29] ibid art 23(3).

[30] FENCA, 'Feedback on the European Commission's Proposal for a Directive on representative actions for the protection of the collective interests of consumers, and repealing Directive 2009/22/EC' (FENCA, 21 June 2018) 7 <https://fenca.eu/images/pdf/Publications/20180620_FENCA_Response_COM_Directive_Representative_Action.pdf> accessed 27 June 2023.

[31] Cătălin Gabriel Stănescu, 'Is There a Scandinavian Model for Regulating Abusive Informal Debt Collection Practices?' in Caroline Heide-Jørgensen, Ingrid Lund-Andersen, and Jesper Lau Hansen (eds), *Festskrift til Linda Nielsen* (Djøf Forlag 2022), 384–85 and n 115, 116.

[32] Romanian Court of Auditors, 'Raportului de audit asupra activității privind protecția consumatorilor pentru perioada 2015-2018 (Audit Report of Consumer Protection Activity 2015-2018)' (*Romanian Court of Auditors*, October 2020) <https://cdn.cursdeguvernare.ro/wp-content/uploads/2020/12/Curtea-de-conturi-raport-ANPC-Sinteza-_20201008.pdf> accessed 18 January 2023.

credit purchaser; any previous infringements; and the actual or potential systemic consequences of the breach.[33]

While these evaluation criteria are beneficial, the lack of clear and harmonized guidelines concerning what constitutes infringement will likely result in significant differences in approaches across MS, leading to inconsistency in the directive's application across the EU. Such inconsistency will create varying consumer protection standards, which, coupled with the jurisdiction of the home MS for enforcement purposes, will increase the likelihood of forum shopping.

The listed factors ensure that any administrative action taken against an infringing subject will be gradual and balanced, in line with the pyramid of 'responsive regulation' advanced by John Braithwaite.[34] Despite this, they allow the beneficiaries of the debt market to operate with a considerable degree of impunity. Empirical evidence from MS supports this observation. For instance, in response to a private inquiry, the Romanian National Authority for Consumer Protection revealed that between 2017 and 2021 it admitted 108 consumer complaints regarding abusive debt-collection, imposed five fines, and issued 'numerous' written notices.[35] Similarly, the Regional State Administrative Agency of Southern Finland reported no temporary or permanent revocations or terminations of registration for engaging in abusive informal debt-collection.[36]

16.1.2.3 The dissuasiveness requirement

The concept of dissuasiveness is even more complicated to apprehend. There is significant concern that the criteria outlined in the directive may result in the imposition of sanctions with limited deterrent effect despite using the annual turnover of the abusive credit servicer to calculate sanctions, as per the recommendations of the Enforcement Directive.[37]

[33] CSCPD (n 1) art 23(4).

[34] John Braithwaite, *Responsive Regulation* (Oxford University Press 2002) 30–34. Braithwaite's theory of 'responsive regulation' presents a dynamic framework for regulatory enforcement, advocating for a flexible approach that adjusts based on the conduct of the regulated entities. At its core, it is a model in which regulation begins with persuasion and cooperative measures, escalating only when necessary to more punitive actions, culminating in criminal penalties or licence revocation for non-compliance. This framework is encapsulated in a 'regulatory pyramid', which underscores the preference for cooperation over punishment but with the capacity for deterrence when voluntary compliance proves insufficient. Braithwaite's theory thus seeks to balance effective enforcement with avoiding over-regulation, ensuring a responsive and proportionate regulatory strategy. Sadly, this approach appears ill suited to counter the effects of abusive informal debt-collection.

[35] Based on the information gathered from the NACP, the numbers of complaints filed against debt-collectors are: 2017—359; 2018—175; 2019—257; 2020—258; 2021—221. Out of these, the number of complaints solved in favour of the debtor is miniscule: 2017—17; 2018—29; 2019—22; 2020—28; 2021—12. When discussing the fines applied, the numbers do not inspire confidence in their deterrent effect: three fines of approximately 6,000 euros, one fine of approximately 4,000 euros, one fine of approximately 500 euros, and numerous written notices.

[36] Letter from the Regional State Administrative Agency for Southern Finland to the author (May 27 2021).

[37] Directive (EU) 2019/2161 amending Council Directive 93/13/EEC and Directives 98/6/EC, 2005/29/EC and 2011/83/EU of the European Parliament and of the Council as regards the better enforcement and modernisation of Union consumer protection rules.

This concern aligns with Braithwaite's theory of responsive regulation.[38] Despite the focus on the proportionality principle and 'dissuasive' penalties, there is a risk of encouraging misbehaviour. Braithwaite's emphasis on cooperation was founded on the possibility of withdrawing the operational licence. Yet, empirical evidence indicates that this is seldom applied in practice,[39] allowing wrongdoers to escape with minor sanctions.

16.1.2.4 Procedural guarantees and potential for abuse

These principles are accompanied by procedural guarantees of fairness and access to justice, including the right to be heard before any decision regarding administrative penalties or remedial actions, well-reasoned decisions, and the right to appeal.[40] However, these guarantees also create the potential for abuse. Credit servicers and credit purchasers can exploit these procedural guarantees to prolong and transfer disputes to the courts, allowing them to further suspend and postpone any measures that might impact their interests or activities. Consequently, many penalties or remedial actions may exist only on paper, lacking practical effectiveness.

Another crucial aspect is the provision allowing MS to eliminate the option of combining administrative and criminal enforcement under national law. On the one hand, this entails the risk that actions falling under criminal law would be shifted to the criminal system, with all its hurdles. Empirical evidence indicates that criminal investigations throughout the EU typically take considerable time, which could further postpone sanctions or result in no action being taken if the breach is deemed non-severe. This raises the possibility of acting with impunity by flying under the criminal radar. On the other hand, it also introduces the potential for regulatory arbitrage because jurisdictions adopting such options would become more appealing to credit servicers and purchasers.

16.2 Enforcement by Home Rule: The Trouble with the Country-of-Origin Principle

The foundation for administrative supervision is the country-of-origin principle. This principle requires MS to ensure that credit servicers and credit service providers comply with national transposition measures *on an ongoing basis* and that those activities are subject to *adequate supervision by the competent authorities of the home MS*.[41] While this works well for credit purchasers and credit servicers

[38] Braithwaite (n 34) 29–44.

[39] For example, in a letter dated 26 April 2021, the Finnish Financial Supervisory Authority also reported that it has never sanctioned or taken any other enforcement action against a financial institution for abusive informal debt-collection practices.

[40] CSCPD (n 1) art 23(6) and (7).

[41] CSCPD (n 1) art 21(1).

operating in their home MS, it presents three types of issues in cross-border scenarios, as identified by Michaels in 2006: substantive, institutional, and methodological conflicts.[42]

16.2.1 Substantive issues

There is a significant substantive conflict between the CSCPD's country-of-origin principle and traditional private international law. Tasking the home MS's competent bodies with supervision and enforcement implies an inherent choice of law. It is unreasonable to expect a home MS authority to apply the laws of another (host) MS in these circumstances. The host MS's authorities are expected to cooperate, but any information concerning the alleged unlawful behaviour of credit servicers that they will transmit is likely to be treated as mere evidence in the home MS.

Moreover, private international law often designates the law of the country of destination as applicable in instances such as torts (i.e. the place of the injury) or consumer contracts (i.e. the passive consumer's habitual residence).[43] This does not align with the country of origin for a foreign credit servicer, further highlighting the conflict with consumer protection rules.

Recital 49 of the CSCPD emphasizes this conflict by stating that

> The provisions concerning infringements of this Directive are without prejudice to a Member State's right to intervene in case of infringements of national law relating to, for example, consumer protection, to borrower rights, or criminal activities. In such cases, the competent authorities of the host Member State and of the Member State where the credit was granted are competent to decide whether there has been an infringement of national law and thus, their powers are not limited by this Directive.

A notable absence to consider is that of a similar reassurance or distinction from the CSCPD's Articles. The powers of the host MS's competent authorities seem to be conditioned and subordinated to those of the home MS, raising institutional concerns and creating challenges in determining and assessing the severity of the credit servicer's unlawful actions committed outside of the home MS's territory. Consequently, the supervision of such actions depends on cooperation with the host MS's competent authorities, which in turn depends on their willingness, competence, and available resources.

[42] Ralf Michaels, *EU Law as Private International Law? Re-Conceptualising the Country-of-Origin Principle as Vested Rights Theory* (Duke Law School Legal Studies Paper No 122, 2006) <http://dx.doi.org/10.2139/ssrn.927479> 12–14.

[43] ibid 12.

16.2.2 Institutional issues

Under Article 14(8), (9), and (12) of the CSCPD, authorities in host MS have the right to independently conduct checks, inspections, and investigations into credit-servicing activities carried out within their jurisdiction by a credit servicer authorized in a home MS. However, the findings of such checks, inspections, or investigations must be promptly provided to the competent authorities of the home MS.

If the authorities in the host MS have evidence that a credit servicer conducting credit-servicing activities within its jurisdiction is violating the relevant regulations (including obligations stemming from national provisions implementing the CSCPD), they are required to share this evidence with the competent authorities of the home MS and request appropriate action. Nevertheless, they are empowered to impose suitable administrative penalties and corrective measures, but only under the following conditions:

1) They have already informed the competent authorities of the home MS.
2) The credit servicer continues to violate the applicable rules.
3) The credit servicer has not taken reasonable and practical steps to address the violation within a reasonable timeframe.
4) There is an urgent need for immediate action to address a severe threat to the collective interests of borrowers.

In addition, the authorities of the host MS have the authority to prohibit the further activities of a credit servicer that violates the applicable rules until the competent authority of its home MS makes an appropriate decision or the credit servicer takes steps to rectify the violation.

The directive's wording speaks for itself. In a cross-border setting, the role of the host MS's competent authorities is to provide assistance through investigation and communication. Direct measures, such as injunctions, penalties, or remedial actions, are possible but temporary and exceptional (conditional). For a host MS's competent authorities to act against a foreign credit servicer, the infringement must be 'systemic' and 'repeated', representing a severe threat to collective interests and ongoing non-compliance.

This effectively translates into selective enforcement. Most infringements affecting individual borrowers are likely to go unnoticed and unpunished. Even when measures are taken, they will face significant delays due to mandatory communications between competent authorities, leading to a convoluted supervision system that enables unethical and abusive practices. This system is evidently designed to malfunction and consume valuable time and resources, impairing the ability of competent authorities, even when willing and adequately resourced, to take prompt and effective action.

16.2.3 Methodological issues

Further problems emerge from the CSCPD's provisions. The directive mandates MS to designate competent authorities responsible for carrying out the functions and duties under the national transposition instrument. MS may choose multiple competent authorities, but they must clearly define their roles and responsibilities and appoint one as a central point of contact for exchanges with the competent authorities of the home and host MS.[44]

MS' freedom to select their competent authority could lead to a diverse network of institutions at the national level. Empirical data from 2021, predating the CSCPD, already highlighted this trend.[45] The situation is likely to worsen with the transposition of the directive into national law due to the absence of a precise and unique legal characterization of debt-collection at the national level.

Furthermore, MS can divide supervision, creating a complex and overly fragmented institutional framework. Notably, there is an existing division of supervisory tasks as specific professional categories involved in debt-collection, such as credit institutions, attorneys, notaries, and bailiffs, are governed by their own legal frameworks and supervisory bodies.[46] These parallel regimes, combined with the exclusions of several categories of creditors and credit servicers from the CSCPD's scope, further compound the complexity and the legal blind spots faced by borrowers (in general) and consumers (in particular) when seeking redress.

The implementation of the country-of-origin principle poses a more general methodological problem. Michaels highlighted the EC's efforts to promote legislative competition and limit the capacity of MS to discriminate against nonnationals in line with their market creation and development goals. At the same time, he added, MS might favour private international law rules, allowing them to retain some regulatory competencies.[47] In the case of the CSCPD, regulatory competition favours the debtor market's primary beneficiaries, credit purchasers and credit servicers, offering them a simplified EU-wide authorization procedure and supervision founded on the country-of-origin principle, which shields them from most national behavioural rules.

Conversely, MS are 'free' to design their own behavioural rules (under the guise of regulatory freedom), but they have limited authority over actions conducted on their territories by foreign credit servicers, reducing their ability to adequately protect their borrowers from the abusive behaviour of foreign entities. This regulatory freedom can lead to diverse protection regimes for borrowers and creates potential

[44] CSCPD (n 1) art 21(3) and (4).

[45] Cătălin Gabriel Stănescu, 'Regulation of Abusive Debt Collection Practices in the EU Member States: An Empirical Account' (2021) 44(1) Journal of Consumer Policy 179.

[46] CSCPD (n 1) art 2(5) and (6) and recital 23.

[47] Michaels (n 42) 13.

for regulatory arbitrage because credit servicers are likely to register in the MS with the most lenient laws.

16.3 Summary

The last three chapters critically examined the CSCPD and its implications for the EU's approach to NPLs and debt-collection regulation. Given that the directive is not a consumer protection instrument, it is unsurprising that it does not prioritize consumer protection. However, as these chapters revealed, the CSCPD's implementation will tremendously impact MS policies vis-à-vis informal debt-collection. It will likely trigger three sets of events. First, it will streamline and simplify debt-collectors' access to the entire EU market by harmonizing licensing requirements, facilitating data access, and standardizing the contractual provisions used by the industry. Second, its transposition into national law will lead to greater legal fragmentation in debt-collection regulation due to the lack of clear guidelines for permitted and prohibited debt-collection activities, leaving policy choices to the MS. Third, it will increase complexity for consumers and reduce enforcement efficiency by favouring home state agencies. The overall outcome is an imbalance between the benefits for the debt-collection industry and the challenges in protecting consumer-debtors.

XVII
IN LIEU OF CONCLUSIONS

So far, the book has addressed the failure of the European Union's (EU) legislators to implement sectoral legislation to regulate abusive informal debt-collection practices and revealed that the existing legal framework is insufficient to tackle them adequately. It also presented evidence suggesting that the failure to regulate was purposeful, mainly due to the influence of the powerful lobby of financial institutions. In addition, the previous chapters showed that fragmentation will deepen once the Credit Servicers and Credit Purchasers Directive (CSCPD) is fully transposed into national legislation.[1]

Instead of merely summarizing the book's findings, this final chapter takes the arguments further by examining the pros and cons of harmonizing informal debt-collection practices through sectoral regulation. This approach is proposed as an alternative explanation for the EU's failure to do so. To this end, the chapter will draw on the elements of economic analysis of legal rulemaking developed by Ehrlich and Posner[2] half a century ago.

In 1974, Ehrlich and Posner introduced a legal process theory suggesting that 'the desire to minimise costs is a dominant consideration in the choice between precision and generality in the formulation of legal rules and standards'.[3] They simplified the 'specificity-generality continuum' by framing it as a choice between 'rules' and 'standards'.[4] Ehrlich and Posner defined a 'standard' as a general criterion of social choice, such as reasonableness or fairness, which remains open-ended and does not list all the relevant circumstances but serves as the criterion for judging specific circumstances presented in a case.[5] To illustrate, a standard of behaviour was adopted through the Scandinavian debt-collection laws, which refer to 'good debt-collection practice',[6] and the CSCPD, which requires credit servicers to treat debtors 'fairly'.[7] In contrast, 'a rule excludes one or more relevant circumstances from the decision maker's consideration, as compared to a standard'.[8] For

[1] Directive (EU) No 2021/2167 on credit servicers and credit purchasers [2021] OJ L438 (CSCPD).

[2] Isaac Ehrlich and Richard A Posner, 'An Economic Analysis of Legal Rulemaking' (1974) 3(1) The Journal of Legal Studies 257.

[3] ibid 280.

[4] ibid 258.

[5] ibid 258.

[6] Cătălin Gabriel Stănescu, 'Is There a Scandinavian Model for Regulating Abusive Informal Debt Collection Practices?' in Caroline Heide-Jørgensen, Ingrid Lund-Andersen, and Jesper Lau Hansen (eds), *Festskrift til Linda Nielsen* (Djøf Forlag 2022) 376–378.

[7] CSCPD recital 20.

[8] Ehrlich and Posner (n 2) 258.

EU Informal Debt-Collection Regulation. Cătălin-Gabriel Stănescu, Oxford University Press.
 DOI: 10.1093/oso/9780198966159.003.0017

Ehrlich and Posner, the distinction between a rule and a standard is a matter of degree, that is, of level of precision.[9]

They also contend that when a legislature decides to enact a set of precise rules or a standard, it essentially chooses between legislative and judicial rulemaking. If a general legislative standard necessitates clarification, it becomes the responsibility of the courts to address this through the litigation process, resulting in the creation of rules particularizing the legislative standard. While the result may be similar, differences in the costs and benefits associated with legislative versus judge-made rules are likely. Thus, these factors should be considered when evaluating the efficiency of a legislative choice.[10]

Considering the above, legislators may opt for precise rules (e.g. sectoral legislation outlining the most egregious debt-collection practices) and vague ones (e.g. general standards of behaviour asking debt-collectors to observe good debt-collection practices) based on a careful evaluation of costs. This evaluation should encompass financial considerations and a thorough assessment of the advantages and disadvantages of each option. The debate over whether to implement precise regulations for informal debt-collection, as in the 2002 Consumer Credit Directive (CCD) proposal, or no or general rules, as reflected in the 2021 compromise text of the CSCPD, could benefit from an analysis using Ehrlich and Posner's theory. This may shed light on whether the choice of the EU legislators was justified by factors other than the interests of financiers.

Ehrlich and Posner's theory posits that the optimal balance between rules promulgated by the legislative, executive, and judicial branches of government aims to minimize social costs, assuming no externalities in the production of those rules.[11] Social loss is identified as relevant and encompasses losses from activities or outcomes that society wants to prevent (e.g. the consequences of violent or misleading behaviour vis-à-vis consumer-debtors), from the undesired deterrence of activities society wants to promote (e.g. unethical debt-collectors reaping more benefits than ethical ones), the enforcement costs of public rules, including the costs incurred by courts in the production of judge-made rules (e.g. the case-by-case application of general standards such as the obligation to treat debtors fairly), and the costs of producing statutory and administrative rules.[12]

According to Ehrlich and Posner, the precision of a law can be quantified based on 'the number of elementary situations or circumstances that are identified by that law to be either included or excluded from the universe of circumstances to which a sanction applies'.[13] In essence, precision is more about the *information* provided by the law than the *number of provisions*.[14] For example, a debt-collection

[9] ibid 258.
[10] ibid 261.
[11] ibid 281.
[12] ibid.
[13] ibid.
[14] ibid.

law could prohibit contacting the debtor at inconvenient times, during working hours, or between 8 p.m. and 7 a.m. Precision does not stem from the number of provisions so much as from the clarity and specificity of the content, which effectively defines what constitutes inconvenience for all parties involved.

To evaluate the optimum level of precision for legal obligations—that is, the choice that maximizes the excess of benefits over costs—Ehrlich and Posner examined the benefits and costs associated with various options, from precise rules to highly general standards. In their view, 'the fewer and simpler the facts to which definite legal consequences attach, the more precise is a legal obligation'.[15]

The *first* benefit of rules deals with *primary behaviour*: a fully detailed and comprehensive set of rules brings society closer to achieving its desired resource allocation by discouraging socially undesirable activities and promoting socially desirable ones.[16] This is accomplished by increasing the subjective probability of punishment for engaging in undesirable activities and reducing it for engaging in desirable ones. As Ehrlich and Posner explain, the cost of an activity includes the anticipated cost of punishment, which is the product of the subjective probability of the participant being apprehended and convicted. The probability of apprehension and conviction, in turn, depends on the likelihood that the activity will be deemed illegal and that the person engaging in it will be charged and convicted. The more precise and detailed the applicable substantive standard of the rule, the higher the probability that an activity will be considered illegal if it is undesirable and the lower the probability if it is desirable.[17] Thus, Ehrlich and Posner suggested that increasing specificity in rules would significantly deter undesirable activities by reducing variations in the outcomes associated with those activities.[18]

This perspective emphasizes the need to regulate and harmonize informal debt-collection legislation at the EU level. If EU legislators and member states (MS) are genuinely concerned about eradicating abusive debt-collection practices and ensuring a high level of consumer protection, establishing a unified and minimal set of clear rules outlining unacceptable behaviour by debt-collectors is essential. Rules such as those of the 2002 CCD proposal or the European Parliament's (EP) amendments to the CSCPD would have protected consumers and businesses. Furthermore, these rules would have facilitated the identification and penalization of unwanted behaviour by courts and supervisory agencies, especially in a cross-border setting such as the single market. Ultimately, they would have created a level playing field for all stakeholders and eliminated variations in protection across MS.

15 ibid 261.
16 ibid 262.
17 ibid.
18 By forcing non-compliant members to invest more resources in the activity than they could expect to gain: ibid.

To illustrate, in Spain, debt-collectors are still allowed to use fake hearses to shame debtors into paying due to the absence of sectoral legislation and the tolerance of practices that are not explicitly banned. In contrast, these tactics are forbidden in Denmark, where case law has clarified that such antics would contradict 'good debt-collection practice'.[19] These discrepancies in the treatment of Spanish and Danish consumers are difficult to justify and accept, especially in the context of the single market, but they remain possible. Had the EU legislator prohibited such practices through a specific rule in the CSCPD, debt-collectors would have been deterred from using them anywhere within the Union, and the variations in outcomes still prevalent across MS would have been reduced.

Ehrlich and Posner note that the precision of legal obligations significantly impacts primary behaviour. They argue that statutory rules are more influential in shaping behaviour than judge-made rules due to their broader scope.[20] This is particularly evident in civilian jurisdictions, where judges have limited rulemaking powers. As a result, general standards of behaviour established by statutory rules such as the CSCPD may have a restricted effect and hinder progress if they must be continually interpreted at the MS level on a case-by-case basis. This could lead to fragmentation and diverse interpretations of the standard.

These points clearly show why the EU should have incorporated the EP's amendments to the CSCPD regarding prohibited debt-collection practices. Without a well-defined set of rules, the EU's decision, in the 2021 compromise text of the CSCPD, to transfer regulatory responsibilities for debtor protection to MS only perpetuates fragmentation. Additionally, it indicates that the EU either lacks a clear understanding of which debt-collection activities are socially undesirable and warrant sanctions regardless of context and location or intentionally allows ambiguity, ultimately benefiting the industry. By rejecting the EP's proposal for a minimal list of banned practices that would have ensured greater precision and harmonization, the EU made a calculated and deliberate choice.

The *second* benefit concerns *legal-system behaviour*, under which Ehrlich and Posner address the effects of precision on behaviour within the legal system. Their analysis brings to light several noteworthy ideas. The starting one is that 'an increase in precision increases the probability of convicting the guilty and acquitting the innocent'.[21] Here, 'guilty' designates those engaged in socially undesirable activities (non-compliant), and 'innocent' refers to those engaged in socially desirable activities (compliant). From an economic perspective, this effect can also enhance the marginal productivity of the resources used by (public or private) law enforcers in prosecuting the guilty. In simpler terms, clear and precise rules enable

[19] Hans Gammeltoft-Hansen, *The Danish Ombudsman 2005—50 Years—50 Cases* (Folketingets Ombudsman 2005) 139–40.
[20] ibid 264.
[21] ibid 264.

enforcers to allocate resources more effectively towards prosecuting offenders rather than engaging in the litigation process to obtain the interpretation of a vague standard, which could go either way.

The next idea is that precise rules decrease the number of cases brought to court, thus reducing the total overall resources devoted to legal dispute resolution. This is because 'a rule withdraws from a lawsuit many of the issues that would have been litigable were the case decided under a standard'.[22] In essence, legal precision increases the *efficiency* of the legal system. This raises the question of why the EU legislator would introduce a solution that contradicts enforcement efficiency, particularly when compared to the simplicity and efficiency of the system established for creditors, debt buyers, and debt-collectors. The book's suggestion that the dichotomy between the advantages offered to the debt-collection industry and the deficiencies of consumer protection rules was deliberate seems to be supported by the lack of enforcement efficiency fostered by the current wording of the CSCPD.

Another idea to consider is *predictability* because 'the fact that the outcome of the dispute[,] if it is litigated, will be determined by the application of a rule rather than a standard should make it easier for the parties to predict the outcome'.[23] However, the EU's decision to reject a list of prohibited practices has diminished predictability and increased uncertainty in litigation outcomes for consumers. This uncertainty will disproportionately impact debtors, who typically have fewer resources and may be less inclined to act. The unpredictable nature of the outcome could generate even greater expense and hardship for consumers compared to those caused by being subjected to abusive practices, ultimately favouring the industry.[24]

Swiftness is another factor that would benefit from greater precision. As Ehrlich and Posner point out, 'the choice of rule versus standard affects speed, and hence indirectly the costs and benefits of legal dispute resolution'.[25] Generally, a decision based on a standard prolongs the time between the occurrence of the incident leading to the dispute and the final judicial resolution because the more matters are litigated, the likelier the trial is to last longer. This primarily results in heightened costs due to delays in the event of a legal error. Conversely, a decision based on rules tends to be quicker and, therefore, should minimize the expenses involved.

Since the CSCPD features only vague standards for debtor protection, one might argue that the resolution of disputes between aggrieved debtors and abusive

22 ibid 265.

23 ibid.

24 The best counterexample comes from the US, where the federal Fair Debt Collection Practices Act not only includes a non-exhaustive list of banned practices but also allows consumers to complain about technical violations of the act (rule breaches) and claim a fixed monetary compensation for each of them, which incentivizes them to take action against debt-collectors. See Fair Debt Collection Practices Act (FDCPA), Section 813, <https://www.ftc.gov/legal-library/browse/rules/fair-debt-collection-practices-act-text> accessed 22 July 2024.

25 Ehrlich and Posner (n 2) 266.

debt-collectors is severely delayed. This is further complicated by the enforcement mechanism, which prioritizes home state rules in administrative enforcement, making delays more of a certainty than a mere possibility. Once again, this situation contrasts starkly with the efficiency and expediency characterizing the rules governing the debt-collection profession.

Precise rules tend to summarize what has been learned in prior adjudications.[26] Thus, rules also increase **homogeneity**. In the case of the EU, establishing a properly functioning internal market with a high level of consumer protection requires at least a basic level of homogeneity. Concerning debt-collection, this fundamental homogeneity could have been determined by studying the existing sectoral legislation of the MS and finding their common denominator. As research showed, despite specific differences, there is significant convergence in what is deemed acceptable in informal debt-collection,[27] which could have been used to design minimal rules of behaviour at the EU level. By rejecting the precise rules proposed in the EP's amendments, the CSCPD triggered the opposite effect, namely, heterogeneity. Because sectoral regulation is delegated to the MS, the probable outcome is increased fragmentation and variety, an extended version of the pre-CSCPD situation.

Given that 'decision according to rule facilitates the social control of decision makers',[28] it increases **accountability** and reduces the likelihood of mistakes and misuse by adjudicators. According to Ehrlich and Posner, when the correct outcome of litigation is highly uncertain due to the numerous factors to be considered and the uncertain weight of each factor in evaluating a standard, it becomes more challenging to detect incompetence and corruption. In essence, implementing rules increases the predictability of litigation, simplifies the role of judges, and allows society to assess their competence and fairness. Conversely, the absence of clear rules creates opportunities for arbitrariness and corruption. Once again, the EU legislator has allowed for discretionary and divergent outcomes by failing to establish clear rules of conduct for debt-collectors operating across the EU and delegating this task to the MS.

The third benefit pertains to *deterrence*. Ehrlich and Posner argue that 'one method of increasing deterrence is to specify the prohibited conduct more exactly'.[29] This approach increases the likelihood of conviction by clearly defining the changes in behaviour needed to avoid punishment.[30] Although the CSCPD emphasizes the need for deterrent sanctions for unlawful behaviour by

[26] ibid 266.

[27] Cătălin Gabriel Stănescu, 'Regulation of Abusive Debt Collection Practices in the EU Member States: An Empirical Account' (2021) 44(1) Journal of Consumer Policy 179.

[28] Ehlrich and Posner (n 2) 267.

[29] Assuming that the loophole effect (underinclusion) is avoided by backing up the specific prohibition with a general prohibition: ibid 275.

[30] ibid 276.

debt-collectors, it does not clearly define the specific behaviours that should be deterred. By delegating this task to the MS, the directive inadvertently leads to the emergence of different types and levels of deterrence.

Despite the advantages of precise rules outlined above, the associated costs may have discouraged EU lawmakers from embracing them. The next paragraphs explore the various expenses related to enhancing the precision of a legal obligation.

First, according to Ehrlich and Posner, 'obtaining and correctly evaluating information concerning the various combinations of events or circumstances under which the general standard that the set of rules is designed to implement should be activated are costly'.[31] This means that the cost is likely higher when the conduct to be regulated is more heterogeneous. Still, this can hardly explain informal debt-collection regulation in the EU.

The observed heterogeneity primarily arises from two sources. The first is the absence of sectoral regulations in some countries, such as Spain, as opposed to the presence of sectoral regulations in others, such as Denmark. This contrast allows debt-collectors to utilize public shaming tactics in the former but prohibits them from doing so in the latter. The second source is the legislative and institutional decisions made by national lawmakers. For example, Denmark and Sweden have opted for open-ended behavioural standards, such as 'good debt-collection practice'. In contrast, Belgium and Romania rely on specific rules of conduct and standards. Heterogeneity can also emerge in legal systems based on similar standards that are interpreted and applied by different state agencies, such as the police, the Consumer Ombudsman in Denmark, and the Data Protection Authority in Sweden (until the adoption of the CSCPD).

However, there is no heterogeneity in conduct given that the informal debt-collection business model still relies on extensive data collection and communication with the debtor to convince them to repay all or part of the debt. Respect for the debtors' privacy, physical integrity, and human dignity cannot be deemed heterogeneous and too costly to harmonize.

A *second* possible explanation is the political cost. However, Ehrlich and Posner restrict political cost to politically controversial topics, which typically involve extensive negotiation among legislators.[32] It is difficult to determine whether informal debt-collection constitutes a controversial topic. Even if the legislators involved engaged in multiple rounds of negotiations that resulted in the compromise text of the CSCPD, the absence of precise rules of behaviour was not due to transaction costs. Instead, it stemmed from a power struggle, a 'game of interests' between the financial lobby (backed by the Directorate-General for Financial Stability, Financial Services, and Capital Markets Union [DG FISMA] and the MS via the Council of the European Union) and consumer interests (championed by

31 ibid 267.
32 ibid.

a few members of the EP). The 'compromise' involved the introduction of several general standards of behaviour for debt-collectors but lacked the specificity and precision of the rules put forward by the EP. This outcome is an improvement on the original proposal, which did not include such standards.

The *third* reason why precise rules may not be adopted is the risk of over- and under-inclusion. Because the human capability for prediction is limited and given the ambiguity of language, it is difficult for legislators to accurately and exhaustively account for all circumstances.[33] Under-inclusion can be addressed by supplementing rules with a standard, as seen in the EU's general provision in the Unfair Commercial Practices Directive. In contrast, over-inclusion is often managed by allowing for ad hoc exceptions at the enforcement level, which involves official discretion. Nevertheless, these solutions come at the cost of some of the benefits of governance by rules.[34]

According to Ehrlich and Posner, the problems of under- and over-inclusion are more serious the more significant the heterogeneity (or ambiguity or uncertainty) of the targeted conduct.[35] While this may hold in some contexts, it seems less applicable to informal debt-collection. The amendments proposed by the EP represented a bare minimum accepted by most MS with sectoral legislation (and some without, if their case law is any indication). In this light, under-inclusion may have been a more pressing concern than over-inclusion. Nonetheless, during the debates, the contention was never that the proposed rules were insufficient; instead, they lacked empirical justification and, thus, were unnecessary. Coincidentally, the same argument led to the removal of the rules governing debt-collection from the final version of the 2008 CCD. This suggests that stakeholders were not focused on the quantity of rules but on their potential impact on their business.

The issue of obsolescence, or the cost of adapting rules to keep up with economic and technological developments, is closely related. Ehrlich and Posner argue that standards are 'relatively unaffected by changes over time in the circumstances in which they are applied since a standard does not specify the circumstances relevant to the decision or the weight of each circumstance, but merely indicates the kinds of circumstance that are relevant'.[36] Furthermore, they contend that 'the more detailed a rule is, the more often it will have to be changed', making the meticulousness of precise rules an additional source of costs, including uncertainty brought about by legal changes.

The arguments against adopting precise rules are valid. However, they do not align with the concerns raised by EU legislators regarding the amendments proposed by the EP, which aimed to establish specific rules of conduct for

[33] ibid 268.
[34] ibid.
[35] ibid 270.
[36] ibid 277.

debt-collectors. In the discussion we had, FISMA acknowledged the potential future implementation of such rules. Additionally, the risk of obsolescence could have been mitigated by establishing a basic set of rules unaffected by technological or economic advancements, particularly those related to safeguarding consumers' well-being, privacy, and dignity, which would likely remain unchanged over time. The industry's significant efforts to avoid clear limitations on debt-collectors' conduct underscore the significance of such rules.

As for the potential need to revise the detailed rules frequently, this cannot be deemed an explanation because the EU has not averted this risk. On the contrary, delegating the regulation of informal debt-collection to the MS at the national level could lead to the issue persisting and being compounded across twenty-seven different jurisdictions. Because the likelihood that legal changes would occur at the same pace, time, and shape in all MS is low, more fragmentation would occur, favouring businesses. In this scenario, implementing a set of harmonized rules at the EU level would have decreased any costs associated with law-making and increased related benefits, whereas passing the task to the MS multiplies costs and increases uncertainty and variation at the expense of society.

A *fourth* type of cost involves hiring experts, such as lawyers, to provide guidance and advice on legal compliance, operate tribunals, and represent parties before them in legal disputes. According to Ehrlich and Posner, if rules are precise, legal uncertainty decreases, reducing the demand for experts to interpret them. Conversely, using standards instead of rules may increase the demand for lawyers' services.[37] However, there is no conspicuous indication that the EU legislator considered this in its decision to adopt standards instead of rules for informal debt-collection.

Ehrlich and Posner also discuss a *fifth* reason why adopting precise rules may not always be justified. So far, the assumption was that increasing the specificity of a legal prohibition always increases the certainty of the prohibition. Yet, that is not always the case: in some instances it may reduce certainty, imposing costs that are usually associated with standards.[38] This is because precision can only be measured with reference to the addressee of a rule. Therefore, a rule may be precise to one group (adjudicators) and imprecise to another (potential wrongdoers).[39] However, such precision effects are more likely to impact consumer-debtors. Debt-collectors are professionals and repeat players. Therefore, even if the rules may seem 'imprecise' initially, they will soon become familiarized with their meaning because they are legally required to comply with them. As with the fourth reason above, there is no indication in the CSCPD or in the discussions surrounding the

[37] ibid 270–71.
[38] ibid 271.
[39] ibid.

EP's proposed amendments that 'imprecision' was considered an obstacle to the amendments' adoption.

One of the fundamental implications of the model advanced by Ehrlich and Posner is that 'anything that increases the benefits or reduced the costs, of legal precision ... will increase the optimum number of precision of rules'.[40] This has not been observed in the revision of the CCD or the adoption of the CSCPD. This does not necessarily invalidate their theory, but testing their hypothesis is beyond the scope of this book.

The EU is not a state; its legislative process is complex, constrained by treaties and influenced by powerful lobbyists. Even if the EU legislators believed that the costs of implementing precise rules at the EU level were too high, these costs might still be incurred at the national level, resulting in varying levels of precision and protection. The cost of these consequences is greater for the EU's legal order, which brings back the question of why harmonization was not realized in the first place. The answer is that the debt-collection industry benefits from fragmentation. The absence of precise rules is not due to cost considerations in law-making but to the deliberate creation of ambiguity and complexity. The failure to implement precise rules for informal debt-collection is intentional.

Another aspect must be mentioned. According to Ehrlich and Posner, statutory rules incur higher marginal costs than judge-made rules because the benefits of statutory rules are typically greater.[41] However, because imperfect specificity contributes to the social cost of any rule, statutory rules are less likely to achieve perfect specificity than judge-made rules.[42] This greater cost of statutory rules would explain why such rules are more difficult to revise or modify than judge-made rules.[43]

Indeed, in EU law, the likelihood of revision is low and would require a significant amount of time. Therefore, once insufficient or improper rules are implemented, they will be difficult to change. Nevertheless, the opposite is also true. Not implementing any rules, with the expectation that this will be done in the future (as FISMA suggested during our discussion), could lead to prolonged periods of heterogeneity, fragmentation, and uncertainty, with significant adverse effects for consumers.

A *sixth* explanation for rejecting precise rulemaking could be an increased delegation of tasks to administrative agencies. Ehrlich and Posner noted that 'the importance of agencies relative to courts, as sources of rules has increased dramatically'.[44] However, that is not the case in the EU, where there is no rulemaking agency at the union level to deal with consumer protection rules. This role remains shared among the EU and national legislatures.

[40] ibid 272.
[41] ibid 273.
[42] ibid.
[43] ibid 274.
[44] ibid 280.

Perhaps the most revealing aspect emerging from Ehrlich and Posner's model is their expectation that 'rules will be more precise the higher the level of economic (or other) activity in the society'.[45] The benefits of detailing a rule are greater the more considerable the amount of activity it governs. Conversely, the costs of detailing a rule will likely be independent of the regulated activity's scale (as opposed to complexity or variety).[46] While theoretically sound, this assertion appears to be contradicted by the way EU legislators handled the idea of regulating informal debt-collection practices.

The apparent contradiction lies not in Ehrlich and Posner's argument but rather in the EU's legislative process. This book has shown the magnitude of the debt-collection market, the debt-collection industry's critical role in the economy and the financial system's stability, its tremendous impact on consumer well-being, and the potential social consequences of unchecked informal debt-collection activities. Ehrlich and Posner correctly assert that factors such as these warrant comprehensive and precise regulation. Yet, this has not been the case. Once again, a pressing question arises: 'why?' The answer is that the interests of those who should have been subject to regulation have prevailed. Despite the clear societal benefits of meticulous governance of a high-impact economic activity such as debt-collection, the industry has evaded, influenced, and controlled the legislative process. Consequently, instead of advancing and safeguarding the welfare of their citizens, EU lawmakers have been more responsive to the interests of businesses, delaying or limiting regulation. As a result, consumer-debtors find themselves waiting for much-needed relief.

[45] ibid 274.
[46] ibid.

Bibliography

Newspaper Articles & Web Sources

BDIU, Die Europäische Datenschutz-Grundverordnung Best Practice Guide 2.0, Leitfaden für den Bereich (20 November 2019) <https://www.inkasso.de/fileadmin/user_upload/mitgliederinformationen/BestPracticeGuideZweiPunktNull_BDIU_DSGVOimForderungsmanagement.pdf>.

BDIU, Stellungnahme Entwurf der Bundesregierung eines Ersten Gesetzes zur Änderung des Bundesdatenschutzgesetzes (9 April 2024) <https://www.inkasso.de/fileadmin/user_upload/stellungnahmen/2024_04_09_BDIU_Stellungnahme_zum_RegE_BDSG_AendG.pdf>.

Bird & Bird, 'CJEU will rule on whether bailiffs can sell databases with personal data in enforcement proceedings' (31 January 2024) <https://www.twobirds.com/en/insights/2024/poland/cjeu-will-rule-on-whether-bailiffs-can-sell-databases-with-personal-data-in-enforcement-proceedings>.

Boeddu G, Chien J, Istuk I, and Lopes L, *Protecting Financial Consumers During the COVID-19 Crisis World Bank Blogs* (8 May 2020).

Brown JM and Smith R, 'Europe's debt collectors face own loan concerns' *Financial Times* (22 November 2017) <https://archive.is/20220322074448/https://www.ft.com/content/1bc35d86-c9e9-11e7-aa33-c63fdc9b8c6c>.

Bundesverband Deutscher Inkasso-Unternehmen (BDIU), 'Targeted consultation on improving transparency and efficiency in secondary markets for non-performing loans (NPLs)' (8 September 2021) <https://www.inkasso.de/fileadmin/user_upload/stellungnahmen/2021_09_08_BDIU_Targeted_Consultation_Data_Hub.pdf>.

Caldweel S, Richardson J, and Hakes RM 'EU Directive for NPLs sets new standards for investors and servicers' (7 February 2022) <https://www.reedsmith.com/en/perspectives/2022/02/eu-directive-for-npls-sets-new-standards-for-investors-and-servicers>.

Campbell D, 'Aggressive debt collectors raise risk of suicide' *The Guardian* (3 December 2018) <https://www.theguardian.com/society/2018/dec/03/aggressive-debt-collectors-raise-risk-of-suicide>.

Carsten D, 'Säumige Kunden sind ein Warnsignal für Konjunkturprobleme' *Die Welt* (22 June 2016) <https://www.welt.de/print/die_welt/wirtschaft/article156438246/Saeumige-Kunden-sind-ein-Warnsignal-fuer-Konjunkturprobleme.html>.

Cloutier E, 'Non-performing loans: early signs point towards an increase next year' (November 2022) <https://kpmg.com/xx/en/home/insights/2022/11/non-performing-loans-early-signs-point-towards-an-increase-in-2023.html>.

CMS, 'A global overview of coronavirus (COVID-19) related moratorium on corporate and retail loans' *CMS* (9 April 2020) <https://cms.law/en/media/local/cms-dsb/files/a-global-overview-of-coronavirus-covid-19-related-moratorium-on-corporate-and-retail-loans>.

Croatian Personal Data Protection Agency, 'Debt collection agency EOS Matrix d.o.o imposed with an administrative fine in the amount of 5.47 million EUR' *AZOP* (5 October 2023) <https://azop.hr/debt-collection-agency-eos-matrix-d-o-o-imposed-with-administrative-fine-in-the-amount-of-5-47-million-euros/>.

Dey D, Heuer D, Landsbert V, Rubinoff J, and Seifman L, 'Covid-19 and the State of the European NPL Market' (April 2021) <https://www.whitecase.com/insight-our-thinking/covid-19-and-state-european-npl-market>.

Duncan E and Ramnarayan A, 'Debt collectors' awkward moment: their own debt is now sinking' *Bloomberg* (23 June 2023) <https://www.bloomberg.com/news/articles/2023-06-23/debt-collectors-awkward-moment-their-own-debt-is-now-sinking?embedded-checkout=true>.

EOS, 'EOS worldwide' (*EOS*) <https://eos-solutions.com/worldwide-companies>.

EOS, 'Homepage' (*EOS*) <https://de.eos-solutions.com/en/eos-deutschland-b2c>.

EOS, 'Our responsibility 2022/23' *EOS* (July 2023) 8 <https://eos-solutions.com/en/dam/jcr:40ca1401-7c57-4d18-8e4f-734b10853cc1/EOS%20Our%20Responsibility%202022-23.pdf>.

European Commission, 'Statistics' (*European Commission*) <https://commission.europa.eu/topics/statistics_en>.

European Commission, 'Transposition status—Credit Servicers and Credit Purchasers Directive' (*European Commission*) <https://finance.ec.europa.eu/credit-servicers-and-credit-purchasers-directive_en>.

European Council and Council of the European Union, 'EU budget for 2022' (*European Council and Council of the European Union*) <https://www.consilium.europa.eu/en/policies/eu-annual-budget/2022-budget/>.

Eurostat, 'Households—statistics on financial assets and liabilities' (*Eurostat*) <https://ec.europa.eu/eurostat/statistics-explained/index.php?title=Households_-_statistics_on_financial_assets_and_liabilities#Structure_of_assets_and_liabilities>.

Federation of European National Collection Associations (FENCA), 25 years of FENCA—How this all started <https://fenca.eu/news/25-years-of-fenca-how-this-all-started>.

FENCA, '2008 Code of Conduct' (FENCA) <https://juliorosonvsbbva.files.wordpress.com/2010/05/fenca-code-of-conduct.pdf>.

FENCA, 'About FENCA' (*FENCA*) <https://fenca.eu/#>.

FENCA, 'Affiliate members' (*FENCA*) <https://fenca.eu/members/affiliate-members>.

FENCA, 'Code of Conduct' (*FENCA*) <https://fenca.eu/images/pdf/FENCA_Code_of_Conduct.pdf>.

FENCA, 'Comments of Fenca (Federation of European Collection Associations) on the ePrivacy Regulation concerning the respect of private life and the protection of personal data in electronic communications' (*FENCA*) <https://fenca.eu/images/pdf/FENCA-Position-on-ePrivacy.pdf>.

FENCA, 'Comments on the European Commission draft Regulation on Data Protection COM(2012) 11 final' (2015) <https://fenca.eu/images/pdf/2015/fenca_data_protection_com.pdf>.

FENCA, 'Congress 2018. FENCA adopts Code of Conduct for GDPR and elects new Board' (2018) <https://fenca.eu/news/fenca-congress-2018>.

FENCA, 'Declaration on COVID-19' (22 April 2020) <https://fenca.eu/news>.

FENCA, 'EU General Data Protection Regulation Threatens Work of Collection Companies' <https://fenca.eu/news/eu-general-data-protection-regulation-threatens-work-of-collection-companies>.

FENCA, 'Feedback on the European Commission's Proposal for a Directive on credit servicers, credit purchasers and the recovery of collateral' (8 June 2018) <https://fenca.eu/images/pdf/Publications/20180608_FENCA_Response_COM_Directive_Proposal_Credit_Servicers_and_Purchasers.pdf>.

FENCA, 'Feedback on the European Commission's Proposal for a Directive on representative actions for the protection of the collective interests of consumers, and repealing Directive 2009/22/EC' (21 June 2018) <https://fenca.eu/images/pdf/Publications/20180620_FENCA_Response_COM_Directive_Representative_Action.pdf>.

FENCA, 'FENCA is working on a pan-European Code of Conduct' <https://fenca.eu/news/federation/fenca-is-working-on-a-pan-european-code-of-conduct>.

FENCA, 'FENCA welcomes European Commission announcement of COVID-19 Best Practices' (14 July 2020) <https://fenca.eu/news>.

FENCA, 'Position paper on the Data Protection—Recast' (11 April 2013) <https://fenca.eu/images/pdf/2013/position-paper-on-data-protection.pdf>.

FENCA, 'Response to European Commission Consultation' (20 October 2017) <https://fenca.eu/images/pdf/Publications/20171020_FENCA_Response_NPL_Consultation.pdf>.

FENCA, 'Survey no 6: debts referred to member associations' (August 1999) <https://www.fenca.org/images/pdf/surveys/6.debts_referred.pdf>.

FENCA, 'White paper on the requirements of the GDPR to business activities of debt collection agencies' <https://fenca.org/images/pdf/NL_Summer_17/BDIU_White_Paper_GDPR.pdf?acm=2891_46>.

FIGEC, 'Nos Missions' (*FIGEC*) <https://www.figec.com/nos-missions/>.

Financial Services User Group (FSUG) *Nonperforming Loans (NPLs)—Letter to the European Commission* (2018).

FitchRatings, 'Rating action commentary: Fitch Affirms Intrum at BB/Stable' (11 July 2022) <https://www.fitchratings.com/research/non-bank-financial-institutions/fitch-affirms-intrum-at-bb-stable-11-07-2022>.

Fleming S and Brunsden J, 'EU banks urged to prepare for bad loans as pandemic hits economy' *Financial Times* (1 November 2020) <https://www.ft.com/content/3c6b4eb0-5b3d-4a37-87e5-d83da8de217d>.

Hager E, 'Debtors' prisons, then and now: FAQ' *The Marshall Project* (24 February 2015) <https://www.themarshallproject.org/2015/02/24/debtors-prisons-then-and-now-faq>.

Harley G and Petkova S, 'What happens if you don't pay your bill? Lessons from Central and Eastern Europe' *World Bank Blogs* (18 July 2017) <https://blogs.worldbank.org/europeandcentralasia/what-happens-if-you-don-t-pay-your-bill-lessons-central-and-eastern-europe>.

Huertas M and Schelling H, 'European Union: the EU's new credit servicers directive—Where are we now' *Mondaq* (19 March 2020) <https://www.mondaq.com/germany/dodd-frank-consumerprotection-act/904974/the-eu39s-new-credit-servicers-directive-where-are-we-now>.

IMY, 'Elkunder ersätts för dubbla inkassokostnader' *IMY* (12 November 2012) <https://www.imy.se/om-oss/arkiv/nyhetsarkiv/elkunder-ersatts-for-dubbla-inkassokostnader/>.

International Monetary Fund, 'Romania: Letter of Intent, Memorandum of Economic and Financial Policies, and Technical Memorandum of Understanding' (10 June 2013).

Intrum, 'About our company' (*Intrum*) <https://www.intrum.com/about-us/company-info/about-our-company/>.

Jungmann N, 'Dutch debt collection system requires major reform, experts say' *NL Times* (5 October 2023) <https://nltimes.nl/2023/10/05/dutch-debt-collection-system-requires-major-reform-experts-say>.

Koltay G and Lorincz S, 'Industry concentration and competition policy' *Competition Policy Brief* Issue 2021/02 (November 2021) <https://competition-policy.ec.europa.eu/system/files/2021-12/Competition%20Policy%20Brief%202-2021_Industry%20concentration%20and%20competition%20policy.pdf>.

Listflix, 'Inkassounternehmen Statistik Deutschland' (*Listflix*) <https://listflix.de/statistik/inkassounternehmen/>.

Macchiarelli C, Giacon R, Georgosouli A, and Monti M, 'Why nonperforming loans are still putting the European banking union' *LSE Blogpost* (27 March 2019) <https://blogs.lse.ac.uk/europpblog/2019/03/27/why-non-performing-loans-are-still-putting-the-european-banking-union-at-risk/>.

Manning AJ, 'Thinking of jailing debtors as Dickensian? Think again' *The Harvard Gazette* (19 September 2023) <https://news.harvard.edu/gazette/story/2023/09/how-common-is-debt-imprisonment-in-u-s-today/>.

Mazuir B, 'Le recouvrement à travers l'Histoire—Partie 1' (2016) <http://www.leblogdurecouvrement.com/le-recouvrement-a-travers-lhistoire-partie-1/>.

NVI, 'Uitspraken klachten voor Wki' (*NVI*) <https://nvi.nl/uitspraken-inzake-klachten>.

Olsen JB, 'Købmandstandens OplysningsBureau' <https://denstoredanske.lex.dk/Købmandstandens_OplysningsBureau>.

Penty C, 'Debt collectors in hearses are a rare booming business in Spain' *Bloomberg* (13 December 2022) <https://www.bloomberg.com/news/articles/2022-12-13/for-debt-collectors-driving-fake-hearses-business-is-booming>.

Pirolo A, 'Decade ends with lowest NPL levels on European bank balance sheets since 2010' *Debtwire* (13 January 2021) <https://events.debtwire.com/decade-ends-with-lowest-npl-levels-on-european-bank-balance-sheets-since-2010>.

Popescu A, 'Sunteti hartuit de recuperatorii de creante? Un avocat va spune ce trebuie sa faceti' *DC Business* (20 September 2022) <https://www.dcbusiness.ro/sunteti-hartuit-de-recuperatorii-de-creante-un-avocat-va-spune-ce-trebuie-sa-faceti_648279.html>.

Reuters, 'Debt collectors make Europe's bad loans pay again' (14 June 2017) <https://www.financialexpress.com/policy/economy-debt-collectors-make-europes-bad-loans-pay-again-717307/>.

Sainsbury D, 'Eugène-François Vidocq and the birth of the detective' (7 February 2024) <https://publicdomainreview.org/essay/eugene-francois-vidocq-and-the-birth-of-the-detective/>.

The Draft Common Frame of Reference, Book III, Chapter 5, Section 1 <https://www.trans-lex.org/400725/_/outline-edition-/>.

The Principles of European Contract Law, Chapter 11 <https://www.trans-lex.org/400200/_/pecl/>.

Trading Economics and European Central Bank, 'Euro Area consumer credit' (*Trading Economics*) <https://tradingeconomics.com/euro-area/consumer-credit>.

Trustpilot, 'EOS solutions' (*Trustpilot*) <https://www.trustpilot.com/review/de.eos-solutions.com>.

Trustpilot, 'Intrum' (*Truustpilot*) <https://www.trustpilot.com/review/intrum.com>.

Trustpilot, 'Transparency Report 2022' (*Trustpilot*) <https://cdn.trustpilot.net/trustsite-consumersite/trustpilot-transparency-report-2022.pdf>.

Tsouni R, 'The NPL situation in Europe for Q3 2022 and beyond' <https://www.exus.co.uk/blog/the-npl-situation-in-europe-for-q3-2022-and-beyond>.

UNIREC, 'Buone Prassi' (*UNIREC*) <https://unirec.it/buone-prassi>.

Za V, 'Europe's debt collectors face reckoning as bad loans vanish' *Reuters* (20 March 2023) <https://www.reuters.com/markets/europe/europes-debt-collectors-face-reckoning-bad-loans-vanish-2024-03-20/>.

Contributions to Edited Books

Belvederesi-Kochs R, Moral or Modern Marketing? Sparkassen and Consumer Credit in West Germany, in Logemann J (ed), *The Development of Consumer Credit in Global Perspective: Business, Regulation, and Culture* (Palgrave Macmillan 2012).

Caponi R and Novak JT, 'Access to Justice' in Hess B and Law S, *Implementing EU Consumer Rights by National Procedural Law. Luxembourg Report on European Procedural Law: Vol II* (Beck Hart Nomos 2019).

Cohn TH, 'The Effects of Regulatory Capture on Banking Regulations: A Level-of-Analysis Approach' in Hira A, Gaillard N, and Cohn TH (eds), *The Failure of Financial Regulation. Why A Major Crisis Could Happen Again* (Springer 2019).

Holtz HM, 'Regulation of Abusive Informal Debt Collection Practices: Sweden' in Stănescu CG (ed), *Regulation of Debt Collection in Europe: Understanding Informal Debt Collection* (Routledge 2023).

Isidro MR, 'Assignability/Assignment of Claims' in Basedow J, Ruhl G, Ferrari F and De Miguel Asensio P (eds), *Encyclopedia of Private International Law*, Vol 1 (Edward Elgar 2017).

Kaprou E, Abusive Informal Debt Collection Practices in Greece, in Stănescu CG (ed), *Regulation of Debt Collection in Europe: Understanding Informal Debt Collection* (Routledge 2023).

Kepinski J, Regulation of Abusive Informal Debt Collection Practices: Poland, in Stănescu CG (ed), *Regulation of Debt Collection in Europe: Understanding Informal Debt Collection* (Routledge 2023).

Leone C and van Duin J, 'Doubling Down on Debt?' in Stănescu CG (ed), *Regulation of Debt Collection in Europe: Understanding Informal Debt Collection* (Routledge 2023).

Lurger B, 'Assignment' in Smits JM, Husa J, Valcke C and Narciso M (eds), *Elgar Encyclopedia of Comparative Law* (Edward Elgar 2023).

Mak V, 'Financial Services and Consumer Protection' in Twigg-Flesner C (ed) *Research Handbook on EU Consumer and Contract Law* (Edward Elgar 2016).

Markworth D, 'Debt Collection Services in Germany. A Sector in Turmoil' in Stănescu, CG (ed), *Regulation of Debt Collection in Europe: Understanding Informal Debt Collection* (Routledge 2023).

McFarlane B, 'Assignment and Novation' in Beale H (gen ed), *Chitty on Contracts*, Vol 1 General Principles (23rd ed, Sweet and Maxwell 2023).

Mikuš M, 'Making Debt Work: Debating and Devising Debt Collection in Croatia' in Hann C and Kalb D (eds) *Financialization: Relational Approaches* (Berghahn Books 2020).

Poretti P, 'Regulation of Abusive Informal Debt Collection in Croatia' in Stănescu CG (ed), *Regulation of Debt Collection in Europe: Understanding Informal Debt Collection* (Routledge 2023).

Porter T, 'Risk Models and Transnational Governance in the Global Financial Crisis: The Cases of Basel II and Credit Rating Agencies' in Helleiner E, Pagliari S, and Zimmermann H (eds), *Global Finance in Crisis: The Politics of International Regulatory Change* (Taylor and Francis 2010).

Posner RA, 'The Concept of Regulatory Capture. A Short, Inglorious History' in Carpenter DP and Moss DA (eds), *Preventing Regulatory Capture: Special Interest Influence and How to Limit It* (CUP 2014).

Ramsay I, 'Changing Policy Paradigms of EU Consumer Credit and Debt Regulation' in Leczykiewicz D and Weatherill S (eds), *The Involvement of EU Law in Private Law Relationships* (Hart Publishing 2013).

Ringe W-G, 'The Law of Assignment in European Contract Law' in Gullifer L and Vogenauer S (eds), *English and European Perspectives on Contract and Commercial Law. Essays in Honour of Hugh Beale* (OUP 2014).

Rochemont S, 'The Payments Revolution. Toward Financial Exclusion or Inclusion' in Stanescu CG and Gikay AA (eds), *Discrimination, Vulnerable Consumers and Financial Inclusion. Fair Access to Financial Services* (Routledge 2021).

Sein K, 'Abusive Debt Recovery Practices in Estonia' in Stănescu CG (ed), *Regulation of Debt Collection in Europe: Understanding Informal Debt Collection* (Routledge 2023).

Stănescu CG, 'Digital Debt Collection. Opportunities, Abuses and Concerns' in Stănescu CG and Gikay AA (eds) *Discrimination, Vulnerable Consumers and Financial Inclusion. Fair Access to Financial Services and the Law* (Routledge 2021).

Stănescu CG, 'Is there a Scandinavian Model for Regulating Abusive Informal Debt Collection Practices?' in Heide-Jørgensen C, Lund-Andersen I, and Hansen JL (eds), *Festskrift til Linda Nielsen* (Djøf Forlag 2022).

Stănescu CG, 'Regulation of Informal Debt Collection. An Introduction' in Stănescu CG (ed), *Regulation of Debt Collection in Europe: Understanding Informal Debt Collection* (Routledge 2023).

Stănescu CG and Albanezi A, 'Romania's Struggle to Regulate Informal Debt Collection Practices' in Stănescu CG (ed), *Regulation of Debt Collection in Europe: Understanding Informal Debt Collection* (Routledge 2023).

Books

Akos R-T and Alya G, *Plastic Money. Constructing Markets for Credit Cards in Eight Postcommunist Countries* (Stanford UP 2014).

Beck TR, *Inkassounternehmen und der Erfolg beim Forderungseinzug* (Springer 2013).

Ben-Menahem H and Hecht NS, *Topics in Jewish Law* (The Open University of Israel Publishing House 1993).

Braithwaite J, *Responsive Regulation* (OUP 2002).

Brown S, *The Regulation of Consumer Credit. A Transatlantic Analysis* (Edward Elgar 2019).

Calder L, *Financing the American Dream. A Cultural History of Consumer Credit* (Princeton UP 1999).

Comparato G, *The Financialisation of the Citizen: Social and Financial Inclusion through European Private Law* (Hart Publishing 2018).

Deville J, *Lived Economies of Default: Consumer Credit, Debt Collection and the Capture of Affect* (Taylor and Francis 2015).

Drezner DW, *The System Worked. How the World Stopped Another Great Depression* (OUP 2014).

Farrow TCW, *Civil Justice, Privatisation and Democracy* (University of Toronto Press 2014).

Ferretti F, *Comparative Aspects of Consumer Over-Indebtedness. A View from the UK, Germany, Greece, and Italy* (Eleven International Publishing 2016).
Ferretti F and Vandone D, *Personal Debt in Europe* (CUP 2019).
Finlay S, *Consumer Credit Fundamentals* (Palgrave Macmillan 2005).
Fuchs D, *Business Power and Global Governance* (Boulder and London, Lynne Rienner 2007).
Gammeltoft-Hansen H, *The Danish Ombudsman 2005: 50 Years—50 Cases* (Folketingets Ombudsman 2005).
Gardner J, Gray M, and Moser K, *Debt and Austerity: Implications of the Financial Crisis* (Edward Elgar 2020).
Gelpi R-M and Julien-Labruyere F, *The History of Consumer Credit. Doctrines and Practices* (Palgrave Macmillan 2000).
Gleeson S, *The Legal Concept of Money* (OUP 2018).
Goode R and McKendrick S, *Commercial Law* (Penguin 2016).
Graeber D, *Debt: The First 5,000 Years* (Melville House 2014).
Hiilamo H, *Household Debt and Economic Crisis. Causes, Consequences, Remedies* (Edward Elgar 2018).
Hillairet J, *Gibets, piloris et cachots du vieux Paris* (Paris éditions de Minuit 1956).
Hohfeld WN, *Fundamental Legal Conceptions as Applied in Judicial Reasoning and Other Legal Essays* (Yale UP 1923).
Hosley M, *Dark Side of Prosperity. Late Capitalism's Culture of Indebtedness* (Routledge 2016).
Hudson A, *The Law of Finance* (Sweet & Maxwell 2009).
Intrum, 'Leading the Way to a Sound Economy Since 1923', Business History Publishing (September 2023).
Johnson S and Kwak J, *13 Bankers* (Pantheon Books 2010).
Koch W, *Das Abzahlungsgeschäft in Handel und Industrie und seine Finanzierung* (Springer 1931).
Levitin AJ, *Consumer Finance Law: Markets and Regulation* (Aspen Publishing 2018).
Levy J, *Ages of American Capitalism. A History of the United States* (Random House 2021).
Lissowska M, *Consumer Credit in Europe* (Palgrave Macmillan 2021).
Lukes S, *Power: A Radical View* (Macmillan 1974).
MacDonald SB and Gastman AL, *A History of Credit & Power in the Western World* (Routledge 2017).
Micklitz HW and Domurath I, *Consumer Debt and Social Exclusion in Europe* (Taylor and Francis 2016).
Montgomerie J, *Should We Abolish Household Debts?* (Polity 2019).
Muldrew C, *The Economy of Obligation: The Culture of Credit and Social Relations in Early Modern England* (Basingstoke 1998).
National Consumer Law Center, *Fair Debt Collection. Volume 1: Chapters and Index* (9th Edition 2018).
Pistor K, *The Code of Capital* (Princeton UP 2019).
Reifner U, Niemi-Kiesiläinen J, Huls N, and Springeneer H, *Overindebtedness in European Consumer Law: Principles from 15 European States* (Books on Demand 2012).
Rizoiu R, *Garantii reale mobiliare. O abordare functionala* (Universul Juridic 2011).
Rock P, *Making People Pay* (Routledge 1973).
Smail DL, *Legal Plunder: Households and Debt Collection in Late Medieval Europe* (Harvard UP 2016).
SoRelle ME, Democracy Declined. The Failed Politics of Consumer Financial Protection (University of Chicago Press 2020).
Spanogle JA and others, *Consumer Law: Cases and Materials* (4th edn, West Academic Publishing 2013).
Spooner J, *Bankruptcy: The Case for Relief in an Economy of Debt* (CUP 2019).
Stănescu CG, *Self-Help, Private Debt Collection and the Concomitant Risks. A Comparative Law Analysis* (Springer 2015).Stănescu CG (ed), *Regulation of Debt Collection in Europe: Understanding Informal Debt Collection* (Routledge 2023).
Tajti T, *Comparative Secured Transactions Law* (Akademiai Kiado 2002).

Warren E, Westbrook JL, Porter K, and Pottow JAE, *The Law of Debtors and Creditors. Text, Cases, and Problems* (7th edition, Aspen Casebook Series 2021).
Woll C, *The Power of Banks* (Speri, University of Sheffield 2013).
Zimmermann R, *The Law of Obligations. Roman Foundations of the Civilian Tradition* (OUP 1990/1996).

Reports and Studies

Alliance for Lobbying Transparency and Ethics Regulation (ALTER EU), *A captive Commission—the role of the financial industry in shaping EU regulation* (5 November 2009).
ALTER-EU, *Corporate interests dominate EU lobbying on financial services* (20 February 2017).
ANGECO, Estudio anual sobre el Sector de la Gestión de Crédito y la Morosidad (2023).
ANGECO, Estudio de mercado sobre el sector de la gestión del crédito y la morosidad en España (2022).
BDIU, Stellungnahme zum Referentenentwurf eines Kreditzweitmarkt-gesetzes (KrZwMG) (9. August 2023).
BEUC, *European Commission's Report on the Application of the Unfair Commercial Practices Directive* (BEUC Position Paper X/2013/049, 24 June 2013) <https://www.beuc.eu/sites/default/files/publications/2013-00457-01-e.pdf>.
CEO, *Banking on the revolving door: rules full of loopholes for former finance officials* (23 January 2013).
CEO, *Corporate interests continue to dominate key expert groups. New rules, little progress* (14 February 2017).
CEO, *Corporate lobbying influence over the Council of the EU* (6 December 2017).
CEO, *Financial regulators and the private sector: permanent revolving door at DG FISMA* (11 April 2018).
CEO, *How the financial lobby won the battle in Brussels* (13 September 2018).
CEO, *Open door for forces of finance at the ECB* (3 October 2017).
CEO, 'Participants in the ECB advisory groups' (*CEO*) <https://corporateeurope.org/sites/default/files/attachments/table_of_ecb_advisory_groups_and_its_members.pdf>.
CEO, *The financial industry employs 1.700 lobbyists and spends €120 million a year to influence the EU—at least* (9 April 2014).
CEO, *The fire power of the financial lobby. A survey of the size of the financial lobby at the EU level*, published by CEO, The Austrian Federal Chamber of Labour (Arbeiterkammer) and The Austrian Trade Union Federation (ÖGB) (April 2014).
CEU, 'Banking: Council sets out action plan for non-performing loans', Press release (11 July 2017).
CEU, 'Council conclusions on Action Plan to tackle non-performing loans in Europe', Press Release (11 July 2017).
CEU, 'Report of the FSC Subgroup on Non-Performing Loans', Brussels, 31 May 2017, 9854/17, EF 113, ECOFIN 481.
CEU, 'Statement of the Council's Reasons: Modified proposal for a Directive of the European Parliament and of the Council on credit agreements for consumers and repealing Council Directive 87/102/EEC' Brussels, 9948/2/07, REV 2 ADD 1, 2002/0222 (COD) (20 September 2007).
CEU, 'Strengthening the Banking Union—presidency progress report' (OR. En) 14354/1/19 REV 1.
CEU, 'Voting result, Brussels' 13688/21, 9 November 2021.
Civic Consulting, *Study for the Fitness Check of EU consumer and marketing law. Final report Part 1*, Main report (May 2017).
Civic Consulting, *Study on the application of Directive 2005/29/EC on Unfair Commercial Practices in the EU, Part 1—Synthesis Report*, Final Report (2011).
Civic Consulting, *The Over-indebtedness of European Households: Updated Mapping of the Situation, Nature and Causes, Effects, and Initiatives for Alleviating Its Impact. Final Report, Part 1: Synthesis of Findings* (2013).

Commission, '2018 Consumer Markets Scoreboard. Consumers remain positive about key markets but trust in services still lacking' (October 2018).

Commission, 'Second Progress Report on the Reduction of Non-Performing Loans in Europe', COM(2018) 133 final.

Commission, 'Communication on the application of the Unfair Commercial Practices Directive: Achieving a High Level of Consumer Protection. Building Trust in the Internal Market, Brussels, 14.3.2013, COM(2013) 138 final.

Commission, 'Consumer Conditions Scoreboard: 2023 Edition' (March 2023).

Commission, 'Consumer Financial Services Action Plan: better products, more choice' Brussels, COM(2017) 139 final.

Commission, 'Consumer vulnerability across key markets in the European Union—executive summary' (January 2016).

Commission, 'Coronavirus Response: Commission welcomes 'Best Practices' to provide relief for consumers and businesses', Press Release, Brussels (14 July 2020).

Commission, 'First Report on the application of Directive 2005/29/EC of the European Parliament and of the Council of 11 May 2005 concerning unfair business-to-consumer commercial practices in the internal market and amending Council Directive 84/450/EEC, Directives 97/7/EC, 98/27/EC and 2002/65/EC of the European Parliament and of the Council and Regulation (EC) No 2006/2004 of the European Parliament and of the Council ('Unfair Commercial Practices Directive')', COM(2013) 139 final.

Commission, 'Guidance on the implementation/application of Directive 2005/29/EC on unfair commercial practices' of 25 May 2016 [SWD (2016) 163 final] (2016 Guidance).

Commission, 'Guidance on the Implementation/Application of Directive 2005/29/EC on Unfair Commercial Practices, Accompanying the document Communication from the Commission to the European Parliament, the Council, the European Economic and Social Committee and the Committee of the Regions: a comprehensive approach to stimulating cross-border e-commerce for Europe's citizens and businesses', COM(2016) 320 final, Brussels, 25.5.2016, SWD(2016) 163 final.

Commission, 'Guidance on the interpretation and application of Council Directive 93/13/EEC on unfair terms in consumer contracts' (2019/C 323/04) OJ C 323.

Commission, 'Post-Programme Surveillance Report. Greece, Spring 2023', Institutional paper 203 (May 2023).

Commission, 'Report on the implementation of Directive 2008/48/EC on credit agreements for consumers', COM(2014) 259 final.

Commission, 'Report on the operation of Directive 87/102/EEC for the approximation of the laws, regulations and administrative provisions of the Member States concerning consumer credit', COM (95) 117 final.

Commission, 'Study on European consumers' over-indebtedness, and its implications. Final report' (June 2023).

Commission, 'Study on measuring consumer detriment in the European Union' (February 2017).

Commission, 'Study on possible impacts of a revision of the CCD. Final report' (May 2021).

Commission, 'Tackling non-performing loans in the aftermath of the COVID-19 pandemic', COM (2020) 822 final.

Commission, 'Targeted consultation on improving transparency and efficiency in secondary markets for non-performing loans—Summary report' (December 2021).

Commission, 'Towards a common operational European definition of over-indebtedness' (February 2008).

Commission, Consumer Commissioner Kuneva welcomes member states decision to back new rules on consumer loans, Press Release, Brussels (22 May 2007).

Commission, Guidance on the interpretation and application of Directive 2005/29/EC of the European Parliament and of the Council concerning unfair business-to-consumer commercial practices in the internal market' C/2021/9320, OJ C 526.

Corporate Europe Observatory (CEO), *EU Financial Lobby Power Must Be Curbed* (14 April 2010).

Council of Europe, 'Legal solutions to debt problems: Recommendation Rec (2007)8 and Explanatory Memorandum' (September 2008).

Curtea de Conturi a Romaniei (Romanian Court of Auditors), *Raportului de audit asupra activităţii privind protecţia consumatorilor pentru perioada 2015–2018 (Audit Report of Consumer Protection Activity 2015–2018)* (October 2020).

Datainspektionens rapport 2014:1, *Elbolags indrivning av konsumenters obetalda elfordringar* (2014).

Dieckelmann D and Metzler J, *Household Inequality and Financial Stability Risks: Exploring the Impact of Changes in Consumer Prices and Interest Rates* (November 2022).

EBA, 'Consumer Trends Report 2014' (28 February 2014).

EBA, 'Consumer Trends Report 2015' (18 June 2015).

EBA, 'Consumer Trends Report 2018/2019' (20 February 2019).

EBA, 'Consumer Trends Reports 2020/2021' (10 March 2021) (EBA/REP/2021/04).

EBA, 'Report on Consumer Trends. Supervisory concerns regarding consumer protection issues in 2012/2013' (Consumer Trends Report 2012–2013) (18 March 2013).

EBA, 'Report on NPLs. Progress made and challenges ahead' (2019).EBA, 'Risk Dashboard data as of Q4 2020' (2020).

ECB, 'Opinion of 20 November 2018 on a proposal for a directive on credit servicers, credit purchasers and the recovery of collateral' (CON/2018/54), OJ C 444, 10.12.2018.

ECB, 'The Eurosystem Household Finance and Consumption Survey', Eurosystem Household Finance and Consumption Network (2013).

ECB, 'What are non-performing loans (NPLs)?' 12 September 2016 (updated 14 January 2021).

ECB, 'What are provisions and non-performing loan (NPL) coverage?' 21 December 2020.EOS, 'Annual and Sustainability Report (ASR) 2022/2023' (August 2024).

EOS, 'Our financial year 2022/2023' (August 2024).

European Credit Research Institute, '2002 Consumer Credit in the European Union Report' (2002).

European Data Protection Supervisor (EDPS), 'Formal comments of the EDPS on the Proposal for a Directive of the European Parliament and of the Council on Credit Servicers, Credit Purchasers and the Recovery of Collateral' (24 January 2019).

European Data Protection Supervisor, 'Formal comments on the Draft Proposal for a Commission Implementing Regulation laying down Implementing Technical Standards for the Application of Article 15(1) of Directive (EU) 2021/2167 with regard to the Templates to be used by Credit Institutions for the provision to Buyers of Information on their Credit Exposures in the Banking Book' (25 July 2023).

European Economic and Social Committee (EESC) (2018) 'Opinion on Proposal for a Directive of the European Parliament and the Council on credit servicers, credit purchasers and the recovery of collateral' 2018/C 367/09.

European Economic and Social Committee, 'Opinion on Proposal for a Regulation of the European Parliament and of the Council on amending Regulation (EU) No 575/2013 as regards minimum loss coverage for non-performing exposures' [COM(2018) 134 final — 2018/0060 (COD)] Proposal for a Directive of the European Parliament and of the Council on credit servicers, credit purchasers and the recovery of collateral [COM(2018) 135 final — 2018/0063 (COD)] OJ C 367, 10.10.2018.

European Financial Management Association, 'Retail banking in CEE—debt collection in times of crisis, summary of study findings', Zagreb (31 May 2011).

European Parliament, 'Application of the Unfair Commercial Practices Directive. Overview of the Commission's May 2016 Guidance document', PE 595.888 (January 2017).

European Parliament (EP), Committee on economic and monetary affairs, 'Amendments 204-468' (Draft Report), 2018/0063A (COD) (7 January 2020).

European Parliament, 'I Draft Report on the proposal for a European Parliament and Council directive on the harmonisation of the laws, regulations and administrative provisions of the Member States concerning credit for consumers' (COM (2002) 443 – C5-0420/2002 – 2002/0222 (COD)) Committee on Legal Affairs and the Internal Market, Provisional A5-0310/2003 Rev1 of 23 September 2003.

European Parliament, 'II Second Report on the proposal for a European Parliament and Council directive on the harmonisation of the laws, regulations and administrative provisions of the

Member States concerning credit for consumers' (COM (2002) 0443 – C5-0420/2002 – 2002/0222(COD).

European Parliament, 'Report on the proposal for a Directive of the European Parliament and of the Council on credit servicers, credit purchasers and the recovery of collateral' (COM (2018)0135 – C8-0115/2018-2018/0063A(COD).

Finance Watch, 'Tackling causes of over-indebtedness in the EU consumer credit market' (March 2022).

Finance Watch, *Consumer Credit Market Malpractices Uncovered. An In-depth Study of Consumer Credit Markets in Spain, Romania and Ireland and What It Means for the Consumer Credit Directive Review* (February 2021).

Finance Watch, *From Debtor Prisons to Being Prisoners of Debt. Making the Case for Harmonised EU Consumer Insolvency Rules* (January 2022).

Finance Watch, *Non-Performing Loans Plan: EU Must Protect Taxpayers and Vulnerable Borrowers* (7 June 2018).

Finance Watch. *Is the Human Dignity of Individual Debtors at Risk?* Bruxelles (2020).

GfK Belgium, *Consumer Market Study to Support the Fitness Check of EU Consumer and Marketing Law. Final Report* (May 2017).

Heys R, Hope K, Ladher R, Lane M, Pasik K, Ramada P, Sinn M, and Suter J, 'Study on means to protect consumers in financial difficulty: personal bankruptcy, datio in solutum of mortgages, and restrictions on debt collection abusive practices', final report, Contract no. MARKT/2011/023/B2/ST/FC, London Economics (2012).

Intrum, *Annual and Sustainability Report (ASR) 2021* (2022).

Intrum, *ASR 2022* (2023).

Intrum, *ASR 2023* (2024).

Intrum, *ECPR 2022* (2023).

Intrum, *ECPR 2023* (2024).

Intrum, *European Consumer Payment Report (ECPR) 2021* (2022).

Jungmann N and Moerman A, *Schulden klein houden en perspectief bieden* (2023).

KPMG, *Non-Performing Loans—Setting Expectations to Meet SSM Priorities* (9 May 2016).

Parliamentary question - E-002334/2021 'Loans under moratoria and associated risks in Europe' (29 April 2021).

Rancoita E, Grodzicki M, Hempell H, Kok C, Metzler J, and Prapiestis A, *Financial Stability Considerations arising from the Interaction of Coronavirus-related Policy Measures*, Financial Stability Review (November 2020).

Royal Commission into the Robodebt Scheme, *Full Report* (7 July 2023).

Stanford University—Computational Policy Lab, *The Stanford Debtors' Prisons Project* (2024).

World Bank—Financial Sector Advisory Center, 'COVID-19 and Non-Performing Loan Resolution in the Europe and Central Asia region. Lessons learned from the global financial crisis for the pandemic', policy note (December 2020).

World Bank (International Finance Corporation), *Responsible Debt Collection in Emerging Markets* (2012).

World Bank and Ministry of Foreign Affairs of the Kingdom of the Netherlands, *Towards Effective Enforcement of Uncontested Monetary Claims: Lessons from Eastern and Central Europe* (June 2017).

World Bank, *Good Practices for Financial Consumer Protection*, 2nd edition (2017).

World Bank, *World Development Report 2022: Finance for an Equitable Recovery* (2022).

Articles

Amit N, Ismail R, Zumrah AR, Mohd Nizah MA, Tengku Muda TEA, Tat Meng EC, Ibrahim N, and Che Din N, 'Relationship Between Debt and Depression, Anxiety, Stress, or Suicide Ideation in Asia: A Systematic Review' (2020) 11 Frontiers in Psychology 1-17.

Baker A, 'Restraining regulatory capture? Anglo-America, Crisis Politics and Trajectories of Change in Global Financial Governance' (2010) 86(3) International Affairs (Royal Institute of International Affairs) 647-663.

Balakrishnan S, 'The Jailhouse Divergence: Why Debtors' Prisons Disappeared in 19th Century Europe and Flourished in West Africa' (2022) 24(5) Punishment & Society 807-823.

Balgova M, Nies M, and Plekhanov A, 'The Economic Impact of Reducing Non-Performing Loans' [2016] EBRD Working Paper no 193, 1-45.

Barnett M and Duvall R, 'Power in International Politics' (2005) 59(1) International Organization 39-75.

Bell S and Hindmoor A, 'Taming the City? Ideas, Structural Power and the Evolution of British Banking Policy Amidst the Great Financial Meltdown' [2014] 20(3) New Political Economy 454-474.

Claustre J, 'La dette, la haine et la force: les débuts de la prison pour dette à la fin du Moyen Âge (2007) 4 Revue historique (no 644) 797-821.

Del Granado JJ, 'The genius of Roman Law from a Law and Economics Perspective' (2011) 13 San Deigo International Law Journal 301-350.

Domurath I, Comparato G, and Micklitz H-W (eds), 'The Over-indebtedness of European Consumers—a View from Six Countries' (2014) EUI Working Paper LAW 2014/10, ERC-ERPL-08.

Drozd LA and Serrano-Padial R, 'Modelling the Revolving Revolution: The Debt Collection Channel' (2017) 107(3) The American Economic Review 897-930.

Efrat R, 'The Evolution of Bankruptcy Stigma' (2006) 7(2) Theoretical Inquiries in Law 365-393.

Ehrich I and Posner RA, 'An Economic Analysis of Legal Rulemaking' (1974) 3(1) The Journal of Legal Studies 257-286.

Engelen E, 'The Case for Financialization' (2008) 12(2) Competition & Change 111-119.
259.

Fabian K, Andhov A, and Stănescu C-G, 'Is Self-Help Repossession Possible in Central Europe?' (2011) 4(1) The Journal of Eurasian Law 83-108.

Fedaseyeu V, 'Debt Collection Agencies and the Supply of Consumer Credit' (2020) 138 Journal of Financial Economics 193-221.

Goldberg L, 'Dealing in Debt: The High-Stakes World of Debt Collection after FDCPA' (2006) 79 Southern California Law Review 711-752.

Hardy DC, 'Regulatory Capture in Banking' (2006) IMF Working Paper WP/06/34, 1-23.

Hartley T, 'Basic Principles of Jurisdiction in Private International Law: The European Union, The United States and England' (2022) 71(1) International & Comparative Law Quarterly 211-226.

Kastner L, 'From Outsiders to Insiders: A Civil Society Perspective on EU Financial Reforms' (2019) 57(2) Journal of Common Market Studies 223-241.

Kim J, 'Propertization: The Process by which Financial Corporate Power Has Risen and Collapsed' (2018) 1(3) Review of Capital as Power 58-82.

Kriebel J and Yam K, 'Forecasting Recoveries in Debt Collection: Debt Collectors and Information Production' (2020) 26 European Financial Management 537-559.

Lall R, 'From Failure to Failure: The Politics of International Banking Regulation' (2012) 19(4) Review of International Political Economy 609-638.

Lowery D and Gray V, 'A Neopluralist Perspective on Research on Organized Interests' (2004) 57(1) Political Research Quarterly 163-175.

Mak V, 'What Is Responsible Lending? The EU Consumer Mortgage Directive in the UK and the Netherlands' (2015) 38 Journal of Consumer Policy 411-430.

Makkai T and Braithwaite J, 'In and Out of the Revolving Door: Making Sense of Regulatory Capture' (1992) 12(1) Journal of Public Policy 61-78.

Mantovani M, 'Notaries and their Debt-collection Writs under the Brussels I Regulation. A Difficult Characterisation' (2019) 15(2) Journal of Private International Law 393-417.

Michaels R, 'EU Law as Private International Law? Re-Conceptualising the Country-of-Origin Principle as Vested Rights Theory' (2006) Duke Law School Legal Studies Paper No. 122, 1-45.

Micklitz H-W, 'An Expanded and Systematized Community Consumer Law as Alternative or Complement?' (2002) 13 European Business Law Review 583-598.

Monnet E, Pagliari S, and Vallee S, 'Beyond Financial Repression and Regulatory Capture: the Recomposition of European Financial Ecosystem after the Crisis' [2019] 147 LEQS Paper, 1-32.
Monnet E, Pagliari S, and Vallee S, 'Europe Between Financial Repression and Regulatory Capture' [2014] 8 Bruegel Working Paper, 1-17.
Mügge D, 'Reordering the Marketplace: Competition Politics in European Finance' (2006) 44(5) Journal of Common Market Studies 991-1022.
Pagliari S, 'Financial Industry Power and Regulatory Policies: What Lessons from the Global Financial Crisis' (2015) 2 Rivista Italiana di Politiche Pubbliche 209-232.
Peebles G, 'Washing Away the Sins of Debt: The Nineteenth-Century Eradication of the Debtors' Prison' (2013) 55(3) Comparative Studies in Society and History 701-724.
Poretti P, 'Debt Collection Practices under Croatian Enforcement Law—Is There a Way Out for Over-indebted Consumers?' (2018) 7(6) Journal of European Consumer and Market Law, 233-240.
Quaglia L, 'Setting the Pace? Private Financial Interests and European Financial Market Integration' (2008) 10(1) British Journal of Politics and International Relations 46-63.
Romeo C and Sandler R, 'The Effect of Debt Collection Laws on Access to Credit' (2021) 195 (C) Journal of Public Economics.
Scholte JA, 'Civil Society and Financial Markets: What Is Not Happening and Why' (2013) 9(2) Journal of Civil Society 129-147.
Sousa MD, 'Bankruptcy Stigma: A Socio-Legal Study' (2013) 87(4) The American Bankruptcy Law Journal 435-482.
Spooner J, 'The Quiet-Loud-Quiet Politics of Post-Crisis Consumer Bankruptcy Law: The Case of Ireland and the Troika' (2018) 81(5) Modern Law Review 790-824.
Stănescu C-G, 'Is the Unfair Commercial Practices Directive Fit to Effectively Tackle Abusive Debt Collection? A Critical Evaluation' (2020) 9(6) Journal of European Consumer and Market Law 235-247.
Stănescu CG, 'Regulation of Abusive Debt Collection Practices in the EU Member States: An Empirical Account' (2021) 44(2) Journal of Consumer Policy 179-216.
Stănescu C-G, 'The Enforcement of Consumer Financial Protection in Romania. Thirty Years Later—An Empirical Evaluation' (2023) 12(3) Journal of European Consumer and Market Law 102-112.
Stănescu CG, 'The Impact of the Credit Servicing Directive on Regulating Abusive Informal Debt Collection in the European Union: A Step Forward or a Missed Opportunity?' (2023) 12(1) Journal of European Consumer and Market Law 4-15.
Stănescu CG and Bogdan C, 'Regulatory Arbitrage and Non-Judicial Debt Collection in Central and Eastern Europe—Tax Sheltering and Money Laundering' (2021) 11(2) Accounting, Economics and Law: A Convivium 119-160.
Stănescu C-G and Kepinski J, 'Regulating Abusive Informal Debt Collection via Codes of Conduct. Evidence from FENCA Members' (forthcoming).
Stiegler GJ, 'The Theory of Economic Regulation' (1971) 2(1) The Bell Journal of Economics and Management Science 3-21.
Sullivan TA, Warren E, and Westbrook JL, 'Less Stigma or More Financial Distress: An Empirical Analysis of the Extraordinary Increase in Bankruptcy Filings' (2006) 59(2) Stanford Law Review 213-256.
Vassalos Y, 'Le pantouflage financier à la Commission européenne' [2017] 3 Savoir/Agir (No 41) 49-57.

Official Correspondence

Letter from the Regional State Administrative Agency for Southern Finland to the author (27 May 2021).

Index

For the benefit of digital users, indexed terms that span two pages (e.g., 52–53) may, on occasion, appear on only one of those pages.